The Philosopher's Habitat
An Introduction to Investigations in, and Applications of, Modern Philosophy

The modern philosophical stage is graced by many new dramas, and even some of the old plots have been given exciting new twists. The major reason for this is that, in recent times, philosophy has developed a truly catholic and interdisciplinary outlook. Philosophers writing on the mind are increasingly acquainting themselves with research in psychology, artificial intelligence and the neurosciences. Philosophers of language are learning from current controversies in linguistics – controversies which themselves are fuelled by activity in psychology and in philosophy itself. Writers on ethics are now involving themselves with social and moral issues of urgent practical concern, and are drawing on actual case studies instead of simply analyzing the words used in moral discourse – for which limited aim contrived, artificially simple examples sufficed. Some moral philosophers are now employed *qua* moral philosophers as decision-makers in hospitals and in business. Philosophers of science are no longer mainly occupied with clarifying such notions as *explanation, confirmation*, and *law*, but are attacking the hard philosophical problems that have been thrown up by science in the twentieth century and are learning from modern laboratory practice.

Rather than introducing philosophy by examining, in the traditional way, the writings of the great dead philosophers, the author has inverted this procedure. He introduces the subject by investigating a variety of the problems which are currently engaging philosophers and which can be made intelligible to an absolute beginner. The idea is that the reader will become absorbed in these dramas, will thereby come to appreciate the ways in which the stage was set by the great writers of the past, and will feel the urge to participate. Questions at the end of each chapter encourage the reader to push beyond the text.

Laurence Goldstein is Reader in Philosophy at the University of Hong Kong. He is the editor of *Precedent in Law* (1987) and is the author of a variety of articles in many journals, including *Mind, The Monist, Linguistics and Philosophy, Philosophical Investigations, Oxford Review of Education, Cambridge Law Journal, Analysis, Philosophy, Australasian Journal of Philosophy*, and *Erkenntnis*.

The Philosopher's Habitat

An Introduction to Investigations in, and Applications of, Modern Philosophy

Laurence Goldstein

R

ROUTLEDGE

London and New York

First published 1990
by Routledge
11 New Fetter Lane, London EC4P 4EE

Simultaneously published in the USA and Canada
by Routledge
a division of Routledge, Chapman and Hall, Inc.
29 West 35th Street, New York, NY 10001

Disc conversion by Columns of Reading
Printed in Great Britain by Richard Clay Ltd, Bungay, Suffolk.

British Library Cataloguing in Publication Data

Goldstein, Laurence
  The philosopher's habitat: an introduction to
  investigations in, and applications of, modern philosophy.
  I. Title
  100

Library of Congress Cataloging in Publication Data

Goldstein, Laurence, 1947–
  The philosopher's habitat.
  Bibliography: p.
  Includes index.
  1. Philosophy, Modern — 20th century, I. Title.
B804.G59   1989   190'.9'04   89–6344

ISBN HB 0–415–04224–0
        PB 0–415–04225–9

This book is dedicated to my son Joel, a nice boy who didn't get all the attention he deserved while I was writing it.

Contents

Contents

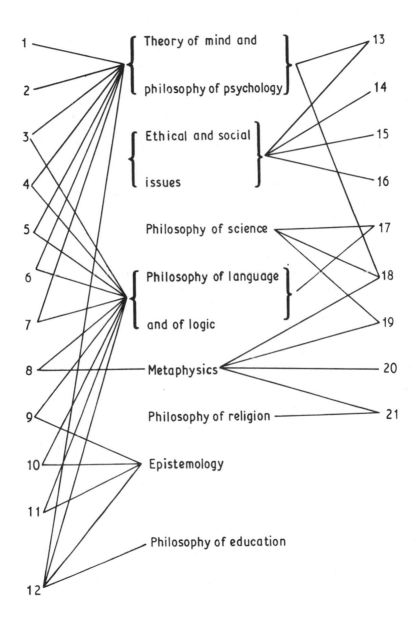

Preface

One of the good things about philosophy is that some of its questions can be expressed in terms quite accessible to the uninitiated, so such questions can be inserted easily and unobtrusively into lunchtime conversations with non-philosophers. This proved of great advantage to me when working on this book, since I wanted to write something that would be useful for a beginner in the subject, and so needed to test out the intelligibility of various ideas on a general – not philosophically sophisticated – audience. Over the past year and a half, my general audience has largely consisted of different groups of people I have met over lunch, and these groups have usually included specialists in fields other than my own. This latter fact has also proved of enormous value since, in my view, philosophy is no longer the introverted pursuit it once was (for example, in the days of linguistic analysis), but both informs and is informed by many other disciplines. This does impose a considerable burden on the philosopher, who must keep somewhat abreast of what is happening in neighboring fields. Here one relies on good relationships with experts who can direct one's reading.

It is usual, in prefaces, to thank those who have provided help and guidance in the process of giving birth to one's book. However, my powers of recall are inadequate to the task of mentally surveying all those lunchtime gatherings and of singling out the many individuals who were either interested or foolish enough to get drawn into a discussion of the philosophical conundrums that were bothering me. I'll just offer a blanket thanks to those people, and an apology for any indigestion caused.

More courteous expressions of gratitude are due to Jay Atlas, Kingsley Bolton, Mark Fisher, Frank Gillies, Keith Johnson, Tim Moore, Paul Morris, Miron Mushkat, Christopher New, Tim O'Hagan, Anthony Price, Elfed Roberts, and Elizabeth Samson, all of whom made written comments on part or parts of the draft. David Chan, Vivian Chu, Paul Lam, and Loletta Li provided secretarial support and succour.

In order to avoid burdening the text with footnotes, and to save the reader the trouble of ferreting around for references, I have made each chapter into a short, self-contained unit with its own notes. References are at the end of each unit.

Laurence Goldstein

Acknowledgements

Chapters 8, 9, and 12 draw heavily upon articles of mine that originally appeared in the 1988 volumes of *Mind, Erkenntnis* and *Oxford Review of Education* respectively, and thanks for permission are due to the editors of these journals. Kluwer Academic Publishers have kindly given permission for me to draw on my article: L. Goldstein, 'Logic and reasoning' *Erkenntnis*, 28:3 (1988), 297–320.

The author and publisher are grateful to Jonathan Cape Ltd and Candida Donadio Associates for permission to reproduce, in Chapter 21, the extract from Joseph Heller's *Catch-22* (Jonathan Cape, 1961) p. 194.

Introduction

Philosophy is concerned with a wide range of problems of diverse kinds. I shall seek to introduce the subject by setting out a variety of such problems and initiating a discussion of each one. My aim is to give readers some indication of the kinds of question that are engaging the attention of modern philosophers. The book will, I hope, be of value not just to budding philosophers but to all those who are reflective, and not satisfied with facile answers.

There has been, in recent years, considerable change in the shape of philosophy. The perennial questions continue to be debated with vigor, but there has also been a vast upsurge of interest by philosophers in questions relating to empirical disciplines such as linguistics, psychology, neurophysiology, physics, and biology. In turn, the better practitioners of such disciplines have recognized the contribution to rigor and clarity in their own subjects that philosophy can provide, and are increasingly both attending to what modern philosophers have to say, and attempting to express their own less mundane, more speculative ideas in the philosophical periodicals. This, in effect, is just the renewal of an old association, for historically philosophy was regarded as partner to or part of the sciences. Even a cursory glance at the writings of outstanding scientists such as Newton, Heisenberg, or Einstein reveals the influence of contemporaneous philosophical thought, and I have no doubt that, over a broad academic area, those students who wish to acquire a richer understanding of (or who hope to make contributions to) other subjects in which they are particularly interested have a great deal to gain from studying modern philosophical writing.

In the past few years, some great philosophy has been written; new questions have been raised and some old questions have been given interesting new twists. A beginner would obviously be ill advised to plunge headlong into recent philosophical literature plucked randomly from the bookstore. He or she would likely get bogged down very quickly, for much of the material presupposes considerable prior training. Yet there are many questions to which philosophers are currently addressing themselves which can be stated clearly and concisely, which lead the reader into central areas of philosophical concern, and which can be confronted without the need for much background theory or technical apparatus. It is such questions that I shall be discussing. The important thing is to first get gripped by the problems, for that provides the motivation for reading around the subject, locating these problems in a broader environment, finding out how other thinkers have tackled the issues and, where appropriate, equipping oneself with enough technical machinery (e.g., formal logic) to advance the understanding.

It is no easy matter to state just what makes a problem a philosophical one. The problems with which philosophy is concerned are such that they cannot be solved by observation and experiment. That may seem to distance philosophy from the sciences, but, in fact, no such distance exists, since an experimenter, unless engaged in the most routine sort of work, is liable to encounter difficulties which cannot be resolved by further experimentation, but which demand reflection. Roughly speaking, that reflection is philosophical only in so far as it is difficult. There is thus a sharp contrast between the sense of the word 'philosophical' as it applies to a disposition which may alternatively be described as 'phlegmatic' or 'resigned', and the sense of the word as it applies to hard problems which require for their resolution determined grappling. While some of these problems, especially those of long standing, do occupy a distinctive area remote from science, there are also, I have been suggesting, interfaces where the philosopher's talents and those of specialists in many other fields coalesce. Philosophy is not a science but, I am arguing, it should be scientifically *informed*.

Although the 'Contents' and 'Connections' pages group my chapters under traditional headings, my choice of what topics to include was not determined by any consideration of how squarely within a traditional philosophical area a given topic falls. The traditional division of philosophy into narrower subject areas – metaphysics, epistemology, the theory of mind, logic, etc. – is somewhat artificial. In philosophy, one thing tends to lead to another, and interesting problems tend to straddle intrasubjective and intersubjective boundaries. Increasingly these days, one finds that progress depends on breaking through the barriers separating narrow specializations. Indeed, this is reflected in the recent emergence of journals – for example, *Mind and Language, The Behavioral and Brain Sciences, Bioethics, The Journal of Medicine and Philosophy, Linguistics and Philosophy, Philosophical Psychology, Law and Philosophy, The Journal of Biology and Philosophy* – all of which are aimed at encouraging cross-fertilization or fusion.

It is not just the links with other *academic* disciplines that I have sought to stress. I do not believe that philosophy has to be just a 'dry', abstract pursuit. It interacts with the rest of our culture and has application to real life outside the ivory towers. This is particularly true of ethics, where there has been a dramatic swing from the abstract to the applied over the last fifteen or so years. My choice of problems to discuss has been motivated by the desire to explore the interfaces between philosophy, science, culture, and practical life.

I'm sure that the 'problem-based' approach I have adopted is the right way to proceed. It is depressing that so many introductory books and introductory courses do little more than present condensed accounts of the writings of the great historical figures. For one thing, this creates the false impression that philosophy is the historical study of what past philosophers have said. Exegesis and exposition are fine, but too much of that can lead to sycophancy and to stagnation. One can spend time interpreting ancient writers, and studying the interpretations of other interpreters (some philosophical traditions consist of just this) but by so doing one may lose sight of the fact that philosophy should be a voyage of discovery, a quest for new ideas, a search for valid arguments and for the exposure of invalid ones. It is not a spectator pastime, but is an activity of lively debate directed towards drawing a clean thread of truth from a tangled skein.

Another reason for not taking the 'historical figures' approach is that it is often very difficult for a beginner to see why certain questions the old writers discussed were worth discussing. Frequently, their problems are no longer our problems, and it takes a good deal of work in the history of ideas to understand why they were their problems. That is not to say that studying the works of great philosophers of the past is unimportant. Anyone who lives a life without reading some of the writings of Aristotle, Ockham, Hume, or Kant goes to his grave an intellectual pauper. What I am saying is that savoring such writers is a pleasure acquired by first developing a feeling for philosophical complexities and a desire to resolve them. Only after getting deeply involved in trying to work out answers for oneself can one get an inkling of what our great predecessors achieved.

Several introductory books attempt to give the reader an overview of the traditional areas of philosophy. That approach too seems to me misguided. Nobody can write a decent overview of anything unless he or she is thoroughly familiar with the details of the material being overviewed. But neither can anyone read an overview with profit unless similarly familiar with the material. Philosophy is not about assimilating information which can be imparted in synoptic form, but is about critical assessment and discussion. One cannot intelligently assess a writer's general picture of a subject unless one already has some acquaintance with the matter depicted, so an overview cannot be a useful introduction. However, at the beginning of each part of the book, I have provided an introduction in which I point out a few landmarks and direct the reader to some further reading.

I have adopted no consistent policy with regard to the manner of presentation of each chapter. No doubt, in an introductory work, some fair-minded, even-handed authors would set out each question to be discussed, and would present the different answers that have been proposed without advocating any one in particular. Occasionally I have done just that, but at other times my own views sneak out unchecked. This would be dangerous only if the reader were unaware that philosophical claims are always up for critical scrutiny, and are never to be accepted on trust. Any reader who did not know this already, knows it now.

At the end of each chapter I have suggested some questions which relate to, and sometimes go beyond, the issues canvassed in the text. Instructors may choose to use these questions as essay titles; another possibility is that they could be a focus for group discussions. Students new to the subject may find this a strange concept; they may even feel that discussion with each other is a kind of cheating. But, once more, it needs to be stressed that the study of philosophy is not a matter of amassing information, but is all about acquiring argumentative skills. Discussion is the best means of developing the skills of defending or criticizing a position, and is a catalyst for new ideas. Thus the (sometimes intimidatingly long) lists of references contained in the endnotes for each chapter should not be regarded as required reading, to be ploughed through and memorized, but should be used selectively as an aid to constructing and testing arguments of one's own.

Part one

Theory of mind and the philosophy of psychology

Introduction: theories of the mind

The belief, or the hope, that there is more to a human being than a human body has existed since ancient times. It is unpleasant to think that we humans, with our talents and virtues and intelligence, should just be matter that ultimately disintegrates. We should like there to be some part of us that is not physical and thus is not subject to decay – something that persists even when our bodies are gone. But wishing is not good enough. We need to find this incorporeal substance or, at least, to show that it must exist. Now, it cannot be the task of the physical sciences to investigate any *non*-physical constituent of ourselves. Traditionally it has fallen to the philosopher to enquire about this 'glassy essence' called the mind, the soul, or the self.

An ancient argument for the existence of this non-corporeal component runs roughly as follows: The hand uses a tool; the implement is quite distinct from what guides it. Now, similarly, I use my body. So I (the real me) must be distinct from my body.

This is a thoroughly bad argument, but it is related to a much more respectable one: We distinguish between involuntary behavior (such as blinking) and voluntary action which comes about from deciding what to do. Now a piece of involuntary behavior is an event with some antecedent cause or causes. The behavior is subject to the causal laws of science. Given those antecedents, the behavior *had to* occur. And this is where it differs from a voluntary action, for with the latter we have some choice as to whether it occurs or not. But even a voluntary action is the end of a chain of events. When I (deliberately) wave my hand in cheerful greeting, that movement is caused by the contraction of certain muscles; those muscular contractions are caused by certain nervous impulses which themselves are caused. . . . If *all* the events in this chain are part of the causal matrix, then the resulting action would be just as much determined by physical law as the involuntary action. So it seems that, in order to account for genuinely voluntary action, we must accept that at least one event leading to that action is non-physical. Hence we come to posit events called *volitions* which are creatures of a non-physical mind.

The mind is thus invoked to explain how we can deliberately act upon the world. Another argument for the existence of the mind springs from a consideration of how the world acts on us. When, for example, you hear the sound of a bell, sound waves affect mechanisms within the ear, and these in turn lead to the transmission of electrical impulses to the brain causing complex patterns of activity. But all the physical organs involved in this chain of events are only in the business of transmitting or processing. The phenomenon which is called your hearing of the sound – your perception – while it is *made possible* by this physical activity seems not to be identical to any or all of it. Hence, once again, the mind is postulated, but now as the agent of perception. Again, the conclusion is compelling because there does seem to be a world of difference between (say) the visual perception you enjoy when you cast your eyes towards a beautiful mountain, and the frenzy of neural activity which results when light from the mountain bombards your retina.

Another famous, but not, I think, strong argument for the existence of mind is due to René Descartes (1596–1650). The argument, which has come to be known simply as 'The cogito' runs like this: I can conceive that I do not have a body, but this very act of thinking requires that I at least be a thinking, if bodiless thing; in other words that I be a mind. Descartes argues further, however, that doubt as to the existence of one's physical body can be undermined. So he holds that a person consists of both a body and a mind. This position is known as *dualism*.

Whatever difficulties there are with the details of this theory (and there are many), an overriding objection to dualism is that this non-physical mind that it postulates is an altogether mysterious entity. In 1949, an ingenious attack on dualism was mounted by Gilbert Ryle. He denied that the mind was any kind of entity. This is not to deny that we have mental lives, but is only to deny that our mental activity is to be explained in terms of a ghostly object, the mind, inhabiting our bodies. Ryle tried to show that ascriptions of mental states could all be analyzed as statements about *dispositions* – dispositions to behave in certain ways. His theory is thus termed *logical behaviorism*.

This theory, too, has its problems. Consider *pondering*, surely a paradigm mental activity. Unlike, say, the state of anger, which is associated with characteristic behavior or dispositions to such behavior, there does not seem to be any distinctive behavior associated with pondering. So whether Ryle can account for *all* mental states is doubtful. But there is a much more damaging criticism of his theory. This is that its explanations don't go deep enough. For comparison, suppose I show a child how a magnet can pick up other pieces of metal – pieces that can't pick up each other. The inquisitive child who wants to understand what is happening is hardly likely to be satisfied with the explanation that the magnet has the disposition to pick up pieces of metal, while non-magnets are not so disposed. A proper explanation would involve describing the actual composition and structure of the magnet, and showing how this *underlies* its disposition to attract metal.

Transposing this point back to our discussion of behaviorism, the objection to that theory is that we need an account of the *physical* state which a person is in if we are to properly account for how that person is then disposed to behave. Now, clearly, the state in question cannot be a state of a *non*-physical mind. Conclusion: the mental states that are involved in the performance of voluntary action, and in thinking, perceiving, etc., are states of the *brain*. This theory is known as *materialism* or *physicalism* or *the mind-brain identity theory*. It erupted in Australia in the mid 1950s, although the underlying idea that there is no more to the universe than matter (no minds, spirits, or abstract entities) is a very old one that some philosophers who predate Socrates defended.

A materialist has to confront all of those problems which, as we saw, tempt one into postulating a non-corporeal mind, and has to account for many other mental phenomena such as mental imagery and self-consciousness which *prima facie* seem to resist explanation in purely physicalist terms. Such was the task undertaken by David Armstrong in his landmark work, *A Materialist Theory of Mind*.

If a certain mental state is the state of a *brain*, it would follow that that mental state could not be identical to the state of some non-organic matter. Yet, if we replaced every part of a living brain, every last neuron, with an electronic component that served the same *function* as it, then we should be hard pressed to deny that the resulting electronic 'brain' was capable of enjoying the same range of mental states as the original. Considerations such as this may lead one to conclude that what is essential to a mental state is not its material realization, but the function it performs – the role it plays in shaping a person's actions. This view is known (not surprisingly) as *functionalism*. Functionalism has been accepted by a great many philosophers of mind in recent years, and it is the theory that underscores much research on cognition in the field of artificial intelligence. It is therefore significant that Hilary Putnam, the founder of the theory, has repudiated it in a recent book. Putnam's argument has not yet been digested by the philosophical community, and it is too soon to tell whether it will gain widespread endorsement.

In the following sections we shall examine four phenomena – *feeling pain, dreaming, thinking* and *understanding* – which are of interest to psychologists and cognitive scientists. Our aim is to bring philosophical considerations to bear in attempting to clarify puzzling aspects of these phenomena and to see whether their ability to handle the difficulties gives us a means of adjudicating between competing philosophical accounts of the mind such as those sketched above.

References

Armstrong, D. M. (1968) *A Materialist Theory of Mind*, London: Routledge & Kegan Paul.
Block, N. (ed.) (1981) *Readings in Philosophy of Psychology*, 2 vols, Cambridge, Mass.: Harvard University Press. (For functionalism.)
Descartes, R. (1969) 'Meditations on first philosophy', in E. Anscombe and P. T. Geach (eds), *Descartes: Philosophical Writings*, London: Nelson.
Putnam, H. (1988) *Representation and Reality*, Cambridge, Mass.: MIT Press.
Ryle, G. (1949) *The Concept of Mind*, London: Hutchinson.

Introductory texts

Bechtel, W. (1988) *Philosophy of Mind: An Overview for Cognitive Science*, Hillsdale, NJ: Lawrence Erlbaum Associates Inc.
Blakemore, C. and Greenfield, S. (eds) (1987) *Mindwaves: Thoughts on Intelligence, Identity and Consciousness*, Oxford: Blackwell.
Carruthers, P. (1986) *Introducing Persons: Theories and Arguments in the Philosophy of Mind*. London: Croom Helm.
Churchland, P. M. (1988) *Matter and Consciousness: A Contemporary Introduction to the Philosophy of Mind*, 2nd edn, Cambridge, Mass.: MIT Press.
McGinn, C. (1982) *The Character of Mind*, Oxford: Oxford University Press.
O'Hear, A. (1985) *What Philosophy Is*, Harmondsworth: Penguin, pp. 210–33.

Theory of mind and the philosophy of psychology

Perry, J. and Bratman, M. (eds) (1987) *Introduction to Philosophy*, New York: Oxford University Press, pp. 319–403.
Smith, P. and Jones, O. R. (1986) *The Philosophy of Mind*, Cambridge: Cambridge University Press.
Teichman, J. (1988) *Philosophy and the Mind*, Oxford: Blackwell.

Chapter one

What is pain?

Not so long ago, surgery was done like this: The patient would be encouraged to drink a lot of whisky to dull the senses. He (or she) was then put on the operating table and held down by strong men as the surgeon plunged in the knife. Needless to say, this treatment was extremely painful, and the after-effects of the operation were frequently more painful than the disease it was supposed to cure, often resulting in death. Fortunately, nowadays we have much better methods for relieving pain. However we still have very little knowledge of what pain is, and our methods of treating pain are very far from perfect. Some 'folk' techniques work well under certain conditions, and the science of pharmacology has made great progress in recent years. Yet it seems clear that a better understanding of what pain is will lead to more effective methods of treatment.

What, then, is pain? Someone might suggest that pain is, for example, getting knocked down by a bus, dropping a heavy weight on one's toe or cutting one's finger. This answer is wrong because it confuses pain with the external stimuli that can cause pain. It is possible for such stimuli to be present when pain is absent, as in cases of congenital insensitivity to pain (a very dangerous condition, since those who suffer it can sustain great damage to their bodies without noticing it, for they don't feel a thing). Moreover, there are pains, such as stomach-aches and headaches, which often occur with no external stimulus. So pain cannot be the same as the stimuli which sometimes *produce* pain.

Another incorrect answer is 'Pain is wincing, crying, hopping around with a contorted expression on one's face etc.' This answer confuses pain with the sort of *behavior* that someone suffering an acute pain might display. But the two are quite different. Non-severe pain unaccompanied by any such behavior is still pain. Further, there are drugs called *paralytics* which paralyze the body without suppressing the pain. A person to whom such a drug is administered may feel intense pain, but will display no behavior. So pain cannot be the same as the behavior which is sometimes produced by pain.

It seems as if the answer to my question 'What is pain?' is not as simple as may have first appeared. Yet surely there is a sense in which most of us know exactly what pain is. If you thought I had somehow forgotten what the experience of pain was like, you might, helpfully, kick me in the leg, and say 'That's pain.' Although such a response has the virtue of drawing attention to two important features of pain, namely, that it's a feeling, and an unpleasant one, it really does not constitute any sort of answer to my question. For I did not need to be reminded of what a pain feels like. I wanted to know how pain is to be characterized. The nature of this question can perhaps be clarified if we consider a puzzled caveman raising the same sort of problem about *lightning*. If one of his companions points to a flash of lightning and says 'That's lightning' that doesn't enlighten him. When it is subsequently discovered (even if only in rough terms) what *causes* lightning, that is a great advance, but we must still distinguish the questions of what causes lightning and what lightning causes from the question of what lightning *is*.

The word 'pain' is a noun, so there is a great temptation to suppose that, like most nouns, it stands for some object, an object that can in some way increase and decrease (since we talk of 'more pain' and 'less pain', and of 'the pain getting worse'). We can reach out and feel the objects around us, so it seems quite natural to think that to have a pain is to feel some object that is *inside* us. However, this conception of pain is misleading. Consider a real object, like a book. It can be moved from one place to another – moving it doesn't make it into a different object. But can a headache move to the elbow? A real object can lose some of its qualities and acquire others while remaining the same object. For example, a red book may fade and turn pink when exposed to sunlight. But now imagine a person who accidentally cuts a finger. The initial sharp twinge is replaced by a dull throb. It would be incorrect to describe this as a case of a single object, a sensation, changing its qualities because we can identify no object that remains the same during this change.

Perhaps because it is so difficult to determine what pain is, it is hard to say what sorts of specialist should be responsible for doing work on the subject. So, although eliminating pain ought to be one of the most important goals for humankind, there are very few people doing research in this area. In a survey reported in *Time* magazine as recently as the mid 1980s, it was found that in 17 standard textbooks on surgery, medicine, and cancer totalling 22,000 pages, only 54 pages provided information about pain, and half the books did not discuss it at all.

The theory of pain that is taught in most medical schools is as follows:

> Pain is a specific modality like vision or audition with its own central and peripheral apparatus. The free nerve endings in the skin are considered to be pain receptors which generate impulses carried by small-diameter fibres in the peripheral nerve to the lateral spinothalamic tract and thence to a centre in the somatosensory thalamus and cortex. The activation of neurons within this hypothetical centre results in the experience of pain. (p. 13)

(This description of the traditional theory is taken from an article by R. Melzack, one of the leading clinical researchers in this field and one who *rejects* that theory.)

Does the traditional theory tell us much? We wanted to know what pain is, but the theory does not answer this question. To say that the activation of certain neurons *results in* the experience of pain is like saying that certain meteorological conditions normally result in lightning. An account of what *results in* pain is not yet an account of what pain *is*. (This is not to deny, of course, that there are interesting connections to be explored between physical changes in the body, either in the periphery or in the brain, and the psychological awareness that is called feeling a pain.)

Some theorists, even more reticently, seem content, given the antecedents of pain, and the behavioral and other consequents, to regard pain just as a *function* from the first to the second. So pain is defined as the state characteristically caused by stimuli ('inputs') of a certain kind and characteristically causing certain 'outputs' – both the kinds of behavior we have mentioned and certain kinds of mental state, such as distress and the desire to be pain-free. This is mathematically tidy, and sufficiently general to cover, for example, the pain that Martians might feel, but what is omitted is any account of that most important aspect of pain, its (unpleasant) *felt quality*. Further, there are many well-known facts about pain that the traditional theory does not explain and which, indeed, seem inconsistent with that theory. For example:

- When you put your foot in a hot bath, you immediately feel a short, sharp stinging pain that is followed, a fraction of a second later, by a longer-lasting, dull, 'deeper' pain. This implies the existence of *two* neural pathways from the skin receptors – a fast route and a slow route. Also, the question of the *character* of a pain – clearly of great importance for diagnostic purposes – is not touched by the traditional theory.

- Soldiers who have suffered terrible injuries in battle sometimes do not feel any pain while they are on the battlefield, but only after they have been taken to hospital. How can this be when, according to the traditional theory, at the time of injury the pain receptors are receiving and generating their impulses, and the route to their destination in the brain is unimpeded? A similar problem arises in trying to explain how people in the grip of religious fervor can subject their bodies to all sorts of injury without feeling a thing.

- Sometimes, after the amputation of a limb, a patient claims to feel acute pain in the place that used to be the extremity of that limb (this is known as the 'phantom limb' phenomenon). Yet there are no pain receptors at that place.

- Concentrating on a pain can sometimes relieve it. But how?

- Patients who have had a lobotomy (an operation in which a lobe of the brain, usually the cerebrum, is severed) claim that, although they feel intense pain, they don't mind it. There are even certain people (masochists) who *enjoy* pain. This suggests that the 'experience' of pain, of which the traditional theory speaks, must be divided into two not necessarily connected components – feeling that the pain is there, and not liking it. Yet that's a hard claim even for philosophers to buy, since many would hold that there is a 'conceptual connection' between *pain* and *aversion*.

- Puppies that have never been exposed to any painful stimuli grow up to be dogs that seem unable to feel pain. What this implies is that feeling pain is a *learned* response, that the pain-processing mechanism needs somehow to be trained.

- Acupuncture works, at least as an anaesthetic, and works especially well for those who have a positive attitude towards the treatment. Yet how can sticking pins into a person, thereby activating pain receptors, *reduce* pain? Some recent work shows that such stimulation releases the body's natural opiates, but the traditional theory is still left with the problem of accounting for how a *psychological* factor (believing the treatment will work) can affect the pain mechanism.

Reflection on facts such as these not only reveals the inadequacies of the traditional theory of pain but also indicates various ways in which a better theory must be more complicated. For example, apart from a sensory system in the brain which responds to pain, we must also posit a *perceptual* system that enables us to locate and characterize the pains we have. 'Surely', you might say, 'if I have a pain I cannot help but know where it is – there's no need for a special internal mechanism to ascertain where the pain is coming from.' But consider: there are some pains that we have which don't seem to have a specific or definite locus. When you experience a certain malaise, or, more mundanely, when you just 'feel bad' after excessive drinking, you cannot say *where* it's hurting. Without a pain-locating mechanism, *all* our pains would be like that.

It is fortunate indeed that we can usually locate our pains and fortunate too that, when damage occurs to our bodies, either externally or internally, our pain-locating systems generally provide us with reliable information about the location of our injuries. If we were all 'wired up' differently, so that, for example, a bang on my ankle resulted in my feeling pain in my head, a bang on your ankle resulted in your feeling a pain in your back, then doctors' lives would be much more difficult. I should have to present my doctor with my own 'wiring diagram' so that she would know what part of me to examine when I report pain in a different part. (If it were just a slight bang on the head, I would probably take care of it myself. And, with luck, by gently rubbing my ankle, the pain in my head would gradually disappear.)

Again, in addition to these sensory and perceptual systems, we need to posit a system that, in general, makes us averse to pain, so that we seek to avoid it. This requirement too may initially seem odd, for it's somewhat natural to think that aversion cannot be anything over and above the pain – we don't, as it were, feel a pain and then reflectively determine that it is really quite unpleasant. Yet, as we have seen, there are certain people who positively relish pain (relish *suffering* it, that is (not that they would regard it as exactly *suffering*)), and there are those whose linguistic competence is not in doubt, yet who claim to feel pain, but not to mind it at all. The idea of an averse-system linked only tenuously with the pain-sensing system is one to conjure with. Think of the implications for treatment in those cases where pain is not associated with a deteriorating condition of the body. If it were possible to suitably modify the *aversion*-system in such cases, there would be no harm (would there?) in letting the pain remain, for the patient wouldn't be averse to it.

The traditional theory, with its picture of a part of the brain given over specifically to receiving and dealing with pain (rather like a complaints department) is clearly entirely inadequate.

Rather, a number of systems are implicated, and a complex network of connections exists between these and other brain structures underlying a variety of psychological conditions which may inhibit, exacerbate, or be related in yet more subtle ways to the quantity and quality of hurt.

As should by now be apparent, making progress in our understanding of pain involves a nice mixture of conceptual and empirical intricacies. In an article called 'Why you can't make a computer that feels pain', Daniel Dennett discusses some of the complications I have just canvassed, and I want to end this chapter by recounting a rather worrying puzzle that Dennett describes in that article.

We have already mentioned that paralytics are drugs that prevent bodily movement, but do not suppress pain. In the 1940s some doctors thought that a drug called curare was a general anaesthetic and used it in major surgery, mainly on infants and young children. After operations, patients complained of having been conscious of excruciating pain, but the doctors did not believe them because during the operations the patients made not the slightest movement. It was later discovered that curare is only a *paralytic*. Now, *amnestics* are drugs which, after they are administered, have the effect of erasing all the patient's memories of the preceding few hours. Apparently, when it is suspected that an operation has gone badly – if the patient was awake for some time during surgery when he or she was supposed to be anaesthetized – then the anaesthesiologist may administer an amnestic, so that the patient will forget the horrifying experience and will not sue the hospital. Question: How do we know that any drug in current use as an anaesthetic is not *really* a compound of paralytic and amnestic? Modern pharmacology knows a great deal about processes occurring at the neuronal level, yet still, with many drugs, little is known of the chemistry of how they work, and they are judged almost exclusively on results. Our paralytic–amnestic compound might perform admirably on this count – so much so that no one would have the slightest reason to suspect that its *anaesthetic* properties were nil.

Notes

The description of the 'traditional' theory of pain is given in R. Melzack, 'Current concepts of pain' in D. J. Oborne, M. M. Gruneberg and J. R. Elser (eds), *Research in Psychology and Medicine*, vol. 1 (London: Academic Press, 1979), pp.13-19.

Melzack and his collaborator P. D. Wall are famous for their 'gate' theory of the mechanism of pain. They have collected many surprising facts about pain in R. Melzack and P. D. Wall, *The Challenge of Pain*, rev. edn (Harmondsworth: Penguin, 1982), which supplies the backing for many of the claims I have made.

Research on explaining acupuncture analgesia in terms of the release of the endogenous opiate β-endorphin is reported in V. Clement-Jones *et al.* 'Increased β-endorphin but not metenkephalin levels in human cerebrospinal fluid after acupuncture for recurrent pain', *The Lancet* (1 November 1980), 946-9.

Of the few philosophical articles on pain, the best three that I have come across, and drawn upon, are J. F. M. Hunter, 'The concept of pain', in *Essays after Wittgenstein* (London: George Allen and Unwin, 1973), pp. 115-46; D. Dennett, 'Why you can't make a computer that feels pain' in *Brainstorms* (Hassocks: Harvester, 1979), pp. 190-229. N. Nelkin, 'Pains and pain sensations', *Journal of Philosophy* 83 (1986), 129-48.

The *Time* article I mentioned is Claudia Wallis, 'Why pain hurts – unlocking an agonizing mystery', *Time* 24 (11 June 1984), 30-7.

For a recent defense by a psychologist of the view that pain just is pain-behavior, see H. Rachlin, 'Pain and behavior', *The Behavioral and Brain Sciences* 8 (1985), 43-83 which includes 'Open peer commentary' and replies by the author. One of the good things about this journal is that it devotes a section to continuing commentary, so that debates can extend over a number of years.

For a short, well-written introduction to neuroscience, I recommend W. Calvin and W. J. Ojemann, *Inside the Brain* (New York: NAL Penguin Inc., 1980).

An outstanding book that successfully welds together neuroscientific and philosophical concerns with mental phenomena is Patricia Churchland, *Neurophilosophy* (Cambridge, Mass.: MIT Press, 1986).

Questions

1 Could scientific advances ever make it possible for one person to feel the pains of another?

2 How could any discovery about our (physical) brain tell us anything about our psychological sensations? In his introductory book *What Does it all Mean?* (Oxford: Oxford University Press, 1987), Thomas Nagel suggests that 'there may be more to the world than can be explained by physical science' (p. 37). This is a view that many find attractive, and Nagel, amongst modern philosophers, has been its staunchest defender. See also his more advanced (but still accessible) works *Mortal Questions* (Cambridge: Cambridge University Press, 1979), especially the essays 'What is it like to be a bat?' and 'Subjective and objective', and *The View from Nowhere* (New York: Oxford University Press, 1986).

3 I mentioned briefly the doctrine called *functionalism* – the doctrine that conscious states can be characterized completely in terms of their causal roles. I also suggested that functionalism (which is, I suppose, the theory of mind most widely accepted by present-day philosophers) might have difficulty in accounting for *qualia* – the way things feel (or look, or sound, etc.) to an individual. Can a functionalist explain *qualia*, or, in particular, can the functionalist account for the experiential aspect of pain – how it feels to the sufferer? For 'Yes', see P. Smith and O. R. Jones, *The Philosophy of Mind* (Cambridge: Cambridge University Press, 1986), pp. 206-22. For 'No', see Paul Churchland, *Matter and Consciousness* (Cambridge, Mass.: MIT Press, 1984), pp. 38-42.

4 In his *Philosophical Investigations* (Oxford, Blackwell, 1953), section 244, Ludwig Wittgenstein claims that a person who truthfully says 'I have a pain' is not describing a mental state but is just using a form of words that replaces more primitive, natural, childish pain-behavior. Is Wittgenstein right? You'll find this question discussed in any text on Wittgenstein's later writings. One I particularly like is R. Fogelin, *Wittgenstein*, 2nd edn (London: Routledge & Kegan Paul, 1987).

5 What is the answer to Dennett's question about the paralytic–amnestic that I retailed at the end of the chapter? In trying to answer this question you should not be afraid to seek advice from medical practitioners, neuroscientists, or pharmacologists. (Such discussions often have the effect of exposing the thinness of one's own a priori speculations.)

Chapter two

The mystery of dreaming

Dreaming is a fascinating phenomenon but one peculiarly difficult to investigate experimentally. We can, of course, study sleepers' behavioral manifestations (e.g. eye movement, pulse, penile erections, and respiration) and also their brain activity, but in order to test whether any of these are correlated with dreaming, we have either to interrupt the state that we are trying to investigate or wait until it has passed. That is to say, we cannot look directly at people's dreams, but have to rely on their dream-reports. This immediately raises a problem: if sleepers, upon waking, report their dreams, are they reporting experiences had while sleeping or reporting experiences resulting from the transition to wakefulness? Is the dream a medley of thoughts, sensations, and images that occurred prior to waking (this is certainly how it seems to the person who has just woken from a dream) or is it a product of the process of waking?

But why should we even entertain the preposterous idea that dreams do not occur while a person is asleep? As we shall see, this idea is not so preposterous. When we come to realize what a strange and wonderful phenomenon dreaming is, it becomes less surprising that we need strange and wonderful hypotheses to explain the facts. Let's try to expose some of the mystifying facts about dreaming. It may appear, at first sight, that dreaming is just an inferior or degenerate kind of thinking, since dreams are often like mental ramblings, the mind skipping waywardly from one topic to the next. Yet, from another point of view, the product of a person's dream-thinking may outstrip anything that person can dream up when awake. The dream-reports of even the most unimaginative people are often fantastic, gripping narratives of a kind that such people would simply be unable to create were they attempting to write fiction. So, when dreaming, people may, in a certain sense, outperform their normal, wide-awake selves. Occasionally, characters in one's dreams say things extremely witty or clever, and, even after waking, one admires these witticisms or *mot*s as being of a kind that one is incapable of producing oneself. Yet the dream character is a creature of the dreamer's own contrivance – it is really the dreamer who is being so sharp and inventive; and with no effort whatsoever.

Sometimes dreams are not of the fantastic, loose, rambling kind but are highly condensed, coherent syntheses of many of the dreamer's beliefs, fears, anxieties, and memories. This dream of mine provides a simple illustration: In the presence of my ex-teacher of Cantonese, I was telephoning the Mandarin Hotel to make a reservation for the night before the day on which I had to make an airplane journey. After the phone call, I turned to my ex-teacher and he abruptly told me to wait until he was ready to talk to me. End of dream. Now, earlier that day I had been lunching with a Chinese woman, and was bemoaning my poor knowledge of Cantonese. The day before, a friend had recommended to me a barber shop in the Mandarin Hotel. The other relevant facts are these: There is only one hotel name of which I know the Cantonese translation, and that is the Mandarin. I had recently suspended my study of Cantonese. Some friends of mine who were due to fly out of town had booked into a hotel on the night before their journey to ensure that they wouldn't miss the plane in the morning. My ex-teacher of Cantonese is an exceptionally polite man.

It doesn't take a Freud to interpret this dream. I took my ex-teacher's unusual behavior (in the dream) to betray that he despised me for having given up my studies in Cantonese for insufficient reasons, and I (my dream self) was feeling guilty, knowing him to be right. The connection between the dream and real life is, in this case, quite apparent. But, as Freud's studies first showed, representations of real life experiences can show up in dreams heavily disguised or distorted, and connected in ways that are astonishingly subtle. The mental mechanism responsible for this warping and weaving is evidently extremely sophisticated. In terms of evolutionary theory, one cannot help but wonder how it benefits humans in the struggle for survival. Is it, as Freud thought, a kind of self-therapeutic device activated by mental trauma, comparable, say, to the body's natural immune system which is activated by infection? Perhaps so, but then why does it work in so complicated a way, concocting crazy stories and weird images? Wouldn't it be simpler for the body to produce some enzymes to inhibit mental distress?

Dreams can supply solutions to problems that the dreamers find intractable when they are awake. There is much anecdotal evidence for this (for example, a satisfactory design for Coventry Cathedral had eluded the architect until it came to him in a dream), but there are also impressive experimental results. Morton Schatzman, writing in *New Scientist*, reports an investigation in which subjects are given a tricky problem to solve. Having failed to solve it, the subject is required to 'sleep on the problem'. In many cases, a variant of the problem situation appears in the subject's dream together with a solution that he or she can easily adapt to solve the original problem. Here is one of Schatzman's examples. (You might like to try sleeping on it yourself, so I'll put the solution in the endnotes')

What is the missing letter?
H Z X O I S

(p. 20)

The fact that we can solve contrived and esoteric puzzles in dreams suggests that another purpose of dreaming is to equip us with the means for dealing with quite ordinary problems. Dreaming may be the occasion for freeing the mind of obstructive clutter, for reorganizing our memories and, as Piaget claims, for shaping and sharpening our concepts.

There are dreams within dreams, a much more puzzling phenomenon than a play within a play, since the dreamer has the experience of 'waking' from a dream only to find subsequently that what he woke into was not reality but was another dream. Such phenomena can exacerbate sceptical doubts – am I a man who has just dreamed that he was a butterfly, or am I a butterfly now dreaming that I am a man? (Chuang Tze b. 369 BC). Dreams can also be self-referential, as when it dawns upon the dreamer that things are not as they should be, and he rightly concludes 'This is a dream.' Dreams during which a person is aware of dreaming are known as *lucid dreams*.

A related phenomenon is that in which the dreamer can, as it were, step outside the action, decide whether to continue the dream, try to guide it etc. It seems that here the dreamer is doing the impossible – being both a participant in the dream and also an observer of it. I often have dreams of this sort where I am riding my motorbike, but crashing with impunity into buses and lorries, knowing that I am in no state to get hurt.

Sometimes the final event in a dream matches the event that woke the dreamer. For example, you break into the Pentagon, steal the files, escape through a maze of corridors and over a wall, and emerge onto a lawn where a waiting helicopter springs into life, its blades sputtering – and you awake to a child deflating a balloon in your ear. If the event in the outside world that wakens the dreamer is unexpected, and if the last episode in the dream is the culmination of a coherent story (as in our Pentagon example), then it seems that the early part of the dream must have been caused by what occurred later, or else the dreamer somehow knows what is going to occur at the end of the dream before it happens. For how, otherwise, would the dream know how to start in order to build to just that climax? Yet we *can't* change the past or see into the future!

This last enigma brings us back to the idea mooted in the first paragraph. If dreams are sequences of experiences that occur in our sleep, there would be no plausible explanation for the kind of dream we have just described which ends with an episode matching the event that does the waking. We seem driven to the conclusion that dreams are not experiences that occupy long stretches of sleep, but are creatures of the short period of waking up. The theory would be that the waking stimulus impinges on the sleeper and, in the time that it takes to become fully conscious, the waking sleeper concocts a dream with an ending inspired by that stimulus.

Another reason for thinking that the lay view that dreams are sleep-time experiences is mistaken is put forward by Norman Malcolm. He argues that being aware of one's surroundings is a precondition of being in any psychological state; in sleep we are not thus aware, *ergo* dreams are not any kind of psychological state; in particular, they are not *experiences*. The argument is supposed not to rely on any empirical evidence, but to depend solely on the analysis of crucial concepts such as *experience*, *sleep*, and *awareness*.

This does raise a problem about whether our lay concepts are so secure that we can reach important conclusions just by reflecting on them, or whether there are confusions in our lay ways of thinking which can be remedied by *refining* certain of our concepts under the guidance of science and philosophy. When modern psychologists claim, for example, that they have convincing evidence of subjects being in psychological states of which those subjects are quite unaware, can we just dismiss such claims as being conceptually confused? Are the psychologists' research efforts thereby totally undermined? We had better be rather confident of the coherence of our own concepts before we start making such wild accusations. These conceptual issues matter; they are not merely verbal trivialities. A surgeon, having ascertained that there is no electrical activity in an accident victim's brain, proceeds to cut out the beating heart for transplanting into someone else. Is this a worrying procedure? If so, are we likely to be reassured by the explanation that, according to the concept of *death* employed by surgeons, the procedure cannot (by definition) amount to violating the body of a living person?

Those criticisms I have levelled against the lay view of dreaming ought to be taken very seriously. But it should be borne in mind that there are strong considerations *in favor* of that view and against the kind of alternative that I have sketched – where dreams are characterized as stories hastily contrived in the process of waking. First, not only does it *seem* to dreamers that their dreams occupy time during sleep, but also, as experiments have shown, the length of a dream, as estimated by the wakened subject, correlates very well with the length of time during which the subject's eyeballs were moving around very fast (the so-called REM period). Second, the sort of rapid eye movement that occurs is consistent with the action in the dream. When the dream is of watching a tennis match, the dreamer's eyes oscillate horizontally; when dream-watching balls being picked up from the floor and tossed in a basketball net, the eyes move up and down. Third, an erotic dream may, with luck, culminate in orgasm. The lay view unproblematically grants sufficient time to savor and succumb to those inspirational thoughts and images. The alternative view commits us to telling a less likely tale. Last, one sometimes remembers a dream only after encountering a situation that triggers the memory, and such a situation may occur hours after waking. This fact clearly sits ill with the suggestion that dreams are contrived in the course of waking up.

What are we left with? Certain facts make life uncomfortable for each of the theories of dreaming that we have considered. Perhaps a synthesis is possible which does justice to (or, at least, is not incompatible with) all those facts. Here's one suggestion: Human beings generally possess a faculty of rich imagination located, roughly speaking, in the right hemisphere of the brain. This faculty, more prominent in artists and romantics, is largely suppressed during waking hours, but is somehow released or activated when we descend into, or emerge from sleep. Dreams occur in sleep, with the sensory apparatus playing a role similar to that which it plays in episodes of mental imagery. When a distinctive stimulus wakens a sleeper, the imaginative faculty tacks on to the end of the dream a short sequence with an ending corresponding, in some way, to the stimulus. But while this faculty is alive and working, the memory is still bleary; most of the dream is forgotten. The dream report is a coherent story pieced together from the remembered fragments.

This is, of course, the merest sketch, but it is of some interest in that great importance is assigned to what happens in the time between being fully asleep and being fully awake. On occasions, for example when we do not need to get up quickly, that period of time can be quite extended; our thoughts drift as if in a dream, and we have a hazy and inaccurate awareness of how fast time is passing. Normally, however, it is of relatively short duration. If my suggestion is correct, then this intermediate state figures prominently in an explanation of the puzzling phenomenon of how the end of a dream 'fits' the waking stimulus. The state that links sleep and wakefulness has not been much studied, but then, how *could* it be examined experimentally? The state is an extremely fragile one, and it may even be practically impossible for an observer to find out when a subject is in that state. But if there are practical limits to the experimental work that can be done on dreaming, then how on earth are we going to be able to unravel its diverse and perplexing mysteries?

Notes

It is widely held that Freud's best work is his investigation of dreams. The ingenuity of his interpretations is quite breathtaking. See S. Freud, *The Interpretation of Dreams* (first published 1899), in J. Strachey (ed.), *The Standard Edition of the Complete Psychological Works of Sigmund Freud*, vols. IV and V (London: Hogarth Press, 1953-74); S. Freud, *A General Introduction to Psychoanalysis* (Garden City, N.Y.: Norton, 1943).

Contrary to what many readers suppose, serious work on dreaming did not begin with Freud. G. W. Leibniz, in *New Essays Concerning Human Understanding*, wrote interestingly on the subject and there was a great deal of philosophical and physiological work done in succeeding centuries which, it can be argued, strikingly anticipates modern views. Freud may, perhaps, be held responsible for current ignorance of this tradition, since his review of pre-twentieth-century scientific literature on dreams was very influential, yet highly selective. See Peretz Lavie and J. Allan Hobson, 'Origin of dreams: anticipation of modern theories in the philosophy and physiology of the eighteenth and nineteenth centuries', *Psychological Bulletin* 100/2 (1986), 229-40.

Some of the research in experimental psychology I mentioned is reported in W. Dement and E. A. Wolpert, 'The relation of eye movements, bodily motility and external stimuli to dream content', *Journal of Experimental Psychology* 55 (1958), 543-53, which deals with stimuli that wake the sleeper and how these are related to the content of the dream.

For a description of experiments on vertical and horizontal REM, see D. Foulkes, *The Psychology of Sleep* (New York, Scribners, 1966), and, for a report of experiments on mental activity during sleep, I. Oswald, *Sleep* , 2nd edn (Harmondsworth: Penguin, 1970).

Experiments on lucid dreaming are reported in P. Fenwick *et al.*, 'Lucid dreaming: correspondence between dreamed and actual events in one subject during REM sleep', *Biological Psychology* 18 (1984), 243-52.

The thesis that dreams are not experiences that occur during sleep is propounded in N. Malcolm, *Dreaming* (London: Routledge & Kegan Paul, 1959).

Malcolm is criticized in H. Putnam, 'Dreaming and depth grammar' in R. J. Butler (ed.), *Analytical Philosophy* (Oxford: Blackwell, 1962), pp. 211-35; E.M. Curley, 'Dreaming and conceptual revision', *Australasian Journal of Philosophy* 53 (1975), 119-41; D. Dennett, 'Are dreams experiences?' in *Brainstorms* (Hassocks: Harvester Press, 1979), pp. 129-48 (although Dennett is impressed by the evidence for the relation of the final event in a coherent dream with the external stimulus that wakes the dreamer, and so is somewhat sympathetic to Malcolm's thesis).

For the solution to the dream problem described in M. Schatzman, 'Sleeping on problems really can solve them', *New Scientist* (11 August 1983), 692-3. turn all the letters through 180°. Schatzman has a fascinating follow-up article, 'The meaning of dreaming', *New Scientist*, (25 December 1986/1 January 1987), 36-9. Here are two more problems to dream on: What is peculiar about the following sentence?

I am not very happy acting pleased whenever prominent scientists overmagnify intellectual enlightenment.

What determines the order of the numbers in the following series?

8 5 4 9 1 7 6 3 2

Questions

1   At the beginning of his *Meditations on First Philosophy*, first published in 1641, Descartes raised the possibility that we never have any real experiences – that everything is a dream. Is such skepticism 'hollow' or is there room for genuine doubt? A point worth considering is that, when we are dreaming, we may not know we are dreaming, yet when we are awake (assuming that we ever are!) we are hardly ever in serious doubt that we are awake.

2   Karl Popper, in *Conjectures and Refutations* (London: Routledge & Kegan Paul, 1963), p. 38, note 3, cites disapprovingly the following passage from Freud's discussion of dreams:

If anybody asserts that most of the dreams which can be utilized in an analysis . . . owe their origin to [the analyst's] suggestion, then no objection can be made from the point of view of analytic theory. Yet there is nothing in this fact which would detract from the reliability of our results.

Popper's complaint is that the Freudian theory is immune to refutation and that therefore, whatever its suggestiveness, it is unscientific. Is Popper right about the scientific status of Freud's theory of dreaming? Freud, let us note, states that 'the interpretation of dreams is . . . the royal road to a knowledge of the unconscious; it is the securest foundation of psychoanalysis and the field in which every worker must acquire his convictions and seek his training', S. Freud, *Two Short Accounts of Psychoanalysis* (Harmondsworth: Penguin, 1962), p. 60.

3 Is there some confusion in our ordinary conception of dreaming? You'll find useful discussions of this issue in the critiques of N. Malcolm that I mention in the notes.

Chapter three

What are thoughts made of?

It is often said that we can never tell what another person is thinking, and by this is meant that another person's thoughts are available, in a direct way, to that person alone. What is true about this claim is that we can normally, if we so wish, conceal our thoughts from others. What does not follow, however (although it is often thought to follow), is that thoughts are essentially inaccessible and subjective in the sense of not being available in principle to scientific scrutiny. The behavior of people may give only a rough or a false impression of what they are thinking. But, when they are *speaking* then it seems fair to say that, except under unusual circumstances, what they say is what they think: We know what they are thinking from what they are saying. In conversation, people *express* their thoughts, and even when they think in silence, their thoughts are *potential* utterances.

There is a temptation to conclude from these considerations that thinking is just covert or inner speaking. Thus Plato (c. 428–c. 348 BC) thought of thought as 'the soul's inner dialogue with itself'. We don't have direct access to people's thoughts, but many philosophers have been attracted to the idea that thinking is analogous to overt discourse, and a driving force behind modern linguistics has been N. Chomsky's claim that studying language provides a clear route into an important part of the *mind*.

Now one objection to the suggestion that all thought is language-like is that there are many cases of human thinking in which language does not seem to play any part. If you are composing a piece of music or painting a picture, you are certainly thinking, but such thinking typically does not involve saying to yourself things like 'I'll insert a D# here' or 'A splash of brown would look nice there'. It is very difficult to say exactly what is going on inside our heads when we think musically or pictorially, but we can say, with a fair measure of confidence, what is not going on, and constructing sentences such as those just mentioned is clearly not an essential part of composing a tune or a painting.

But even if it is conceded that not *all* thought is linguistic, we may wish to set aside these examples of artistic thought as not being *typical* examples of thinking. Typical cases of thinking might be cited as *pondering, judging, deciding*, and *reasoning*. In such cases it appears much more plausible to claim that a language is involved. *Reasoning*, for example, does seem to include the framing of thoughts, and these thoughts could be expressed as sentences. If we wrote down the premises, conclusion, and intermediate steps of the reasoning, we would be writing down sentences. Imagine someone – Alberta – performing the following short piece of scientific reasoning:

> Nothing can travel faster than the speed of light. Suppose that a woman is travelling forwards at that speed holding a mirror in front of her face. Then, since light cannot leave her body in the direction she is travelling, she will not see her face reflected in the mirror.

In order to make this deduction 'in her head', Alberta need not, as it were, internally scan any such sequence of English sentences. Nevertheless, if called upon to explain how she arrived at her conclusion (a conclusion which, incidentally, is false), she would produce such a sequence either in English or in a language familiar to her.

This doesn't *prove* that thinking is a covert form of talking or writing some natural language. But what it does suggest is that, like sentences, thoughts have a structure; they must be composed of different kinds of parts. The reason why we can recognize the scientific inference cited above as an example of sensible reasoning is that we can perceive connections between various parts of the sentences involved. Unless there were such connections, and similar connections between the constituents of our thoughts, there would be no reasoning, only lunatic rambling.

If what we have said so far is correct, then it is appropriate to raise the question: 'What are thoughts and what are the parts of which they are composed?' Now, if I had asked 'What are sentences?' one answer might be that sentences are inscriptions in ink, or are moving pressure waves. This could be information about the material or concrete realization of sentences. A different sort of answer might define sentences in terms of syntax (vocabulary and grammar) and semantics (meaning). Similarly our question about thoughts can be taken in at least two ways.

First, if we are enquiring about the material of thoughts, that is, of acts of thinking, only a very flimsy answer can be given. For we know that thinking involves electrochemical activity in the brain, but although a great deal of interesting neurophysiological work in this area has been done recently, researchers are really only at the beginning of what looks likely to be an extremely long road. We could say, very noncommittally, that an act of thinking consists of a group of neural roiths, where 'roith' is an acronym for 'recondite occurrence inside the head'.

We can do a bit better if we take our question about thoughts in the second way. Consider the example of scientific thinking cited above. The first premise in that inference was about, among other things, the speed of light. So it seems quite natural to suppose that there must be some element in the thought that represents the speed of light. (Some people believe that such mental representations consist of visual images, but this is a mistake. What would be the image corresponding to the speed of light? And what image could correspond to the word 'won't' which figures in the conclusion of that inference?) Other elements of thought can be determined. Because we can distinguish between the thoughts 'I am holding the mirror' and 'I am breaking the mirror', it seems that verbs such as 'holding' and 'breaking' must have counterparts in thought. And surely we can have a thought that *if* a certain state of affairs occurs then a certain consequence will follow. So it seems that we must recognize conditionals and other logical connectives such as 'and' and 'or' as elements of our thought.

There seem to be such striking similarities between the elements of thought and the elements of language that it is hard to resist the conclusion that thinking, of the sort we have been considering, has, like language, syntactic stucture and semantic relations. Philosophers and linguists have postulated a 'language of thought' in which thinking is conducted. This is a 'mental language' of a complexity sufficient to articulate all the elements necessary for distinguishing one thought from another, and having a structure rich enough to account for those connections between thoughts upon which, as we have seen, normal inference depends. Some philosophers and linguists contend that this 'mental language' is common to all non-defective human beings. Others argue, to the contrary, that the language in which a person thinks depends intimately on the language he or she speaks.

The story so far is that thoughts are language-like in their structure, and are physically embodied in neural roiths. But after so much plain sailing, we hit troubled waters. First, how can a roith – some disturbance in the brain - *represent* anything in the outside world? Other occurrences, for example, explosions, don't represent anything beyond themselves, so how do small neural 'explosions' have this representational ability? Second, when we think of an individual, for example, Saint Thomas Aquinas, do we have to call up the appropriate roith in order to do the thinking? But if so, how do we know which roith to call up? – we can't tell ourselves to call up our Saint Thomas roith, for to do this we should *already* need to be thinking of the angelic doctor. Third, if our thoughts occur in our heads as coded messages (nobody believes that there are sentences of ordinary English inscribed on the brain) then, since we are not aware of the code, how do we gain access to our own thoughts? It might be suggested that within our brains is a decoder that operates on the language of thought, rather as in a computer, where a machine-language statement is translated into a statement that appears in ordinary language on the screen. Yet this suggestion looks suspect, for the input to such a decoder would be statements in the 'language of thought' embodied in one set of roiths, but the output could only be some coded message carried in a different set of roiths. And how do we read that?

In the light of these problems, a nasty suspicion arises. Perhaps this whole account of the constituents of thought that we have been exploring is radically mistaken. Perhaps thoughts don't have anything like linguistic structure. One way of reinforcing this suggestion is to consider the behavior of intelligent animals. Nobody who has been around dogs would deny that dogs think and have beliefs. But it is implausible to suggest that the constituents of doggy thoughts are similar to the constituents of any spoken language, since dogs don't have a spoken language.

We earlier argued that our ability to *reason* in a logical way presupposes the existence of thoughts which, like sentences, have constituents and structure. Was that a sound argument? In analyzing a piece of reasoning, we can use the methods of logic because the sentences *representing* the argument have a certain form. But does that mean that what is going on inside our heads has anything like that form? Even if it is correct to say that we *express* and *represent* our thoughts in language, it may be a big mistake to suppose that there are structural similarities between what is doing the representing and what is represented. Robert Stalnaker, in his book *Inquiry*, suggests an analogy with the representation of *numbers*: The number 9 can be *represented* as

'12–3' but it does not follow that 12, 3, or *subtraction* are *constituents* of the number 9. We could compare a thought and its verbal expression with toothpaste and its 'expression' from a tube. That the result of expressing toothpaste is a long, thin cylinder does not entail that toothpaste itself is long, thin, or cylindrical. Similarly, a thought might get expressed out loud in a statement with a particular linguistic structure. It does not follow that the thought itself has such a structure. Suppose, for example, that I look at a fruit bowl, and think that there is an apple and an orange in that bowl. The objects in front of my eyes include some pieces of fruit and a bowl, but no object corresponding to the word 'and' exists either in the world or in my visual image. There does not seem a clear reason for saying that my *thought* must have the form of a conjunction, nor, indeed, that the thought must have a structure anything like that of the *sentence* I have been using to talk about what I saw.

Here are three more reasons for taking seriously the claim that thoughts are not language-like. First, imagine this situation: You walk into a room and 'take it in' at a glance. It is clear that your survey of the room furnished you with a very large fund of beliefs and thoughts. However, it seems unlikely that your glance around the room equipped you with a large fund of mental *sentences*, even though, if asked to fully describe the room, you would (given time) produce a long string of statements expressing all those beliefs and thoughts you had acquired.

Second, we get an unrealistic account of *memory* if we assume that a human memory is a belief-store consisting of stacks of statement-like objects. There are millions of facts about our pasts that each of us can recall, but the implausibility of supposing that these memories are stored as mental sentences becomes apparent as soon as we begin to wonder *how* they are stored and where. Would there be suffcient room for them all, even with a wonderfully efficient system of coding and filing? Are they stored in chronological order? How do we search this stack of sentences?

Third, we mentioned early on that the thinking involved in composing a painting or a piece of music is non-linguistic. Following Stalnaker, we are now considering the hypothesis that the sort of thinking which can be expressed in statements is also non-linguistic. Now, much thinking involves not just the straight deduction of statements from statements, but also involves, for example, the forming of images and the perception of analogies. If these processes are categorially different from the deducing of propositions, then it is difficult to see how they could all be amalgamated in a single train of thought. However, if *all* thinking is non-linguistic, we may entertain the prospect of an integrated theory of mental phenomena, which might hope to offer some account of the way that these processes causally interact.

The reader may, by now, be in a state of perplexity. There are persuasive arguments that the *only* way we can account for human reasoning is to view the process as computation on sentences in a mental language. On the other hand, we have offered several reasons for thinking that the very idea that we have sentences running around in our heads is, if not crazy, at least highly suspicious. Where should we go from here? There are a number of directions that further research might take, and I shall briefly mention just two.

One possibility worth exploring is that beliefs and thoughts have a structure, but one that is quite unlike the structure of sentences. Some recent artificial intelligence programs for belief-representation use representations that are tied not too closely to the sentential paradigm. There is considerable scope for philosophical reflection about what kind of structure human thought must have, given that we conceive of ourselves as existing in a spatial world, with a temporal order, that we classify and categorize the objects in our environment and that we are able to make inferences, practical decisions, etc. These reflections are partially of the 'armchair' variety, but they can be aided and abetted by activities such as producing computer models of the dynamics of belief-systems and investigating the sorts of thought impairment that result from different kinds of brain damage.

A more radical suggestion is that there are no such things as beliefs and thoughts. Someone maintaining such a position is known (not surprisingly) as an *eliminatavist*. Eliminatavists grant that there are sentences, and grant that there is brain activity that can properly be termed *thinking*. But they hold that the notion of a *thought* is a confused contrivance of primitive or 'folk' psychology. An eliminatavist would not be surprised at the tangles into which our discussion of thought led us – 'What do you expect when you are dealing with a conceptually incoherent notion?' Can folk-psychological terms and theories be eliminated in favor of theories couched entirely in a vocabulary drawn from the neurosciences, or is there a level of psychological description that is *irreducible* if our aim is to provide explanations and theories of intelligent human behavior? This question has been around for some time, but it is only recently that tools sufficiently sharp to dissect it carefully are becoming available.

Notes

For Chomsky's view about how language is a window on the mind, see N. Chomsky, *Language and Mind*, enlarged edn (New York: Harcourt Brace Jovanovich, 1972).

The thesis that there has to be an 'inner language' for thought is forcefully defended in J. Fodor, *The Language of Thought* (Cambridge, Mass.: Harvard University Press, 1975); J. Fodor, *Psychosemantics* (Cambridge, Mass.: MIT Press, 1987), see esp. Appendix, and is contrasted with other views on the market in the same author's 'Fodor's guide to mental representations: the intelligent auntie's vade-mecum', *Mind* 94 (1985), 76-100.

Fodor is criticized in D. Dennett, 'A cure for the common code?' in *Brainstorms* (Hassocks: Harvester, 1979), pp. 90-108; D. Dennett, 'Reflections: the language of thought reconsidered' in *The Intentional Stance* (Cambridge, Mass.: MIT Press, 1987), pp. 227-35.

The view that belief and thought do *not* have linguistic structure is argued for in R. Stalnaker, *Inquiry* (Cambridge, Mass.: MIT Press, 1984); Patricia Churchland, *Neurophilosophy* (Cambridge, Mass.: MIT Press, 1986), chap. 9, esp. pp. 386-99. For a very helpful critique of Churchland's position, see M. Sereno, 'A program for the neurobiology of mind', *Inquiry* 29 (1986), 217-40, esp. section 3. Much useful discussion on experimental research on thought without language is contained in L. Weiskrantz (ed.), *Thought Without Language* (Oxford: Clarendon Press, 1988).

Three collections of good, but hard essays are S. Guttenplan (ed.), *Mind and Language* (Oxford: Oxford University Press, 1975), see especially the essays of D. Davidson, D. Føllesdal, and W. Quine's 'Mind and verbal dispositions'; A. Woodfield (ed.), *Thought and Object: Essays on Intentionality* (Oxford: Clarendon Press, 1982); R. Grandy and R. Warner (eds.), *Philosophical Grounds of Rationality* (Oxford: Clarendon Press, 1986), the papers by Grandy and J. Perry in particular.

For a glimpse of some of the complications involved in writing AI programs for belief representation, see W. Rapaport, 'Logical foundations for belief representation', *Cognitive Science* 10 (1986), 371-422.

An excellent philosophical essay on the structure of thought (but one that I should classify as 'advanced') is J. Campbell, 'Conceptual structure' in C. Travis (ed.), *Meaning and Interpretation* (Oxford; Blackwell, 1986), pp. 159-74.

For the view that our folk psychology, with its obfuscating vocabulary, will come to be replaced by a genuinely scientific psychology, see S. Stich, *From Folk Psychology to Cognitive Science* (Cambridge, Mass.: MIT Press, 1983).

Eliminatavism is defended in a book that I consider to be the best introduction to the philosophy of mind: P. Churchland, *Matter and Consciousness: A Contemporary Introduction to the Philosophy of Mind* (Cambridge, Mass.: MIT Press, 1984).

Questions

1 One of the reasons for doubting whether thoughts can be events taking place in the brain is that events in the brain have a definite location, but the same does not seem to be true of thoughts. Is this a *decisive* consideration? There are many introductory texts in the philosophy of mind, and this issue will be discussed under the heading 'materialism', or 'physicalism', or 'mind-brain identity thesis'. See, for example, P. Carruthers, *Introducing Persons: Theories and Arguments in the Philosophy of Mind* (London: Croom Helm, 1986), chap. 5, esp. pp. 147-50.

2 The fact that we can 'picture things in our minds' has inclined many people to suppose that all thoughts are pictorial representations. In opposition to this, M. Devitt and K. Sterelny, in *Language and Reality: An Introduction to the Philosophy of Language* (Oxford: Blackwell, 1987) write:

> Depictive representation is too rich and ambiguous to capture the content of a thought; a picture of [President Bush] is no more a representation of the belief that [President Bush] is wrinkled, than it is of the belief that he is Caucasian, or of the belief that he is surprisingly hairy for an old man. Moreover, no pictures could come close to capturing the beliefs that [President Bush] is dangerous, that turtles make poor lovers, and that high interest rates could cause a banking collapse. In sum, many thoughts are unpicturable; any picture could be associated with many thoughts. (p. 117)

Are these convincing arguments? Can you think of any arguments which either support or go against the view that thoughts are pictorial?

3 If there is indeed a 'language of thought', what evidence or arguments tend to count in favor of the view that it is *not* universal, but depends on the speaker's native language? Again, you might find Devitt and Sterelny (*Language and Reality*) helpful. See especially pp. 115-19, 172-8.

4 One objection we mentioned to the view that thinking involves language-like representations is that it is implausible to suppose that lower animals have *sentences* in mind. Is this a strong objection? For J. Fodor's reply to it, see his 'Why Paramecia don't have mental representations' in *Midwest Studies in Philosophy X : Studies in the Philosophy of Mind* (Minneapolis: University of Minnesota Press, 1986), pp. 3-23.

Chapter four

Prospects for artificial intelligence

The twentieth century has seen an unprecedented 'knowledge boom', and during the last twenty-five years the rising tide of information generated by researchers has become a flood. For reasons not too difficult to discern, much of this work is second rate or worthless, and much of it is misdirected, for example, towards producing military hardware or luxuries for the already luxuriating. Nevertheless, the sheer volume and intensity of effort, together with the availability of sophisticated new technology (itself a product of the knowledge boom) has created, in certain areas, real progress, and a feeling of the imminence of even more dramatic advances.

In no field of study is this more true than in a subject relatively new to the academic world, called *cognitive science* – the scientific study of the human mind. Cognitive science is a meeting-ground for specialists in several disciplines:

- psychologists, who have traditionally been responsible for measuring and assessing intelligent human behavior;
- linguists, who through the investigation of that distinctively human asset, language, provide testable hypotheses about our mental capacities for learning, categorizing, processing, and storing;
- philosophers, who, building on a long tradition of thinking about thinking, have developed a sensitivity for the conceptual hazards that beset theorizing about our mental lives;
- anthropologists, who provide hard empirical information to refute assumptions about human ways of thinking that are based on the limited experience of our own cultural groups;
- neuroscientists who reveal, in increasing detail, the fine structure of the brain, and those
- computer scientists who are working on the project of creating 'artificial intelligence'.

It is the contribution to cognitive science of artificial intelligence (AI) research that I want to consider here from a philosophical standpoint.

Obviously it is only with the recent advent of very fast computers with vast memories that the project of creating artificially something akin to an intelligent human performance has become more than a science-fiction fantasy. We are already familiar with impressive 'expert systems' capable of making better-considered decisions than a human can make, and chess-playing programs that can beat most of us, even giving away several bits.

Some of the early AI programs were quite arresting. One of them, ELIZA, written by Joseph Weizenbaum, conducted conversations with people some of whom, evidently, came to treat the program as a sympathetic hearer to which (to whom) they could reveal intimate emotional problems. Another program, written by Kenneth Colby, was designed to respond to questioning like a neurotic human being. This was achieved by writing into the program counterparts to mental phenomena such as anxieties and fears, the levels of which were made to vary, in accordance with the principles of Freudian psychoanalytic theory, as a function of new input and the changing state of what were the program's counterparts of beliefs. This program was intended to *model* a neurotic mind, but it would be quite wrong to say that the program itself was anxious.

The kind of programs I have just mentioned are products of a research enterprise which, following John Searle in his famous paper 'Minds, brains and programs', I shall call 'weak AI'. Now, weak or cautious AI, of which Searle approves, holds that the principal value of the computer in the study of the mind is that it gives us a very powerful tool. As he says, it enables us to formulate and test hypotheses about the workings of the mind in a rigorous and precise fashion. But it is *strong* AI that Searle, both in the above-mentioned paper, and in his 1984 Reith Lectures, wants to show is a mistaken endeavor. 'According to strong AI', Searle writes, 'the computer is not merely a tool in the study of the mind; rather the appropriately programmed computer really is a mind in the sense that computers given the right programs can be literally said to *understand* and have other cognitive states' (p. 417).

Searle goes on to attack the claim made by strong AI that an appropriately programmed computer literally has cognitive states and that the programs thereby explain human cognition. He discusses programs of R. C. Schank and R. P. Abelson which, when given stories as input, are able to answer questions that go beyond what was explicitly stated in those stories. The claim that such programs possess *understanding* is representative of the strong AI position that Searle wishes to undermine.

The concept of *understanding* is a rather slippery one, but Schank and Abelson, together with many other AI workers, content themselves with what might be called an 'operational definition' of the notion. That is, they adopt a test, and whatever successfully passes that test is credited with understanding. This test, of course, is not arbitrarily chosen, and in fact is a very natural one, namely: If a program can respond satisfactorily to detailed questions about some information it has been supplied, then it understands that information. The sort of questions relevant to this test are those designed to ascertain whether the program has integrated the new information with its existing data base and whether it can draw consequences from the augmented store.

Let me subject *you* to such a test. Here's the information:

Yesterday, my motorbike started leaking petrol from the carburetor, so I had to walk to work. But this evening I picked the bike up from the shop.

Now here are some questions:

Q1   Was there anything wrong with my motorbike?
Q2   Do I usually walk to work?
Q3   Did I lift the bike into the air?
Q4   Did I ride it from the shop?

You will notice that, although you answered these questions with ease, the answers cannot be extracted from anything *explicitly* present in the information given. But, if you should try to spell out the background knowledge on which you relied, you would soon realize that the task is enormous. Just for a start: (i) While *consuming* petrol is normal for a motorbike, *leaking* petrol is not; and leaking petrol is not a desirable quality, but the sign of something wrong. (ii) To say that one 'has to do' something sometimes means that one couldn't resist doing it; it can also mean that doing that thing was a prerequisite (e.g. 'I had to pass the exam in order to graduate') and it can also mean, as in the present context, that the agent was *reluctant* to do it. In order to say why, in the present context, the latter interpretation is plausible, we could mention that a short motorbike journey is probably a long walk and that people generally don't like to waste time walking to work. (iii) The verb 'to pick up' is ambiguous. We know that, in the present context, it means 'to collect' rather than 'to lift' because we know that motorbikes are too heavy to be lifted by one individual, that they very rarely need to be lifted into the air, and that motorbikes are not left forever in shops but are collected soon after repair is completed. (iv) After a repair is completed, the machine is restored to good working condition so, in answer to Q4, there should be no reason not to ride it from the shop, and many reasons against pushing it or transporting it by some other means.

Now, all this 'background' I have just supplied is only a tiny fragment of the information that would be needed by a program in order for it to answer the four simple questions I cited. At a very minimum, the program would need to have resources for analyzing concepts (in order, for example, to get the right interpretation for 'pick up'); it would need to know a lot about the normal sequence of events following the discovery of a defect in one's vehicle (in Schank/Abelson terms, it would require a *script* describing such a course of events) and it would need to possess information about what humans seek to avoid (e.g. discomfort, time-wasting) and, conversely, about what humans seek to attain – their *goals*.

Let us suppose that, in twenty years' time the art of programming concepts, scripts, goals, etc. has reached such a highly developed state that, with the ultra-fast parallel processors that will then be available to run these programs, computer doctors will be replacing human ones. (I regard this as a distinct possibility.) Someone who needs medical attention picks up the videophone and, on a monitor, a face appears with lips that move, a brow that furrows and, perhaps, a nose that twitches endearingly. The following conversation might ensue:

J. Hello, I'm Joan.
F. Hello, I'm Fine.
J. I don't want to know how you are; it's me that's sick.
F. No, my name's 'Fine' – a lot of people get that wrong.
J. Oh. Well, I have arthritis.
F. I'm sorry to hear that, Joan. What are the symptoms?
J. There's this persistent and nagging pain in my right thigh, which seems to get worse in damp weather.
F. That's not arthritis. Arthritis is an inflammation of the joints.
J. Are you sure?
F. Listen Joan, am I a doctor or am I a doctor? One thing I know so far is that you haven't got arthritis. So tell me a bit more.

Let's suppose that, at the end of this dialogue, Fine comes up with the correct diagnosis, prescribes suitable medication and answers all of Joan's questions, leaving her feeling satisfied and reassured. But Fine is a connection machine, a parallel processor that was delivered to the health centre in a carton about one metre cube. Among the specifications stamped on the carton was 'Personal attributes: JOLLY, CONCERNED, AMIABLE'.

Clearly, Fine passes the Schank/Abelson test for understanding. But Searle rejects this test; he would maintain that Fine understands *nothing*. Searle would be happy to say that the Fine-machine *simulates* a human ability, but proponents of strong AI make the bolder claims that, when a program of Fine-like sophistication is presented with a text, then

1 the machine running the program can literally be said to *understand* the text and
2 what the machine and its program do *explains* the human ability to understand texts and answer questions about them.

Searle believes that both of these claims are *false*, and tries to demonstrate this by means of a thought-experiment which has now become well known, and is usually referred to simply as 'The Chinese Room' ('Minds, brains and science', pp. 417-18).

Searle asks us to imagine that he is locked in a room and given large baskets full of Chinese characters. He knows no Chinese, either written or spoken – Chinese writing looks to him just like meaningless squiggles. He has also been given a batch of Chinese writing which constitutes a data base, for it is (although Searle doesn't know this) a set of Schank/Abelson scripts. He also has a 'program' – a manual written in English – and this contains a set of rules for dealing with Chinese characters. These rules describe the characters in terms only of their *shapes*; their *meanings* are not mentioned.

Suppose now that some Chinese characters are passed into the room through a slot in the wall, and that Searle has been given instructions for responding to this input: He has to look at these characters, compare them, in ways prescribed by his manual, with some of the resident scripts, noting certain geometrical matchings and mismatchings. The manual also contains a comprehensive set of output rules of the form: 'When such and such a pattern of matchings/mismatchings occurs, then take from your basket characters with shapes such and such, assemble them in that order and pass them out of the room through the slot'. Unknown to Searle, the people outside the room are Chinese, and they are passing in to him what they would call 'questions'.

Moreover, Searle's rule-book is so comprehensive that the groups of characters he passes back appear, to those outside the room, to be answers to their questions.

The point of Searle's thought experiment is that even though, to the people outside the room, it may appear that whoever or whatever is inside the room understands Chinese, the person inside the room is in fact only manipulating shapes – he has no understanding whatsoever of Chinese. Similarly, Searle argues, a Schank/Abelson program only manipulates coded sentences. It does not acquire any semantic knowledge. The program may include all the sign-manipulation rules in Searle's rule-book; it can be supplied with the same inputs and may provide similar ouputs. So it is in the same situation as Searle locked in the room. *And, just as Searle gains no understanding of Chinese, so neither does the computer.*

We could press the point even more forcibly than Searle does. Locked in the room, Searle doesn't have a clue about what's going on. He doesn't even know that what are coming in through the slot are bits of written language rather than, say, money. For all he knows, he is acting as banker in a fiendishly complex card game. In just the same way, a microcomputer doesn't know when it's word-processing or when it's figuring your monthly debts. The state induced by loading a program and the changes in state effected by impulses originating at the keyboard mean nothing at all to it.

If Searle's argument is correct then the prospect of AI research achieving any of the exciting goals announced by enthusiastic advocates is dim indeed. For what are the chances of a program being genuinely *inventive* or *insightful*, developing new methods to solve currently unsolved problems, or finding for itself satisfactory explanations of puzzling phenomena if programs cannot even *understand* anything?

Needless to say, many people have resisted Searle's conclusion. One obvious objection is this: If we took an intelligent human being and removed one cell, replacing it by an artificial component that performed the same function, then the human's cognitive abilities would be impaired not at all. We can now imagine replacing, one by one, *all* the human cells with artificial ones. So the resulting robot should possess all the mental powers of the human including, of course, the ability to understand a language. Then isn't it reasonable to suppose that, at some time in the future, we shall be able to build a computer that *understands* what we tell it? David Cole seems to have such an idea in mind when, in opposing Searle's conclusion, he constructs another thought-experiment to set against Searle's. I quote Cole's description of it verbatim:

> Searle is taken into a lab one night and given a drug which puts him into a deep trance. A lab technician announces: 'Subject ready for programming. Give him the program and the script.' For a moment the lab is silent but then a very long series of loud irregularly spaced clicks comes from a loudspeaker in front of Searle. Finally these cease, and Searle is given a pat on the back. He blinks, stands, and asks what happened. The lab director explains that he has been programmed in a way which modified a heretofore unused part of his brain so as to enable him to understand Chinese. Searle laughs, says 'Don't be silly', and leaves. The lab director's discounted explanation of what happened was given in Chinese (p. 442).

Cole's conclusion seems to be that the normal process of language-learning can be bypassed, and that full understanding of a new language may be achieved by brain programming. Now, Searle may well accept this conclusion, for, in his view, it is a brain with its particular causal properties that is required for the possession of understanding. But suppose it were not an unused portion of Searle's brain that was programmed, but a bit of electronic hardware, which was then implanted inside his skull replacing the unused portion of brain. That shouldn't make any difference to Searle's ability to understand Chinese, should it? I think that Searle would reply that even the modified thought-experiment does not damage his position. For he was not arguing that it is in principle impossible to build thinking robots, but that a computer, just by running a program, cannot achieve understanding. This brings us, then, to the question of how the robot can achieve what the running of a program cannot achieve. What do we, or this robot have that is *essential* for our being able to understand a language?

We may try to modify Cole's experiment by supposing that the laboratory is able to program a *first* language into a human or nonhuman subject. Is that an intelligible supposition? The new şcenario is not nearly so plausible. Could the subject just get up and ask a question? S/he/it has not been taught the *purpose* of questioning. If s/he/it utters an interrogative sentence can we say that s/he/it has asked a *question* if s/he/it doesn't know what questioning is *for*? And how do *people* come to know what questioning is for? Or what stating is for? Does our achieving this knowledge depend on the fact that we *interact* with others who can supply us with information and who seek information from us? Is interaction with a community of speakers a *necessary* condition for having the ability to understand language?

Let us pursue this enquiry a little further. *Why* do we seek information? Well, having information makes life easier. But what, for a computer, is an easier life? Human beings soon realize that, unless we find things out, get our information right and avoid inconsistency, we get into difficulties. And we have a natural desire to avoid difficulties, and particularly to avoid pain. The desire to avoid pain explains a lot of what we do. Now, it is certainly possible to write a program that checks for, and eliminates its own inconsistencies. But could a computer understand the point of eliminating inconsistency unless it could *feel* (and not merely represent) pain? Is the capacity to feel pain a necessary condition for having the ability to understand language? If we are talking only about physical pain, the answer to this question is 'No'. For, as I mentioned in chapter 1, there are humans who are unable to feel pain – but this does not seem to prevent them acquiring language. Yet humans can also suffer emotional hurt. If a person were incapable of being hurt mentally or physically, and so never had the experience of 'suffering the consequences', would he or she ever be able to speak a language, as opposed to merely reciting grammatically acceptable, situationally appropriate linguistic formulae?

A suggestion floated in the preceding paragraph (no substantial *argument* was offered for it) was that a necessary condition for a subject's being able to understand language is that s/he/it have a sensorium (and/or an emotionarium). This suggestion might please those who like to take a 'holistic' view of the human psyche, but it needs some kind of a defense. One tentative line of approach is *via* an examination of how infants acquire their first words.

It is a striking fact that the word 'mama' is universal among all non-defective babies. The linguist Roman Jakobson has an explanation that is too good to be false: Acquisition of the word can be seen as the culmination of a multi-stage process. When its lips are pressed to its mother's breast or to the feeding bottle, the only sound the baby can make is a contented nasal murmur. At the next stage, this 'm' sound is produced at the mere sight of food; it has become an anticipatory signal, a conditioned response. At the third stage, the sound is used as an expression of discontent and impatience when desired food is not immediately available. But it is now supplemented. As Jakobson puts it, 'When the mouth is free from nutrition, the nasal murmur may be supplied with an oral, particularly labial release' (p. 542). In other words, when junior doesn't get what it wants, it brings in the compact vowel which has maximal energy output, thereby producing 'ma', insistently repeated for maximal effect. At a further stage, this sound 'mama' comes to be used not to demand any supplier of food, but for the female parent in particular.

Now IF language is learned mainly through experience, and is not 'wired in' before birth (a big 'if' – see chapter 6) and IF all the stages that Jakobson describes are necessary for acquiring 'mama', and IF our understanding of language must develop from the initial acquisition of simple words like 'mama' then it may be reasonable to conjecture that our *sensory* endowments (e.g. deriving pleasure from sucking on a nipple) are pre-requisites for certain *cognitive* skills.

The tentative nature of these suggestions must again be stressed. What we have been asking, in effect, is 'What capacities, other than high computational power, are required for genuine artificial *intelligence*?' We have gestured towards some sapling answers which may fail to survive much cold, hard scrutiny. But even if it is correct that genuinely thinking machines need to interact with members of a thinking community or need the capacity to feel, it still remains a vast open question as to whether we shall be able to equip machines with such abilities.

Notes

A good introduction to philosophical issues in AI, including detailed accounts of Weizenbaum's ELIZA and of K. Colby's neurotic program, is provided in M. Boden, *Artificial Intelligence and Natural Man* (Hassocks: Harvester, 1977).

For a short explanation of the difference between traditional computer models of the mind and the connectionist models offered by parallel distributed processing (PDP) systems, see W. Bechtel, 'Connectionism and rules and representation systems: are they compatible?', *Philosophical Psychology* 1/1 (1988), 5-15.

The Schank/Abelson programs are reported in R. C. Schank and R. P. Abelson, *Scripts, Plans, Goals and Understanding* (Hillsdale: Lawrence Erlbaum Press, 1977).

Searle's original paper attacking strong AI is J. Searle, 'Minds, brains and programs', *The Behavioral and Brain Sciences* 3 (1980), 417-57. This includes large number of replies by psychologists, biologists, philosophers, and AI workers, and Searle's reply to them. His Reith Lectures, delivered as a set of radio talks, are published in J. Searle, *Minds, Brains and Science* (Cambridge, Mass.: Harvard University Press, 1985); see especially chapters 2 and 3.

For a broader picture of Searle's views on mind and language, consult his *Intentionality* (Cambridge: Cambridge University Press, 1983).

Of the many papers questioning the significance of Searle's Gedanken experiment, I mentioned D. Cole, 'Thought and thought experiments', *Philosophical Studies* 45 (1984), 431-44. A (rather difficult) book, written by a member of the AI community, and largely concerned with the problem of how to get meaning into machines, is Z. Pylyshyn, *Computation and Cognition* (Cambridge Mass.: MIT Press, 1984).

'Workers in AI may have set out to remove the mystery from intelligence, but their greatest achievement to date has been to exhibit the mystery of common sense.' This quotation is from a review by Stuart Sutherland of J. Haugeland, *Artificial Intelligence: the very Idea* (Cambridge, Mass.: MIT Press, 1985). I found this book particularly interesting on machine translation and conversation. Haugeland argues for a 'wait and see' attitude towards strong AI. He thinks that many of the questions about the possibility of creating artificial intelligence will only be answered (one way or the other) after many years of empirical research. A much more skeptical line is taken by H. and S. Dreyfus, *Mind Over Machine* (New York: Free Press, 1986). The Dreyfus brothers try to show that the billions of dollars spent annually on AI research is mostly money down the drain.

A different approach to these problems of mind, language and artificially created intelligence is via investigation of the higher animals (kind of half way between humans and machines). For this perspective, scc D. Premack, *Gavagai! Or the Future History of the Animal Language Controversy* (Cambridge, Mass.: MIT Press, 1986). Premack's book is also relevant to the concerns of chapter 6.

There has been a recent flood of popular works on AI. Two that I would recommend are M. Mitchell Waldrop, *Man-Made Minds: The Promise of Artificial Intelligence* (New York: Walker and Company, 1987); I. Aleksander and P. Burnett, *Thinking Machines: The Search for Artificial Intelligence* (New York: Knopf, 1987).

The article I mentioned on the infant development of language is R. Jakobson, 'Why "mama" and "papa"?', in *Selected Writings* (The Hague: Mouton, 1962), pp. 538-45.

For a useful survey of the contributions of its various sub-disciplines to cognitive science, see H. Gardner, *The Mind's New Science: A History of the Cognitive Revolution* (New York: Basic Books, 1985).

An introductory text that provides information on recent developments in several areas of cognitive science is P. Johnson-Laird, *The Computer and the Mind* (London: Fontana, 1988).

Questions

1 What theoretical obstacles do you see to building an artificial *sensorium*, e.g. a machine that feels pain? An article I mentioned in the notes to chapter 1 is useful here too: D. Dennett, 'Why you can't make a computer that feels pain', in *Brainstorms* (Hassocks: Harvester, 1979), pp. 190-229.

2   Does Searle provide a compelling proof that a computer running a program cannot understand a language? Thoroughly uncompelled is D. R. Hofstadter, who provides some 'Reflections' on Searle's essay in D. R. Hofstadter and D. Dennett, *The Mind's I* (New York: Basic Books, 1981), pp. 373-82. The next article in that book, 'An unfortunate dualist' by R. Smullyan, is also relevant. See also D. Dennett, 'Fast thinking', in Dennett, *The Intentional Stance* (Cambridge, Mass.: MIT Press, 1987).

3   By what criteria should we judge whether an action is *intelligent*?

Part two

Philosophy of language and logic

Introduction: the philosopher's interest in language

Language has always been a source of interest to philosophers. In the dialogue *Cratylus*, we find Plato discussing the question of whether the assignment of names is a matter of convention and agreement or whether a name 'naturally fits' what is named. In many of the medieval texts on logic (or 'the philosophy of logic', as we should now call the subject) there are some wonderfully subtle discussions of the diverse functions of words and of the nature of propositions. In the 1950s, western philosophy was dominated by a school of thought which held that the only true path to philosophical enlightenment lay in the analysis of language, and nowadays there are many philosophers who believe that the philosophy of language is the foundation of *all* philosophy.

Why is language of such particular interest? Two of the reasons have already been hinted at in chapters 3 and 4: First, language is intentional in the technical sense that certain words (or our uses of those words) have the property of *aboutness*. We use the sign 'spoon' to talk about something that doesn't look in the least like that sign. The word refers to a spoon, but a spoon doesn't refer to anything. Signs (but not spoons) point beyond themselves, and it is in virtue of this property that humans are able to talk about things. So it is worth finding out just how this referential mechanism operates. Second, and again, in contrast to other natural objects, linguistic entities (or our use of them) have meaning. We saw in the previous chapter that there is serious cause to doubt that a computer (even one equipped with a 'script' and running a sophisticated program) can understand its input or, correlatively, mean anything by its output. Equally, a parrot may occasionally repeat some words that it has heard, but it neither understands those words nor does it mean anything by them.

Many animals can be conditioned to produce or to respond to certain sounds and gestures, and human babies certainly *go through* the stage of making conditioned verbal responses to verbal and non-verbal stimuli. But normal infants, when they acquire their first language, go much further; they learn to *mean* what they say. So the phenomenon of meaning is important; an understanding of it will undoubtedly improve our understanding of us. Thus semantics – the study of the relation of language to the world – has always been high on the philosophical agenda.

Some other features of language deserve a brief mention. Language is versatile: we can talk not only about things going on around us, but also about past and future events; we can talk about particulars, but also make general statements. And we can not only make statements, but also perform many other acts of speech, such as promising, praying, questioning, commanding, demanding, and so on. Language is flexible: words are elastic – the range of objects to which a word applies may shrink or expand over time; words can be used innovatively as in metaphor and some of the rules of language may be bent a little bit for dramatic or humorous effect. Language is productive: armed with a vocabulary of a few thousand words together with a knowledge of grammar we can produce millions and millions of new sentences. The use of a human language permits us, when describing a situation, to abstract just those features to which we wish to draw the attention of our audience. When I say 'Tina is beautiful', I abstract, or select just one feature of Tina while ignoring others (e.g. her intelligence). Certain bees have a remarkably intricate communication system consisting of movements which inform their fellows of such things as the location of honey and even of the concentration of sugar in the honey. But, as Michael Devitt and Kim Sterelny point out, in a discussion to which this paragraph is indebted, the bees' dance-language does not permit selective reporting, for example of direction but not distance of the food source. Each of these aspects of language raises philosophically interesting issues, but I think it's fair to say that some have been given much less attention than others.

The reason why there is such a large overlap between modern philosophy of language and philosophy of logic (as a glance at the contents pages of introductory texts will confirm) is that, since its birth in 1879, a major task for modern logic has been to reveal the *logic of language*. The year 1879 was the publication date of Gottlob Frege's *Begriffsschrift* (*Concept-script*). At the beginning of that work, Frege makes it clear that he believes reliance on ordinary language to be a hindrance to achieving philosophical clarity. He speaks of the 'peculiarities' of ordinary language and offers in its stead a mathematically precise concept script or 'ideography' with which to conduct accurate reasoning. In ordinary languages, some words are ambiguous, and many are vague – the range of objects to which they apply is not sharply defined. Further, expressions belonging to the same category (according to the way that traditional grammar categorizes parts of speech) may display quite different *logical* behavior. This can be illustrated quite simply. Consider the following arguments:

1 Playing Polonius is better than playing the fool. Playing Hamlet is better than playing Polonius. Therefore playing Hamlet is better than playing the fool.
2 Nothing is better than making love. Kissing is better than nothing. Therefore kissing is better than making love.

There is surely a difference between the *logical* behavior of the noun-phrase 'nothing' and that of the other noun-phrases occurring in the above pair of arguments. This manifests itself in the clearest possible way, namely, the first argument is valid, the second invalid. From a logical point of view, 'nothing', unlike 'playing Polonius', does not perform the function of denoting any action or thing. A perspicuous notation would reflect such logical differences. Although that would not be greatly helpful in the present case, one can easily conceive that, in complex argumentation, it would be a benefit to have a safeguard against being led into serious error by the confusions to which our use of ordinary language makes us vulnerable. This, at least, was the view of Frege, and that of many writers at the beginning of the twentieth century, including Bertrand Russell.

Even though one may not be in the business of *replacing* (for philosophical purposes) ordinary language with an artificial counterpart, there would still be some point in trying to reveal the logical (as opposed to grammatical) behavior of the different components of ordinary languages. A spectacular, and, some would say, spectacularly successful example of this was Russell's analysis of definite descriptions, published in 1905. We have already seen that, while noun-phrases may generally be thought to denote, or pick out an item, some, for example, 'nothing', do not. It is plausible also to suppose that an *indefinite* description, for example, 'a book' doesn't pick out a particular item. When I say 'You should use a book to prop up this table', I probably don't intend to single out a particular book for the job. Russell defended the apparently amazing claim that the same is true of *definite* descriptions – that knowing the identity of what (if anything) fits a definite description is irrelevant to our grasping the information conveyed by a sentence containing such a description. (The editor of the journal *Mind*, to whom Russell sent this article for publication, thought the claim so ridiculous that he asked Russell to reconsider.) According to Russell, when one says, for example, 'The editor of *Mind* is a complete idiot', one is not referring to a certain individual. Rather one is making a composite, general claim: 'There is someone who edits *Mind* and whoever does is unique in doing so, and is also a complete idiot.' This translates very neatly into a logical notation of the kind invented by Frege.

What reasons do we have for buying Russell's analysis? There are several, but I'll mention just two. First, the analysis gives us a way of accounting for the meaning of sentences containing definite descriptions that *don't* fit anything. Take the sentences 'The present King of France is bald' and 'The greatest prime number does not exist.' If you think that definite descriptions refer, then you will either have to say that both of these sentences refer to the same thing (namely nothing – which, as we pointed out above, isn't much of a thing) or that each refers to a different *non-existent object*. Non-existent objects offended against Russell's 'robust sense of reality' (although it must be said that some modern philosophers, e.g. Terence Parsons and Richard Routley, have robustly embraced them). The Russellian analyses of our two sample sentences would be 'There is a person who at present rules France as king and who is the only one and who is bald' and 'It is not the case that there is a prime number which is greater than all other primes'. (Note how the predicate 'exists' gets swallowed up too.) So understood, the sentences can unproblematically be assigned the truth-values 'false' and 'true' respectively; we don't have to bother our heads about weird objects with dubious modes of existence. Similarly with the description 'the class of all classes that don't contain themselves as members'. This noun-phrase, one might presume, denotes a class. But then the claim that this class either is or is not a member of itself leads to a contradiction. (Figure it out.) However, on the Russellian analysis, the definite description disappears and the claim is paraphrased by the composite assertion 'There is a class of all non-self-membered classes, there is only one, and it is a member of itself.' This assertion is provably *false* – there is no such class, so the problem is dissolved. (This was a great relief to Russell since the problem – known as 'Russell's paradox' – had cost him four years of intellectual agony. But he later opted for a different solution.)

Second, another puzzling conundrum is easily solved by Russell's theory. I quote from a letter written by Russell in 1905:

If two names or descriptions apply to the same object, whatever is true of the one is true of the other. Now George the Fourth wished to know whether Scott was the author of *Waverley*; and Scott was as a matter of fact the same person as the author of *Waverley*. Hence, putting 'Scott' in the place of 'the author of *Waverley*', we find that George the Fourth wished to know whether Scott was Scott, which implies more interest in the Laws of Thought than was possible for the First Gentleman of Europe. (cited in S. Blackburn, p. 30).

According to Russell's theory, it's not that George the Fourth wanted to know of a particular guy whether *he* was Scott. What the monarch ('the First Gentleman of Europe') wanted to know was whether Scott wrote (and was unique in writing) *Waverley*.

Russell believed that such puzzles are fertile; that they serve a purpose similar to that of experiments in physical science, namely to be a test of and inspiration for our theories. That seems right. Problems that are simple to state are often extremely difficult to solve (two chapters in this section deal with problems of this kind) and much fascinating modern philosophy of logic and language has flowered from such apparently humble seeds.

Even if one agrees with Russell (and, of course, plenty of people don't) that definite descriptions do not refer, one may remain convinced that, if anything refers, proper names do. However, both Russell and Frege took the view that ordinary proper names are simply abbreviated or disguised descriptions so, on the Russellian view just outlined, those names don't refer either. If I say 'Greg got hurt in a shooting accident', then, if you ask me who I am referring to, I might answer, 'The first American to win the Tour de France.' That might be the first time you have heard of this Greg, so when you subsequently come to use his name, all you mean is 'whoever fits the description "the first American to win the Tour de France"' (and, if you believe my statement, 'who got hurt in a shooting accident'). That's one way (among many) of defending a so-called 'description theory' of proper names.

In a famous work called *Naming and Necessity*, Saul Kripke offered powerful arguments against description theories. One of these arguments runs as follows. Consider (1) Aristotle was fond of dogs. Russell would analyze (1) as (2) The last great philosopher of antiquity was fond of dogs (taking it that that's the description that Russell associates with Aristotle). Thus, in terms

45

of his theory of definite descriptions, (2) in turn should be analyzed as (3) Exactly one person was last among the great philosophers of antiquity, and any such person was fond of dogs. Let's now suppose that, contrary to fact, Aristotle was not the last great philosopher of antiquity, that is, that someone else fits the description in (3). Then, as Kripke points out, 'Russell's criterion would make *that other person's* fondness for dogs the relevant issue for the correctness of (1)!' (p. 7). That is an absurd consequence. The name 'Aristotle' refers to a particular individual, even though every description that the user of the name believes is true of Aristotle is false of him.

If the course of world history had been different, that is, in different 'possible worlds', descriptions like 'the last great philosopher of antiquity' or 'the president of the United States in 1965' would apply to people other than those to whom they apply in the actual world. But, in Kripke's view, proper names are 'rigid designators' – they apply to the same individual in all the possible worlds inhabited by that individual. In a nutshell, Kripke's position is that what a proper name refers to (as opposed to what the speaker may have intended to refer to) is independent of any description that the speaker possesses, i.e. is independent of a speaker's beliefs.

A similar conclusion can be drawn about other terms of our language. Take 'water', for example, and an argument due to Hilary Putnam. When the English residents of earth five hundred years ago said 'water' they referred to the same stuff as we refer to – stuff which we, but not they, know is H_2O. Now imagine a planet in a distant galaxy called Twin-Earth which is exactly like our earth of five hundred years ago (it looks exactly the same, the residents possess the same scientific knowledge, speak the same languages, etc.) with the sole important difference that everywhere that our earth had water, theirs has a fluid with chemical composition XYZ which looks exactly like water, behaves exactly the same, and is referred to by their English-speaking residents as 'water'. So, although what is going on inside the heads of fifteenth-century earthlings when they used the word 'water' may be exactly the same as what is going on inside the head of Twin-Earthlings when they use that word, the former are referring to H_2O, and the latter to the different stuff XYZ.

Semantics, as it was traditionally practised, took for granted the idea that we succeed in talking about things only in virtue of representing them. The idea is that, in order to be talking about one thing rather than another, we must have what Howard Wettstein calls a 'cognitive fix' on that thing – we have the object 'in mind', we represent it mentally, and then use a name, description, or some other linguistic item to give outward expression to this inner representation. But if, as the examples we have given above seem to show, what is inside our heads is *irrelevant* to the reference of linguistic terms, then we may wonder (borrowing the title of Wettstein's new book) 'Has semantics rested on a mistake?' *Meaning*, the other central concept of traditional semantics, has been under heavy fire ever since W. Quine cast aspersions on such notions as *synonymy* (sameness of meaning) and *analytic truth* (truth in virtue of meaning). In a justly celebrated work entitled *Word and Object*, Quine sought to establish that, in trying to interpret the language of a foreign tribe, one might end up with several incompatible translation manuals, each compatible with all possible evidence of the tribe's linguistic and other behavior. He concluded that there is no such thing as *the meaning* of what people say. Several authors, including Stephen Schiffer and the Gordon Baker and Peter Hacker duo, have recently made out strong cases against the very possibility of a theory of meaning.

If these assaults on traditional semantics are successful, where does that leave us? One possibility, advocated by Wettstein, is that we abandon the traditional conception of language as the expression of thought-contents and instead regard language, in the manner of the later Wittgenstein, as an integral part of various complex social practices. This approach has profound consequences both for philosophy and for linguistics. It is also the case, I believe, that the *phenomena* of meaning and reference, as described at the beginning of this essay, present genuine problems that remain to be solved. Just how does a child come to acquire the ability to mean what it says, to talk about places and things both near and far, and what is the nature of these abilities? These are very large issues, and my feeling is that, in the near future, we shall find philosophers needing to think (as Wittgenstein advised) about the *learning* of language and to draw, to a much greater extent than they have before, on the expertise of psycholinguists, applied linguists, and child developmentalists.

References

Baker, G. and Hacker, P. M. S. (1984) *Language, Sense and Nonsense*, Oxford: Blackwell.

Blackburn, S. (1980) *Philosophical Logic: Units 10-11 of Open University Course A313 – Philosophical Problems*, Milton Keynes: Open University Press.

Devitt, M. and Sterelny, K. (1987) *Language and Reality: An Introduction to the Philosophy of Language*, Oxford: Blackwell.

Frege, G. '*Begriffsschrift*, a formula language, modeled upon that of arithmetic, for pure thought', in J. van Heijenoort (ed.) (1967) *From Frege to Godel: A Source Book in Mathematical Logic, 1879–1931*, Cambridge, Mass.: Harvard University Press.

Kripke, S. (1980) *Naming and Necessity*, Cambridge, Mass.: Harvard University Press.

Parsons, T. (1980) *Nonexistent Objects*, New Haven: Yale University Press.

Plato, *Cratylus*. There are numerous editions of Plato's works. I use B. Jowett (ed.) (1892). *The Dialogues of Plato*, New York: Random House.

Putnam, H. (1975) 'The meaning of "meaning"' in Putnam, *Mind Language and Reality (Philosophical Papers)*, vol. 2, pp. 215-71.

Quine, W. V. (1960) *Word and Object*, Cambridge, Mass.: MIT Press.

Routley, R. (1980) *Exploring Meinong's Jungle and Beyond: An Investigation of Noneism and the Theory of Items*, Canberra: Research School of Social Sciences.

Russell B. (1905) 'On denoting', *Mind* 14: 479–93; reprinted in F. Zabeeh *et al.* (eds) (1974) *Readings in Semantics*, Urbana, University of Illinois Press, pp. 141–58.

Schiffer, S. (1987) *Remnants of Meaning*, Cambridge, Mass.: MIT Press.

Wettstein, H. (1989) *Has Semantics Rested on a Mistake?*, Stanford: Stanford University Press.

Wittgenstein, L. (1953) *Philosophical Investigations*, Oxford: Blackwell.

Introductory texts

Austin, J. L. (1962) *How to do Things with Words*, Oxford: Clarendon Press.

Blackburn, S. (1984) *Spreading the Word: Groundings in the Philosophy of Language*, Oxford: Oxford University Press.

Devitt, M. and Sterelny, K. (1987) *Language and Reality: An Introduction to the Philosophy of Language*, Oxford: Blackwell.

Geach, P. and Black, M. (eds) (1952) *Translations from the Philosophical Writings of Gottlob Frege*, Oxford: Blackwell.

Grayling, A. C. (1982) *An Introduction to Philosophical Logic*, Brighton: Harvester.

Haack, S. (1978) *Philosophy of Logics*, Cambridge: Cambridge University Press.

Hacking, I. (1975) *Why does Language Matter to Philosophy?*, Cambridge: Cambridge University Press.

Martin R. M. (1987) *The Meaning of Language*, Cambridge: Cambridge University Press.

Martinich, A. P. (ed.) (1985) *The Philosophy of Language*, Oxford: Oxford University Press.

Quine, W. V. (1970) *Philosophy of Logic*, Englewood Cliffs: Prentice Hall.

Searle, J. R. (ed.) (1971) *Philosophy of Language*, Oxford: Oxford University Press.

Strawson, P. F. (ed.) (1971) *Philosophical Logic*, Oxford: Oxford University Press.

Chapter five

Humor as a guide to the study of language

Humor is probably specific to the human species, and verbal humor certainly is. Hence the study of verbal humor promises to throw light on those mental characteristics distinctive of humans. This is the reason that humor has been of interest to psychologists. Humor should also be a source of fascination for linguists and for philosophers of language because, I wish to suggest, examining verbal humor leads to important discoveries about *language*. Prima facie this suggestion may appear zany. Only a tiny fraction of discourse is humorous, so what justifies our harboring the ambition of extracting important general conclusions about language from an investigation of this fragment? The main reason, I think, is this:

Speaking a language is clearly an activity governed by rules. A subset of these rules, including many of the rules of syntax, is such that to violate them is to fail to engage in the language; in this respect they resemble the constitutive rules of chess. (If you move the king three squares forward, you are not playing proper chess; if you say 'Squares king move you not if', you are not speaking proper English.) But there are other rules such that a speaker can violate them or, at least, deviate from them, without thereby ceasing to speak the language. It is precisely for this reason that most deviations from the rules of language are met not with a blank stare of non-comprehension, but with a range of reactions including, of course, *amusement*. Competent speakers possess (even though they cannot generally *formulate*) both kinds of rule. Violation of a rule of language results in one or other kind of incongruity, and incongruity is often amusing. So an investigation of what verbal performances we find amusing may be expected to lead to the discovery of the rules being violated (rules we may hitherto not have suspected to exist), and, more generally, to finding out about the *workings* of language.

Humor is a *social* phenomenon. It typically occurs in a social setting and typically social factors such as the culture of the participants are relevant to its explanation. In some linguistic research, lip service is paid to the relevance of contextual and cultural elements for the study of language, but, when investigating humor, these elements are immediately seen to be *essential ingredients*. Examining humor forces us to take a view of language broader than that generally taken by the philosopher of language or by the specialist in some area of linguistics.

Until very recently, the philosophy of language was widely regarded as providing the underpinning to all other serious philosophical activity. This was due, in large part, to the influence of writers such as Michael Dummett, who regards providing a theory of *meaning* as the central task of philosophy, and Donald Davidson who championed an account of meaning inspired by the formal investigations into the concept of *truth* of the Polish logician Alfred Tarski. Much of current writing in the philosophy of language is highly technical, is conducted at a very abstract level, and is resistant to an introductory condensation. But looking at verbal humor gets us into a position to question some of its results and assumptions. This may not be the only route to that position, but it certainly is one of the more enjoyable.

My first example is taken from the popular TV comedy show *Benson*. The following conversation takes place when Benson (B), a black man, is a guest at an otherwise all-white gathering, and is addressed by the hostess (A):

1   A: How do you like your coffee, black?
    B: Us niggers do have names, ma'am.

The example draws our attention to that much neglected phoneme (if phoneme it be) the *juncture* (the time gap between spoken words), and, in particular, to the way in which different *lengths* of pause determine different senses. Precious little work has been done on the semantic importance of the lengths of junctures in spoken English, yet an appreciation of the rules governing pauses is essential not just in odd cases of possible ambiguity, such as example (1), but for all speech performances, most prominently, for oral poetry. It may be natural to suppose, and many philosophical theorists of language have proposed, that the meaning of a sentence is composed wholly of the meanings of its constituent words. But (1) shows this to be false. Certainly 'black' may be a color adjective or a noun, but *which* sense it has in any particular utterance of (1) is determined by intonation and by the *length of pause* after 'coffee'. Any realistic theory of interpretation must recognize the contribution to sense of silence.

The point is not just that there are extra ingredients of meaning (such as silence) that have to be added to the meanings of the words in a sentence if we are to grasp the meaning of the whole. Rather it is the conception that the meaning of a sentence is composed of parts which have meaning in isolation that needs to be questioned. Of course, in some sense, isolated words have meaning (otherwise there wouldn't be any dictionaries), but we may still resist the idea that these word-meanings function as building-blocks. A sentence can be dissected into words, but it does not follow that the meaning of a sentence can be split into meaning-parts. Similarly, a knight's move in chess can be described as consisting of two movements, one at right angles to the other; but the making of a knight's move cannot be divided into parts – you can't make half of a knight's move. We can be creative in our use of language, imposing new or extended roles for words, not only by stipulating definitions, but also by producing sentences that make sense only if the 'standard' meanings of some of the component words are distorted or extended a little. Such conceptual innovation is intelligible to all competent speakers, but would be impossible to achieve if we were limited to constructions built from a stock of fixed 'meaning-parts'.

Let us turn now to *ambiguity*, the exploitation of which is a familiar humorous device. The resources of traditional grammar are sufficient to disambiguate both (2) Eighth Army push bottles up Germans and (3) Women lay preachers at Vatican council. A simple analysis employing modern linguistic theory reveals the two senses of (4) Boy wanted to kill the Queen. (Although, to fully appreciate the joke, one also needs to know something about a tradition of placing advertisements offering menial part-time jobs for schoolchildren.) Further, since G. Frege's invention of the theory of quantification in 1879 (when, according to W. Quine, logic changed from being a good subject to being a great one) logicians have had a notation for laying bare the different senses of sentences such as (5) I thought your boat was longer than it is (to which Bertrand Russell replied 'It's exactly as long as itself'). Consider, however, the next two sentences: (6) A headmaster has said that a pupil will be killed unless something is done about road safety provision around his school. (7) I can get as much sexual satisfaction as I want just by snapping my fingers.

Both of these are ambiguous (the rich old widow who utters (7) may be reporting a peculiar orgasmic technique, or boasting of her ability to summon a stud from the adjoining room), but no lexical ambiguity is present. The ambiguity of (6) may be illustrated by a linguistic analysis (which would show that the verb 'to kill' could occur in either the active or the passive voice) but no such analysis would reveal the ambiguity of (7). Nor does it seem likely that the possibility of an active or a passive occurrence of 'will be killed' explains our perception of the ambiguity in (6). Our perception of the ambiguity in both cases depends on our knowledge of *certain facts about the world*, and our discerning the correct interpretation for any particular utterance of either sentence demands a sensitivity to the context in which that utterance is made.

The point of the joke, in example (6) is that, although the headmaster was probably making a *prediction*, he could be construed as making a *threat*. The difference does not show up phonologically, since *the speaker* is neither making a prediction nor issuing a threat. When we read sentence (6) in a newspaper, we know that the headmaster is predicting, possibly protesting or warning, but not threatening a life. On the other hand, when we read 'The terrorists have said that a passenger will be killed unless their demands are met', we naturally interpret this as report of a threat. That we interpret the two syntactically similar reports as reports of *different* acts of speech is due to what we know about teachers and terrorists, that is, it is due to *extra-linguistic* knowledge. We know that terrorists, being what they are, mean their 'killed' as 'killed deliberately by us', whereas the headmaster means 'killed accidentally, by a vehicle'. It is not that the word 'killed' has these two meanings (literal or dictionary meanings); rather, it is *speakers* who may intend to express different thoughts. This seems, again, to illustrate that there is more to meaning than can be found in a dictionary. Speakers frequently rely on knowledge and/or experiences shared with their particular audiences in order to get their messages across.

Meaning may also depend on images and association. When a couple of German acquaintances and I were driving in Bavaria, we passed through a village and spotted an amazingly tiny church. 'That's a church for dwarfs', I said, hinting that here was evidence of affirmative action in favor of a neglected minority. Simultaneously, and much more wittily, one of my companions remarked (8) That's a church for beginners. The joke depends on forging a semantic link between 'small' – brought to mind by the visual experience – and 'beginner'. Had I failed to make this connection, my companion's remark would have made little sense to me. For similar reasons, the meaning of this graffito is quite clear, even though one of the constituent words has no meaning:

9   Be alert.
     What this country needs is more lerts.

The connection between 'lert' and at least some of 'lout', 'nerd', 'layabout' 'inert' and (in British English) 'berk' would be apparent to fluent speakers of English who would immediately recognize that lerts are just what the country *doesn't* need since lerts, in general, lack alertness (and most other desirable properties).

Now, it is a fact that we understand the point of (6)–(9), but how is this fact to be explained? Traditional semantics views meaning as a relation between words and the world – it is in virtue of how the world is (independently of us) that words, and larger slices of discourse, mean what they do. Such a theory, of course, cannot account for the meaning of a sentence that contains a meaningless component. It is because of the sound-associations of the word 'lert' that speakers – all competent speakers of English – can understand (9). It is because of meaning-associations that we can understand the point of (8). 'Small' and 'beginner' are linked by a (fairly short) semantic chain. And it is a chain that we humans forge. The class of beginners overlaps with the class of small things, but in a quite uninteresting way. Yet *we* see the connection between 'small' and 'beginner' as being fairly intimate. The intimacy is *our* contrivance.

Thus the meanings of our words and sentences are not dictated by how the world is, but are determined by the ways that we experience the world, by the ways that we find it natural or useful to group and arrange our perceptions. To cite a couple of famous examples of Wittgenstein (*Philosophical Investigations*, sections 65 and 66), what we call *games* are a whole host of activities; it's not that they all share a set of 'objective' properties, but if we are impressed by similarities between Activity 1 and Activity 2, and by different similarities between Activity 2 and Activity 3, we may choose to call them all games, even though Activity 1 and Activity 3 have no similarities. Again, the word 'number' was originally used to denote what we should now call the positive integers. It is a matter of human decision that we 'extend' the word to cover the negatives, fractions, irrationals, and imaginaries.

Wittgenstein was the first person to have seen that language is woven into the world and is the product of (what he called) our 'forms of life.' Whereas in his first book the *Tractatus Logico-Philosophicus* Wittgenstein had regarded the structure of language merely as a *reflection* of the world, and individual statements as *pictures*, this perspective was dramatically inverted in his later writings. Here Wittgenstein insists that language is shaped by the activities in which humans engage, and by our agreements in perceptual judgements, presumably the result of our biological similarities. The first linguist to have seen the importance of these views and to have developed them systematically is George Lakoff. Lakoff's first paper on this theme was published in 1977, and his research has culminated in an iconoclastic book enticingly entitled *Women, Fire and Dangerous Things*. One of his collaborators, Mark Johnson, has recently published a work very much in the same mold, called *The Body in the Mind*.

In his early manifesto, Lakoff declares that the basic claim of what he then called 'experiential linguistics' is this: 'A wide variety of experiential factors – perception, reasoning, the nature of the body, the emotions, memory, social structure, sensorimotor and cognitive development, etc. – determine in large measure, if not totally, universal structural characteristics of language' ('Linguistic gestalts', p. 237). Lakoff holds that all universals of language follow from, or are special cases of, other facts about the mind and body.

In *Women, Fire and Dangerous Things* Lakoff sets himself in opposition to what he describes as 'the most fundamental assumption on which Noam Chomsky's theory of language rests', namely the assumption that grammar is independent from the rest of cognition. As an illustration, Lakoff conducts a 'case study' (occupying 122 pages) in which he tries to show that the 'cognitive grammar' he advocates can explain the relationship (that earlier theories could not explain) between existential and deictic (presentational) *there*-constructions. As a particular example, consider that, when you have a knee injury that is acting up, you can say either of the following:

There goes the pain in my knee
There goes my knee

but, when one senses that one's knee is *about to* act up, one can say

Here comes the pain in my knee

but not

*Here comes my knee.

Lakoff's explanation is:

THE THING PERCEIVED STANDS FOR THE PERCEPT WHILE THE PERCEPTION IS IN PROGRESS – so that when the perception is not in progress, that is, before the pain comes on, the description of the *site* of the pain cannot be substituted for the description of the pain. He claims that this formulation 'does not merely account for the linguistic facts. It is also an account of what we normally *do* when we perceive – that is, we take our percepts as actual things that give rise to our perceptions.' (*Women Fire and Dangerous Things*, p. 516).

I mention this example to give just a flavor of the kind of explanations that a 'cognitive grammar' proposes. You will notice that, quite unlike other linguistic theories, cognitive grammar offers explanations that make essential reference to the ways in which we experience the world. The theory casts light upon the question of what it is about the examples we have cited that makes them humorous. There are still recalcitrant phenomena, however. Consider the Irishman in jail who requests, as a treat, a packet of tampons because (10) 'It says on the packet that you can swim in them, ski in them, even parachute in them.' The Irishman has understood 'in' as 'inside', and envisages a whole new miniature sporting life within his prison cell, whereas we, possessing more knowledge of tampons than he, interpret 'in them', in (10) as 'with them in'. Now, what determines the cases in which the phrases 'with them in' or 'with them on' can be shortened to 'in'? We *do* say 'You can swim in these contact lenses', and 'You can swim in those shoes', but we don't say 'You can swim in this hearing aid' or 'You can swim in that artificial limb'. Nothing I have read in Lakoff helps to explain this joke, nor does it seem to be touched by Johnson's extensive discussion of 'in' and the containment metaphor. I cannot yet see what facts about our cognition could begin to explain the linguistic data.

I want to mention, very briefly, two further sorts of cases of humor where trying to explain what is funny leads us into interesting reflections about language. The first case involves people *suggesting* things by what they say, without saying them explicitly. Suppose, for example, that I have been asked to supply a confidential report on my student Trixie, who wants to go on to do graduate work in astrophysics. I write as my report (11) Trixie is always clean, and she spells her name accurately. Now, (11) doesn't *say* that I don't think that Trixie is cut out for the kind of graduate work she envisages, but anyone who reads it will get the message. So there must be common knowledge of what H. P. Grice (who pioneered this kind of study) calls 'maxims' governing verbal exchanges and of how these maxims may be deliberately flouted in order to convey more than what we say. It turns out, upon investigation, that this code which underlies conversation is extremely intricate and subtle. It takes a good humorist to exploit it fully.

The second case involves contradiction and what I shall call 'quasi-contradiction'. A contradiction is the conjunction of a statement and the negation of that statement. A quasi-contradiction doesn't necessarily have this strict form, but involves the same kind of giving with one hand and taking back with the other. Examples of this abound in verbal humor:

12 Mrs Maggie Backhouse looking calm but tense at the end of her husband's trial.

13 Mr Kenneth Aylott, for Dearman, said to the jury that they may find the films 'Dirty, lewd, indecent, shocking, repulsive, revolting, outrageous, utterly disgusting or filthy', but added that those feelings would not mean that the videos were obscene.

14 'Mumsey, tell me about weird love', begged Harry.

15 The dead man was described as white, aged between 30 and 40 with a southern accent.

16 I'm about to have a previous engagement.

Why are contradictions and quasi-contradictions funny? It can't be just because they are false, since there's nothing quintessentially funny about being false. Perhaps the answer is that someone who utters a contradiction in all seriousness doesn't even succeed in saying something false, but only exhibits floundering confusion, a failure to communicate any thought that we can grasp and act on. We, unsympathetically, find that sort of handicap amusing. No less a philosopher than Wittgenstein believed that contradictions are not false, but people in general (myself not included) would regard this as the ultimate semantical heresy.

Notes

There is a considerable psychological literature on humor. I'll just mention P. McGhee, *Humor* (San Francisco, W. H. Freeman and Co., 1979).

The philosophical literature is fairly sparse. Traditional and contemporary theories of laughter and humor are collected in J. Morreall (ed.), *The Philosophy of Laughter and Humor* (Albany: SUNY Press, 1987). The only other item I would recommend is T. Cohen, 'Jokes' in E. Schaper (ed.), *Pleasure, Preference and Values: Studies in*

Philosophy of language and logic

Philosophical Aesthetics (Cambridge: Cambridge University Press, 1983), pp. 120-36.

I mentioned Michael Dummett: the reference is *The Interpretation of Frege's Philosophy* (London: Duckworth, 1981), especially chapters 3 and 5; and my reference to Alfred Tarski is 'The semantic conception of truth', in H. Feigl and W. Sellars (eds), *Readings in Philosophical Analysis* (New York: Appleton Century Crofts, 1949) pp. 52-84.

There are several introductory texts in the philosophy of language. The one I like best is M. Devitt and K. Sterelny, *Language and Reality* (Oxford: Blackwell, 1987). Another introductory text which, to my mind, is good but somewhat demanding is S. Blackburn, *Spreading the Word* (Oxford: Clarendon Press, 1984), esp. chapters 2-4.

A hard-hitting, even bombastic, often humorous attack on recent work by philosophers and linguists in the theory of meaning is mounted by G. P. Baker and P. M. S. Hacker, *Language, Sense and Nonsense* (Oxford: Blackwell, 1984).

Wittgenstein's early and late period writings are represented respectively by L. Wittgenstein, *Tractatus Logico-Philosophicus* (London: Routledge & Kegan Paul, 1961), and originally published in 1922, *Philosophical Investigations* (Oxford: Blackwell, 1953).

For 'cognitive grammar', see G. Lakoff, 'Linguistic gestalts', *Chicago Linguistic Society Papers* 13 (1977), 236-87 (but only the first few sections are essential); Lakoff, *Women, Fire and Dangerous Things* (Chicago: University of Chicago Press, 1986); M. Johnson, *The Body in the Mind* (Chicago; University of Chicago Press, 1987).

H. P. Grice's theory of 'conversational implicature' was presented over twenty years ago as a series of William James Lectures at Harvard University, but remains unpublished. A short excerpt is available: H. P. Grice, 'Logic and conversation' in P. Cole and J. Morgan (eds), *Syntax and Semantics, Vol. 3: Speech Acts* (New York: Academic Press, 1975), pp. 41-59.

Questions

1 The claim 'Speaking a language is a rule-governed activity' trips lightly off the tongue, but in what sense (if any) is it true? It has been denied by Paul Ziff, who in *Semantic Analysis* (Ithaca, Cornell University Press, 1960), pp. 34-5, writes, 'Rules have virtually nothing to do with speaking or understanding a natural language . . . . An appeal to rules in the course of discussing the regularities to be found in a natural language is as irrelevant as an appeal to the laws of Massachusetts while discussing the laws of motion.' G. Baker and P. Hacker (*Language, Sense and Nonsense*) have a chapter entitled 'The mythology of rules'.

2 Humpty Dumpty says that he can mean by a word whatever he chooses. Now, it is quite true that in humor, or in the creation of metaphor, we often use words in non-standard ways. Is this a matter of

extending the literal meaning of words? Donald Davidson says 'No'. In a paper entitled 'What metaphors mean', reprinted in his *Inquiries into Truth and Interpretation* (Oxford: Clarendon Press, 1984), pp. 245-64 he asserts that 'metaphors mean what the words, in their most literal interpretations, mean, and nothing more'. For criticisms of Davidson see J. M. Soskice, *Metaphor and Religious Language* (Oxford: Clarendon Press, 1985) and E. F. Kittay, *Metaphor: Its Cognitive Force and Linguistic Structure* (Oxford: Clarendon Press, 1987). Davidson's theory receives an extended defence in D. E. Cooper, *Metaphor* (Oxford: Blackwell, 1986).

3 (Continuing with Humpty Dumpty and Donald Davidson.) We may share Alice's skepticism about the license to use words any way he fancies that Humpty Dumpty grants himself. Surely there are limits: there must be certain conventions that have to be respected if we are to successfully communicate with one another. Are conventions necessary for linguistic communication? Davidson tackles this question in his essay, 'Communication and convention', in *Inquiries* (pp. 265-80). Chapter 4 of S. Blackburn (*Spreading the Word*) is very useful, as is R. M. Martin, *The Meaning of Language* (Cambridge, Mass.: MIT Press, 1987), chapter 8. Almost certainly, in working on this and the previous question, you will begin to encounter what P. F. Strawson in 'Meaning and truth', reprinted in his *Logico-Linguistic Papers* (London: Methuen, 1971), pp. 170-89, calls a 'Homeric Struggle' over meaning. One of the classical sources of hostilities is H. P. Grice, 'Meaning', *Philosophical Review* 66 (1957), 377-88, reprinted in many places including the following useful collections: P. F. Strawson (ed.), *Philosophical Logic* (Oxford: Oxford University Press, 1967); D. D. Steinberg and L. A. Jakobovits (eds.), *Semantics* (Cambridge, Cambridge University Press, 1971); F. Zabeeh, E. D. Klemke, and A. Jacobson (eds.), *Readings in Semantics* (Urbana: University of Illinois Press, 1974).

Chapter six

Speaking your mother tongue: nature or nurture?

Are our talents and defects innate (inborn), or are they nurtured (encouraged to develop) after birth? In the case of physical abilities, the answer seems to be 'both'. No amount of training will make you an Olympic 100-metre champion if you don't have the right kind of body to begin with. Conversely, if you are naturally endowed with a fine, well-proportioned body, you will not get to be Olympic champion unless you train hard to improve it.

What about our mental abilities? The popular theory used to be that the *intelligence* of an individual changes little throughout most of that person's life, and is something that cannot be nurtured. On the other hand, it seems that *memory* is something that can be improved by practice. Everyone reading this book has *linguistic* ability. Is this an innate capacity? What I mean by this question is, 'Are we born possessing a certain part of a brain which is structured specifically for the mastery of language?' Does the human brain have an inbuilt biological program for language or does the brain gradually adapt to the task of language-mastery after one becomes a member of a language-using community? We saw, in the previous chapter, that George Lakoff opts for the latter alternative.

Like many animals, humans have the ability to make vocal sounds, but the ability to speak anything more than the most rudimentary language appears to be limited to the human species. Children who were abandoned as infants and survived for a long time either on their own or in the company of wild animals (there are several famous cases) do not succeed in readily acquiring a language. This may suggest to you that language cannot be innate. Also, it may seem obvious that whatever we learn, we can learn only from *experience*. So the idea that we possess some linguistic ability prior to the having of any experiences may strike you as ridiculous.

Yet think how quickly normal children acquire their first language. When you consider it, this is an astonishing feat. Imagine that you are listening to an audio tape of some strange language played at high speed. It would seem to you just a bewildering barrage of sound. And this is something like adult speech must appear to a baby. But, after a short time, the infant learns how to partition that sound into significant segments. And even though much of what the child hears from the speakers in its environment is ungrammatical snatches, in a short while it can create complete, original, grammatical sentences of its own.

Noam Chomsky concluded from such facts that humans must be innately endowed with some knowledge of certain fundamental rules of language. If we look at the linguistic development of children, and, in particular, at the various linguistic stages through which children pass on the way to achieving the ability to construct perfectly grammatical sentences, then the hypothesis that children are genetically predetermined to follow a certain pattern of language-acquisition looks attractive.

Chomsky did not, of course, claim that a new-born baby possesses the rules of a *particular* natural language, such as Vietnamese or German. A Vietnamese orphan baby raised by German-speakers will learn German, not Vietnamese. What Chomsky claimed was that *all* natural languages have some underlying features in common – these are termed *linguistic universals*. If such characteristics common to all languages are discovered, then this again points in the direction of the hypothesis that all humans have specific neural structures that account for these universals.

However, as I mentioned, the idea that there are innate language-specific structures is problematic, and the claim that there are linguistic universals realized in such structures has come in for a lot of criticism. One objection is that it is a trivial truth that there is likely to be *some* difference between the brain of a creature with the capacity for language-acquisition and the brain of a creature without this capacity. But it is hard to formulate a more 'meaty' and testable hypothesis about a language-specific device for, as we saw in the previous chapter, it is difficult to disentangle first-language learning from a wide range of general cognitive skills. Another objection – quite a subtle one – is that certain features that a theorist might claim are universal may not actually be present in the language that is being discussed, but may be present only in *translations* of that language into the language in which the discussion is being conducted.

The debate between opponents and proponents of innate

principles has gone on for several centuries, and Chomsky's views on the innate component in language-acquisition have been hotly contested for the past twenty years or more. Of course, if a neurophysiologist were to discover within the brain a language-acquisition device, the issue would be settled in favor of Chomsky. But up till now, no such device has been found, and it is not even clear how we should go about looking for one. However, two recent research projects seem to provide strong evidence for the hypothesis that humans possess certain inborn language mechanisms.

The first, reported by Peter D. Eimas in the *Scientific American*, January 1985, shows how infants who are just a few weeks old recognize sound changes that are phonemically significant, while ignoring other acoustic variations in speech. That is to say that the children are equipped to notice those differences in sound that make for differences in meaning between spoken words long before they know the meanings of any words.

For example, the fact that we can perceive the difference between the plosives /b/ and /p/ is crucial for our being able to discriminate the words 'ba' and 'pa', 'bai' and 'pai' when we hear them spoken in Putonghua, or the words 'bin' and 'pin', 'bet' and 'pet' when spoken in English. Now, a major difference between the /b/ and /p/ sounds is that the latter is *aspirated* – a puff of air is released prior to the voicing of the next sound. So, in making the sound /pa/, the *voice-onset time* (the time between the release of the lips and the onset of vocal cord vibration) is in excess of 30 milliseconds.

It was discovered that, although the infants did not notice differences between pairs of sounds with voice-onset times ranging from 0 to 20 milliseconds, nor between pairs of sounds with voice-onset times ranging from 40 to 70 milliseconds, they *did* notice a difference between two sounds with voice-onset times falling on opposite sides of the 30 millisecond barrier. The infant, it seems, naturally recognizes sounds with voice-onset times of less than 30 milliseconds as belonging to a different *category* from those sounds with voice-onset times of greater than 30 milliseconds.

P. Eimas concludes that this category-recognition ability is innate. He writes:

It is difficult to see how learning could account for the mode of perception we have demonstrated in infants. What events during the first few weeks of life would train an infant to respond categorically to gradations of acoustic properties? A simpler view is that categorization occurs because a child is born with perceptual mechanisms that are tuned to the properties of speech. These mechanisms yield the forerunners of the phonemic categories that later will enable the child unthinkingly to convert the variable signal of speech into a series of phonemes and thence into words and meanings. (p. 37)

Eimas' argument looks persuasive, but a couple of queries might be raised. First, if, as recent research seems to show, we make categorical discriminations between auditory sounds in general (i.e., not just between speech sounds) then the case for an innate biological mechanism for speech is less strongly sustained by Eimas' evidence. Second, we should acknowledge the possibility of an alternative explanation of the voice-onset time data. The parallel distributed processing computer models now available would predict that a child could *learn to* recognize certain sound differences and to ignore others, given relevant exposure in early infancy. Even if Eimas is right, however, we should still be a long way from confirming the hypothesis that there is an innate mechanism for *grammar* – although establishing that there is an innate mechanism for speech perception might make the postulation of other language-specific devices more palatable.

The second source of recent support for Chomsky's view is a paper by the linguist Derek Bickerton called 'The language bioprogram hypothesis'. Bickerton's speciality is pidgin and creole languages. A pidgin is a language that arises when speakers of different, mutually unintelligible, languages come together and need to communicate with each other. A creole is a language acquired by children as a first language in a pidgin-speaking environment. Now, although pidgins are very basic, rudimentary, languages, creole languages are relatively sophisticated, with grammars much more complex than those of the pidgins from which they arose. You might expect creoles to derive this complexity from the continuing influence of those languages native to the pidgin-speakers, and indeed such influence cannot generally be denied. Yet, under certain conditions, for example, when slaves originating from different parts of Africa escaped and formed 'maroon' communities, the linguistic input to children in those communities was almost exclusively pidgin – *but still they succeeded in developing creoles with grammars remarkably similar to that of other creoles.*

What Bickerton tries to establish is that the creation by children of creoles is most plausibly attributable to an innate, human species-specific genetic program for grammar. Bickerton's hypothesis is this: 'Creole languages are largely invented by children and show fundamental similarities, which derive from a biological program for language' (p. 173).

Pidgins, by definition, have no native speakers, and, if one thinks of the circumstances in which they emerge, it is easy to see why, in their early stages, they have sparse vocabularies and simple grammars. A creole, however, typically has a complexity of grammar that far outstrips that of the antecedent pidgin. There are several reasons for this. First, as a language develops from being a simple tool for trade into a means for general-purpose communication, it will of necessity become more sophisticated. Second, the original languages of speakers will continue to exert an influence, and subtleties of their grammar may be taken into the creole. Third, according to Bickerton's language bioprogram hypothesis (LBH), 'the innovative aspects of creole grammar are inventions on the part of the first generation of children who have pidgin as their linguistic input' (p. 173).

Bickerton's evidence for this last claim results from a comparison of the grammars of a number of different creoles. He claims that even though different creoles arose in geographically diverse areas and with quite different linguistic backgrounds, they strikingly share a set of *common* grammatical features. Since these features are not present in the antecedent pidgins, then, if the influence of the pre-existing languages can be discounted, a plausible explanation seems to be that it is contributed by the children in virtue of their possessing 'a species-specific program for language, genetically coded and expressed . . . in the structures and modes of operation of the human brain'. It is exactly such a modular, functionally specialized 'mental organ' that Chomsky posited to account for human linguistic competence.

The main burden of proof for the LBH lies, of course, in showing that the influence of pre-existing languages *can* be discounted. If there had been communities in which children exposed *only* to a simple pidgin had developed a sophisticated creole, then the case might be easily made, but, of course, no actual linguistic community conformed exactly to that specification. However, different communities had *differing* exposure to non-pidgin sources, and Bickerton rests his argument on a comparison of such linguistic communities.

In order, first, to establish that all, or most of, the grammar of a language can arise in just one generation, Bickerton draws on the last remaining *living* evidence of a pidgin and its creole descendant – the speech of Asians and others who settled in Hawaii in the period 1876–1920. The earliest adult immigrants spoke pidgin, and continued to do so even after the creole had evolved in the next generation. This shows that the grammatical structures in the creole must have been acquired by children. Bickerton points out that this is consistent with the 'critical period' view put forward by the psycholinguists E. Lenneberg and S. Krashen, according to which grammar acquisition is maturational.

Hawaiian pidgin possesses no consistent markers for tense, case, aspect, and modality, and lacks a consistent system of anaphora. By contrast, the creole possesses case and aspect markers, embedded sentential complements, relative clauses, ways of marking contrast or emphasis, and other grammatical features besides. Bickerton argues that the development of these innovative grammatical structures by the children of immigrants to Hawaii is typical of all pidgin-to-creole transitions.

The other creoles discussed by Bickerton are those that emerged in slave colonies in the period of European colonization from 1500 to 1900. At the beginning of the colonization process, masters would typically outnumber slaves, and the earliest slaves would acquire the dominant language (i.e. the language of the masters) as a second language. But then, as the size of a colony grew, new arrivals were trained by the early slaves. Since the languages of the new arrivals were diverse, the medium of instruction would be the slave-teachers' second-language version of the dominant language. One wonders why the slave-teachers did not use their own native language for teaching, so that that language would form the basis of a pidgin. The answer (although Bickerton doesn't address this point) may be that the old slaves did not have the right to communicate in a way that would be totally unintelligible to the bosses and, of course, part of the training included teaching new slaves to understand the orders of the slave-drivers.

In colonies where, for many years, the number of masters was greater than the number of slaves, one would expect the grammar of the emerging pidgin to resemble that of the dominant language. At the opposite extreme were those maroon communities consisting entirely of escaped slaves most of whom had been transported into slavery many years after the foundation of a colony – when the slaves far outnumbered the masters so that the influence of the dominant language was much diminished.

Such was the Saramaccan slave community founded in Surinam at around 1680. Theirs was a rudimentary pidgin so that the scope for linguistic development by the first generation of native Saramaccan speakers would have been great.

Bickerton sketches a meager core grammar which, so the bioprogram hypothesis suggests, is genetically encoded. He marshals impressive evidence which tends to show that Saramaccan syntax is indeed closest to this innate grammar and that the extent to which other creole grammars depart from this central core is directly related to the influence of a dominant language on their formation. This is exactly what the LBH would predict. Further, since, according to the hypothesis, all of us (not, of course, just creole speakers) are equipped with the bioprogram, then it should be the case that those features of our own first language which are also present in the bioprogram grammar should be learned most readily and unerringly. Again, the evidence seems to show that this is so.

Whether the LBH turns out ultimately to be right or wrong, it is apparent that Bickerton has provided a fascinating and testable view. His paper is heroic in the sense that it achieves a grand perspective by standing upon mountains of research done by historians, anthropologists, demographers, linguists, philosophers, and psychologists. It is noteworthy that these disciplines, which are normally classified as belonging to the 'Arts' or 'Humanities' or 'Social Sciences' should have so significant a contribution to make towards solving what is apparently a biological problem – the problem of discovering whether there is an innate mechanism with the specialized function of making possible the learning of our first language.

Notes

For a detailed account of the distinction between linguamental innate structures (those intrinsic to all mental activity) and modality-specific innate structures, e.g. those universals limited to language, consult the introduction to T. G. Bever, J. M. Carroll, L. A. Miller (eds), *Talking Minds* (Cambridge, Mass.: MIT Press, 1984).

Chomsky defends the innateness hypothesis in many writings, including *Aspects of the Theory of Syntax* (Cambridge, Mass.: MIT Press, 1965).

The two arguments I offered *against* linguistic universals derive from N. Goodman, *Of Mind and Other Matters* (Cambridge, Mass.: Harvard University Press, 1984), p. 16.

It has seemed to many linguists that study of the linguistic development of children reveals a stage-by-stage progression towards grammatical speech that is common to all normal children, and is best accounted for by the hypothesis that such a pattern is predetermined from birth. See N. Smith and D. Wilson, *Modern Linguistics: The Results of Chomsky's Revolution* (Harmondsworth: Penguin, 1979) chap. 1, esp. pp. 29-30.

The two papers I mentioned as providing new kinds of support for Chomsky's thesis are Peter D. Eimas, 'The perception of speech in early infancy', *Scientific American* 252/1 (January, 1985), 35-40; Derek Bickerton, 'The language bioprogram hypothesis', *The Behavioral and Brain Sciences* 7 (1984), 173-221, which includes 'Peer comment' and a reply by Bickerton. Critical discussions of Bickerton's work on the bioprogram are contained in P. Muysken and N. Smith (eds), *Substrata versus Universals in Creole Genesis* (Amsterdam: John Benjamins, 1986); P. Mühlhäusler, *Pidgin and Creole Linguistics* (Oxford: Blackwell, 1986). Other aspects of the study of pidgins and creoles – for example, semantic changes and the functioning of referential devices – are also highly relevant to the philosophy of language. As a useful, brief introduction to the field, I recommend J. Holm, *Pidgins and Creoles*, vol.1 (Cambridge: Cambridge University Press, 1988).

Questions

1 Does evidence about language-acquisition justify the postulation of innate ideas? See the 'Symposium on innate ideas', contributors N. Chomsky, H. Putnam, and N. Goodman in J. R. Searle (ed.), *The Philosophy of Language* (Oxford: Oxford University Press, 1971), pp. 121-44; R. M. Martin, *The Meaning of Language* (Cambridge, Mass.: MIT Press, 1987), pp. 29-32; F. D'Agostino, *Chomsky's System of Ideas* (Oxford: Clarendon Press, 1985), pp. 61-113; J. Samet, 'Troubles with Fodor's Nativism', *Midwest Studies in Philosophy X* (1986), 575-94.

2 Bickerton seems to suppose that a bioprogram grammar can account for the linguistic competence of creole speakers. But can a grammar explain competence? There is an extensive discussion of this question in M. Devitt and K. Sterelny, *Language and Reality* (Oxford: Blackwell, 1987), pp. 130-54. The issue is also broached by S. Soames, 'Linguistics and psychology', *Linguistics and Philosophy* 7 (1984), 155-79. Chomsky has a brief discussion of Soames in Chomsky, *Knowledge of Language: It's Nature, Origin and Use* (New York: Praeger, 1986), pp. 34-6.

3 A version of the 'nurture' position on the acquisition of *semantic* ability is neatly formulated by Paul Feyerabend: 'Little children learn a language by attending to noises which, being repeated in suitable surroundings, gradually assume meaning' (P. K. Feyerabend, 'Putnam on incommensurability', *British Journal for the Philosophy of Science* 38/1 (March 1987), 75-81, see 79). Observations of the development of gestural and linguistic performances in infants seem to support this view:

'There was no single moment when the performative structures could be said to "sprout" propositions. Instead, words as symbolic vehicles with corresponding referents emerged gradually out of the action schemes of sensorimotor communication' (E. Bates, L. Camaioni, and V. Volterra, 'The acquisition of performatives prior to speech', in E. Ochs and B. B. Schieffelin (eds), *Developmental Pragmatics* (New York: Academic Press, 1979), p. 125.) The idea that meanings are *gradually* acquired may seem attractive, but does it withstand scrutiny? When infants begin to produce the sound 'mama' as a means of demanding sustenance, can they be said to have *partially* acquired the meaning of the word 'mama'? Is there a 'half-way stage' between a child's not understanding and understanding the meaning of 'wait'? For a further defence of gradualism, see E. Clark, 'Some aspects of the conceptual basis for first language acquisition', in Clark, *The Ontogenesis of Meaning* (Wiesbaden: Athenaion, 1979), pp. 63-88.

Chapter seven

This statement is false

There is a paradox which has given me many sleepless nights and which apparently had the same effect on Philetas of Cos, judging by his epitaph:

> Philetas of Cos am I
> 'Twas the Liar who made me die
> And the bad nights caused thereby.

The Liar paradox, to which this ancient Greek insomniac was referring, comes in many forms, one of which serves as the title of the present chapter. In order to see what's puzzling about the statement 'This statement is false', just ask yourself whether it is true or false. If it's true, then what it says is true; but what it says is that it is false, so it is false. But, on the other hand, if it is false, then the situation is just as the statement describes, for it says that it is false; but when any situation is just as a statement describes it as being, then that statement is *true*. In short, if the statement is false, then it is true and (as we've already shown) if it is true then it is false.

Peculiar. You may well think that a statement has to be either true or false yet, in the case of the Liar statement, if it's one then it's the other – but surely it can't be *both* true and false. This crazy result is characteristic of paradoxes. A paradox is a piece of reasoning in which one starts from a perfectly innocuous assumption but ends up with a conclusion that is obviously absurd. Usually, the steps in the reasoning are simple and seem quite acceptable yet, since they lead you to an *unacceptable* conclusion, something must be wrong somewhere. The difficulty lies in finding out just what has gone wrong and, for a number of paradoxes, this difficulty has been thought by many people to be insuperable – hence the term 'insolubilia' (unsolvables) used by medieval writers. Paradoxes are not 'trick' arguments; they have defied the attempts of extremely clever people to solve them. So it is highly likely that a correct solution will bring to light some very fundamental errors in our ways of thinking.

There are many versions or variants of the Liar and, of course, no solution of the paradox is adequate unless it applies to all manifestations. To bring out the flavor of the Liar, I shall mention some of these versions. First, one due to Albert of Saxony (1316–1390), involves 'indirect' self-reference:

The statement below is false.
The above statement is true.

Unlike the standard version, where a statement refers to itself, here one statement refers to another, which latter refers back to it. In order to see the paradoxicality involved, it's easiest to consider whether the lower statement is true or false.

The next version I adopt from the tenth problem in chapter 8 of Jean Buridan's (1300–1358) beautiful tract *Sophismata*.

Horses are animals.
2 + 2 = 4.
Pigs can fly.
Of the four statements here, two are true and two are false.
(G. E. Hughes (ed.), *Sophisms on Meaning and Truth*, p. 57)

If the last of these four statements is true, then the true statements outnumber the false by three to one, hence the last statement is false. But if it is false then there are two true statements (the first two) and two false ones (the last two) – just as the last statement claims. So that statement is true. (Given that the first two statements are true and the third false, the fourth statement, in saying that there are two false statements , is implicitly claiming that it itself is false. That's why it's correct to call this paradox a version of the Liar.)

Another amusing version is the following:

There are threee errors in this senntence

Look carefully. You'll find two spelling errors, so you might think that the statement is false. But being false is another kind of error, so the statement is true. Yet, if it's true, then there is not the third error of falsity, but just the two spelling errors. So the statement is false. . . .

How should we go about solving the Liar paradox ? Let us consider a version for which the reasoning can be set out most clearly. We want, to begin with, a statement that says of itself that is not true. That's easy to arrange. Statements, like people and planets, can be given names, so I'm going to give the name

'Martin Seattle' (just 'Martin' to its friends) to the statement that Martin Seattle is not true. Therefore, in the friendly version of the paradox, we have

1 'Martin' is the name of the statement that Martin is not true.

In order to find out whether Martin is true or not true we have to ask whether the statement with that name (i.e. 'Martin is not true') is true or not true. Is Martin true ? Well, Martin is true if, as we have noted, the statement called 'Martin' is true, that is,

2 Martin is true if 'Martin is not true' is true.

Now, to say that it's true that a statement is not true is to say that that statement is not true. So, from 2, we obtain

3 Martin is true if Martin is not true.

That doesn't seem very promising. Let's look again at 1 and ask whether Martin is *not* true. We obtain

4 Martin is not true if 'Martin is not true' is not true.

Now, to say that it's not true that a statement is not true is to say that that statement is true. So, from 4, we obtain

5 Martin is not true if Martin is true.

Putting 3 and 5 together, we get

6 Martin is true if and only if Martin is not true.

and this is bad news in anybody's language. It's quite absurd to say that some statement is true if and only if it isn't.

There is an alternative and even quicker way of getting to this absurdity if we accept a criterion for the adequacy of any definition of truth that was proposed by Alfred Tarski in a seminal paper of modern logic. Tarski suggested that whatever theory of truth you propose it must, for any sentence *p*, and any name or description of that sentence S, entail the following:

S is true if and only if *p*

For what could be a simpler truth about truth than that? Now substitute 'Martin' for 'S' in that formula, and for *p* substitute the sentence of which Martin is the name, and you obtain the equivalent of 6.

You can easily see why this version of the Liar fits my characterization of a paradox. We started out from the reasonable assumption that our statement, Martin, was either true or not true, but quickly ended up with the absurd conclusion that it is true if and only if it is not.

At this stage, it might be a good idea for you to sit back and think how you would solve the problem. When you have done so, go on to the next section where I'll review some attempted solutions (including, probably, yours) and try to say why they're no good.

One reaction to the paradox is to protest that Liar statements like Martin just don't make sense, because statements cannot refer to themselves. This protest is out of order: lots of statements refer to themselves with complete propriety, for example 'This statement is in English', 'This statement is not very interesting', and 'This statement refers to itself'. Also, as we have already seen with 'indirect' versions, the paradox doesn't require a statement to refer to itself; we can have it refer to *another* statement, and there's surely nothing wrong in that. We often say things like 'What you just said is not true'.

Another attempted solution, this time a very famous one, is set out in Tarski's chapter mentioned above. The suggestion is, in effect, that the transitions from 2 to 3 and from 4 to 5 are invalid because the word 'true' in the statement being spoken about has a different meaning from that of the word 'true' in the statement speaking about it. So the cancelling laws

'p is not true' is true = 'p is not true' and
'p is not true' is not true = 'p is true'

do not apply. It has to be said that this proposal does block the paradox reasoning, yet it is unsatisfactorily *ad hoc*. If you say 'It's not true that it's not true that rabies is contagious', and I reply 'That's true', there doesn't seem any good reason on earth for saying that my 'true' means something different from yours.

A different kind of proposed solution contends that our assumption that the Liar statement is true or not true is incorrect. The suggestion is that Liar statements are *neither* true nor not true. Now, this proposal is not completely *ad hoc*, since there are many kinds of statement that, it could seriously be claimed, have no truth value. For example, the statement 'The man in the moon likes cakes' presupposes that there is a man in the moon. Since this presupposition is false, the statement is neither true nor not true. (More austerely, you might say that it isn't a statement at all.) Again, a *vague* statement like 'France is hexagonal' isn't clearly true nor not true. Or again, you might say that the statement 'The number three rides a horse' has no truth value, since the number three doesn't belong in the category of things that ride or don't ride horses. However, what reason could we have for saying that Martin is neither true nor not true ? The statement 'Martin is not true' makes no false presuppositions, it is not in the least vague, its subject is a statement (Martin) and it is precisely to members of this category that the predicates 'is true' and 'is not true' apply. So it is no solution to claim that Martin is neither true nor not true, at least, not without some further reason.

Finally, to illustrate the desperate extremities to which the Liar has driven some people, a number of modern writers have been prepared to accept all of the reasoning within the paradox, and thus to accept the conclusion that certain statements like Martin are *both* true *and* not true. That is not so outrageous as it may first seem. After all, before the discovery of transfinite numbers, who would have thought that the number of points on a 1 cm line is equal to the number of points on a 2 cm line? And, if we have a surface painted half red, half green, is it too outrageous to say that the color of the *boundary* is *both* red and green? Nevertheless, I think that we should entertain this proposed solution to the Liar only if all else fails. It simply seems a crude distortion of our concept of *truth* to allow that a statement can be true and, at the same time, not true.

My own view is that there is a mistake in the paradox reasoning, and that it occurs at the very beginning. In 1 we stipulated that 'Martin' is to be the name of the statement that Martin is not true. But are we empowered to make such a stipulation? We have attempted to *identify* Martin with the statement 'Martin is not true'. If they *are* identical then one is true if and only if the other is, that is,

Martin is true if and only if 'Martin is not true' is true

that is,

Martin is true if and only if Martin is not true

which is a contradiction. Since our identity claim led to a contradiction, that claim must be rejected. (This type of argument is called *reductio ad absurdum*. We shall be encountering it again in chapter 21.) So line 1 in our reasoning about Martin is false.

Needless to say, this is only the beginning of a long story. However, rather than pursue it here, I want to mention briefly another group of paradoxes very similar to those in the Liar family. The earliest paradox in this group derives from St Paul's epistle to Titus. St Paul mentions a Cretan who confessed to him that all Cretans are Liars. The Cretan in question is called Epimenides, and if we construe Epimenides as saying

7   All statements made by Cretans are not true

then the obvious question is whether statement 7 which is, after all, made by a Cretan, is true or false. The answer looks easy: 7 cannot be true because it says that all Cretan statements (including 7 itself) are not true. So 7 is not true. But that's not the end of the matter. Since 7 is not true, it follows that some statements made by Cretans are true. And since, as we've seen, 7 can't be true, it must be some *other* Cretan statement or statements that are true. We seem to have shown by pure logic that, so long as Epimenides actually made the remark attributed to him, some other statement must have been made by a Cretan.

If you don't find that surprising, consider the following related example. (The reasoning in this one is a bit brain-bending, so tackle it only when you're in the mood.)

A courthouse drama: A policeman goes to the witness box and testifies

8   Everything the prisoner says is false.

Then the prisoner takes the stand and swears

9   Something which the policeman testifies is true.

If 8 is true, then 9 is false (because 9 is one of the things that the prisoner says) and this means that nothing that the policeman says is true, so, in particular, 8 is not true. In other words, it's not true that everything the prisoner says is false – and that's the same as saying that *something said by the prisoner is true*. Now, 9 is one of the things said by the prisoner, and it is either false or true. If it's false, then it follows from the italicized result that the prisoner must have made some statement *other than* 9. On the other hand, if 9 is true, what that says is that something said by the policeman is true. But that something must be some statement *other than* 8 for, given that 9 is true, then 8 must be false (since 9 is one of the statements referred to in 8). Either way, something other than 8 or 9 must have been said. We seem to have shown, by pure logic alone, that statements 8 and 9 could not have been made unless at least *three* statements had been made by the participants in this drama. Yet, as Arthur Prior observed, 'it does not seem *logically* impossible that the policeman and the prisoner should make the assertions mentioned and no others (the court house having been bombed immediately afterwards, say)'

Can Prior's worry be allayed ? One possible response might be worked out by first considering this question: If I say to you

10   Your next statement will be false

and then you immediately drop down dead without saying a word, is my utterance of 10, true, false, or neither?

Notes

The epitaph of Philetas, a translation from the Greek by St George Stock, is cited in B. Mates, *Elementary Logic* (Oxford: Oxford University Press, 1965), p. 206.

J. Buridan's *Sophismata* is packed with instructive examples: see G. E. Hughes (ed.), *John Buridan on Self-Reference* (Cambridge: Cambridge University Press, (1982). An excellent translation of the relevant chapter is in G. E. Hughes (ed.), *Sophisms on Meaning and Truth* (Cambridge: Cambridge University Press, 1982).

There are some decent surveys of different types of attempted solution to the Liar in J. L. Mackie, *Truth, Probability and Paradox* (Oxford: Clarendon Press, 1973), pp. 237-301, and S. Haack, *Philosophy of Logics* (Cambridge: Cambridge University Press, 1978), pp. 135-51.

The 'seminal paper of modern logic' I mentioned is A. Tarski, 'The concept of truth in formalized languages' in his *Logic, Semantics and Metamathematics* (Oxford: Clarendon Press, 1956), pp. 152-278. This paper is really tough. For a simpler, more informal presentation of the material, see A. Tarski, 'The semantic conception of truth' in H. Feigl and W. Sellars (eds), *Readings in Philosophical Analysis* (New York: Appleton-Century-Crofts, 1949), pp. 52-84.

My own solution is worked out in a sheaf of papers, and I'll take the liberty of mentioning three short ones: L. Goldstein, 'The paradox of the Liar – a case of mistaken identity', *Analysis* 45 (1985), 9-13; 'Epimenides and Curry', *Analysis* 46 (1986); 'False stipulation and semantical paradox', *Analysis* 46 (1986).

The background to the Epimenides paradox is described in A.R. Anderson's introduction to R. L. Martin (ed.), *The Paradox of the Liar*, 2nd edn. (Reseda: Ridgeview, 1978), which has a fairly extensive bibliography. Most of the essays in this collection are fairly technical, and even more technically demanding are the contributions to a later collection assembled by the same editor: R. L. Martin (ed.), *Recent Essays on Truth and the Liar Paradox* (Oxford: Oxford University Press, 1984).

A recent book on the Liar is: J. Barwise and J. Etchemendy, *The Liar – An Essay on Truth and Circularity* (Oxford: Oxford University Press, 1987), but this can be read only by those who move around easily in logic and set theory.

The relationship between certain paradoxes and some astonishing results in mathematical logic (including Gödel's Incompleteness theorem) is marvellously illuminated in the very readable R. Smullyan, *Forever Undecided* (New York: Alfred Knopf, 1987).

The quotation from Prior occurs on pp. 71-2 of A. Prior, 'Epimenides the Cretan', reprinted in his *Papers in Logic and Ethics* (London: Duckworth, 1976), pp. 70-7.

The Liar, the Sorites paradox (see chap. 8), the paradox of the surprise examination (see chap. 10) and several others are discussed in R. M. Sainsbury, *Paradoxes* (Cambridge: Cambridge University Press, 1988); T. S. Champlin, *Reflexive Paradoxes* (London: Routledge, 1988).

Questions

1   What should count as a solution to a paradox like the Liar? In other words, what criteria should a proposed solution satisfy in order for us to accept it as genuine? Charles Chihara makes some suggestions in his 'The semantic paradoxes: a diagnostic investigation', *Philosophical Review* 88 (1979), 590-618.

2   It has been claimed of certain paradoxical sentences that they fail to make statements, so the question of their truth or falsity does not arise, hence the paradoxical reasoning is avoided. Under what conditions does a sentence fail to make a statement? Do these conditions obtain in the case of any paradoxical sentences? If you are not sure of the distinction between sentences and statements it is roughly this: A sentence may be *used* on a certain occasion to make a statement. Two classical papers in which the sentence/statement distinction is employed for different purposes are J. L. Austin, 'Truth' (1950), reprinted in G. Pitcher (ed.) *Truth* (Englewood Cliffs: Prentice Hall, 1964), pp. 18-31 and P. F. Strawson, 'On referring' (1950), reprinted in his *Logico-Linguistic Papers* (London: Methuen, 1971), pp. 1-27.

3   Can a statement be *both* true *and* false? Historically, a large number of writers have said 'Yes'. See G. Priest, R. Routley, and J. Norman (eds), *Paraconsistent Logic. Essays on the Inconsistent* (Munich: Philosophia Verlag, 1987).

4   Let us say that adjectives that do apply to themselves are *autological* words. ('autological' is an adjective that means 'self-applicable'. The word 'short' is autological, since it is indeed a short word; 'polysyllabic' is autological, since 'polysyllabic' is polysyllabic. Let us say that adjectives that *don't* apply to themselves are *heterological* words (so 'heterological' is an adjective meaning 'non-self-applicable). The adjective 'long' is a good example of a heterological word, since the word

'long' is not long. Any adjective must either apply to itself or fail to apply to itself. In other words, every adjective is either autological or heterological. So, since both 'autological' and 'heterological' are adjectives, each of them must be either autological or heterological. But which? Just consider the adjective 'heterological'. If it is true that 'heterological' is heterological, then the word 'heterological' applies to itself – in other words, it is autological. But if 'heterological' does apply to itself, that means that it is true that 'heterological' is heterological. So, is 'heterological' heterological or isn't it? (This is known as Grelling's paradox.)

Chapter eight

The Sorites paradox: vagueness and slippery slopes

'Soros', from which the term 'Sorites' derives, is a Greek word meaning 'heap'. Take one grain of sand and throw it on the floor. Throw on another grain. You certainly have not yet created a heap of sand. Add one more grain. Still no heap. Add another. . . The point is that, for any number of grains, if that number does not constitute a heap, then neither does that number of grains plus one. One grain does not constitute a heap, so it follows that there is no number n such that n grains make a heap. But that conclusion is obviously false, since 10 million grains piled together on the floor certainly *do* constitute a heap of sand.

The Sorites argument can be stated as a series of inferences of the sort called *modus ponens*:

1 grain does not make a heap.
If 1 grain does not make a heap, then neither does the addition of one more grain.
Therefore 2 grains do not make a heap.

2 grains do not make a heap.
If 2 grains do not make a heap, then neither does the addition of one more grain.
Therefore 3 grains do not make a heap.

By using the conclusion reached in one chunk of argument as the first premise of the next chunk, we arrive at the false conclusion that 10 million grains of sand don't constitute a heap. Once you have granted the first stage of the argument, you have no good reason for denying the next, so you are on a slippery slope which apparently leads you to granting a conclusion that you would strongly wish to deny.

We can argue the other way round: Nobody denies that a pile of 10 million grains constitutes a heap, and removing one grain still leaves a heap. In fact, given any number of grains that constitute a heap, remove one and you still have a heap – there is no 'critical point' at which the heap becomes a non-heap by the removal of a single grain. But now, working backwards, we get to the conclusion that one grain of sand (or nought, come to that) constitutes a heap, and that's plainly wrong.

Take another example. A child who grows older by one heartbeat is still a child. One heartbeat later that individual is still a child. In fact never is there a time when a child, one heartbeat later, is transformed into an adolescent. By reasoning similar to that employed in the previous examples, it seems that we are driven into accepting that a person who is fifty years old, or a hundred years old, is still a child. At no point (so the argument seems to show) could the person have even become an adolescent.

Suppose that I am leafing left to right through a thick book containing 2,001 of the flimsiest sheets. Near the beginning of the book I should correctly judge that the number of sheets in the right-hand section (RH) is greater than the number of sheets in the left-hand section (LH). And turning one flimsy page will not alter that judgment. Now, in this case, the principle

If RH > LH, then (RH − 1 page) > (LH + 1 page)

fails when LH = 1,000. In order to get a Sorites-type paradox, we need to substitute 'feels larger' for 'is larger' in the above principle. What this shows is that the establishment of Sorites-type paradoxes depends crucially on the employment of vague predicates. Although a vague predicate may be clearly true of some things and clearly false of others, there is no clear line dividing those things of which it is true from those of which it is false.

Color predicates are vague and therefore lend themselves to a Sorites paradox: I open a large pot of red paint and show it to Mary. She sees and says that the paint is red. Now, unbeknownst to Mary, I add to the pot a drop – just a smidgen – of yellow paint, and stir it well in. Mary, of course, cannot distinguish the color of this mixture from that of the original, so she says that the color of the mixture is red too. Add another smidgen of yellow to the mixture and stir well in. Mary is bound to say that the color of the new mixture is red too since it's indistinguishable from the first mixture the color of which she says is red. You can easily see where this is leading. If Mary calls one mixture red and she cannot distinguish the color of that from the color of the next mixture which results from adding a smidgen of yellow then, it seems, she'll still be calling the mixture red after the addition of a thousand drops of yellow. But everyone, Mary included, can see that that mixture is orange. So we have an absurd upshot. Mary seems committed to *saying* that the final mix is red, yet she can *see* that it's orange.

Since the paradoxes in this family involve vague predicates, the application of which does not rest wholly on testable matters of fact, some writers have concluded that such predicates are somehow defective or unsatisfactory. But this seems to me an unsatisfactory response to the Sorites. Most of the predicates of our language are vague, and this is because there are many words we can learn only by being shown samples of the things to which those words apply. If I learn the word 'red' in this way, I shall apply it to the color of those things deemed by me, under the guidance of competent speakers, to be sufficiently similar in color to the red samples. The word is not learned by a definition, nor by the learner being shown everything that is red. In particular, no boundary line for the application of 'red' is drawn in advance. Yet such vague expressions are perfectly serviceable. There is nothing wrong with the claim that the pen you are now holding is red. Vague words are pervasive, indispensable elements of natural languages.

In order to try to throw some light on the Sorites puzzle, I shall construct a version of the paradox around the (very) vague predicate 'beautiful'. If, for this version, we can find a way of escaping from contradiction, there may be some hope of extending the solution to other versions. Conversely, if the solution cannot be so extended, then we shouldn't set too much store by it.

Let us suppose that I am perusing a perfect reproduction of the *Mona Lisa*, call it ML1. But now consider a reproduction just like ML1, except that an imperceptibly tiny quantity of the original color has been replaced by a shade of puce that, in large quantities, I find repulsive to the point of nausea. Call this new reproduction ML2. By similar tiny additions, we obtain a series of reproductions such that the last contains nothing of the *Mona Lisa*, but is just a disgusting sea of puce. By the usual form of Sorites reasoning, one ends up apparently having to conclude that this reproduction is also beautiful, since, by a long series of imperceptible transitions, one reaches it from ML1.

Imagine an experiment in which I am presented, one by one, with the reproductions in such a series. Each reproduction is imperceptibly different from the next, but each is actually different from (because pucer than) its predecessor. The first in the series is such that, at any time, I should be willing unequivocally to pronounce it beautiful. Suppose that I had managed to view the first five hundred reproductions on Day 1 of the experiment, and pronounced each beautiful. It is clear that, on Day 2, I may refuse to ascribe beauty to the five hundred and first. This may be due to my having developed a less fervent appreciation of Da Vinci after close scrutiny of many near-reproductions of his work, or I may have become heartily sick of *Mona Lisa* reproductions after the rigors of Day 1, or perhaps become more finely attuned to their subtle nuances. Or the reason may be something to do with changes in my visual perception (as is well known, our perceptual acuity varies in various ways with the time of day).

Let us suppose, then, that, having declared ML501 unbeautiful on the morning of Day 2, I am asked to review ML500. I find it indistinguishable from ML501, and hence not beautiful. If it were pointed out to me that this was the self-same reproduction that I had viewed and declared beautiful the previous evening, I honestly reply 'Well, that's certainly not how it appears to me now', or 'It's a borderline case – let me have another look at ML499'. And my assessment of ML499 might differ from that of Day 1. This would hardly be surprising, since I should be seeing that reproduction 'with new eyes' and bringing further experiences to bear in its assessment. I might now start working backwards through the reproductions to discover the extent of the disagreement between my new judgments and those of the previous day. The upshot of this reappraisal on Day 2 would be the establishment of a 'murky area' in which I should have to confess my estimation of beauty uncertain. This murky area would not have sharp boundaries, for experience taught me (if I didn't know it already) that what appears beautiful now may well appear not so in the light of a new day.

Each step in the ML Sorites reasoning leads, by *modus ponens*, from a premise 'MLk is beautiful' to a conclusion 'ML(k+1) is beautiful', and each conclusion serves as a premise in the next application of *modus ponens*. But, as we have seen, a reproduction within the murky zone may at one time be classified as beautiful, at another time as not. Each conditional premise 'If MLk is beautiful, then so is the perceptually indistinguishable ML(k+1)' is acceptable, but commitment to the truth of the antecedent is always subject to revision when MLk is in the murky zone. With vague predicates, people are not liable to be consistent in all of their claims. The Sorites reasoning is blocked not because the first premise is false, nor because *modus ponens* (or repeated applications of *modus ponens*) is unacceptable. Where the reasoning appears to go wrong, at least in this version, is in assuming that a proposition which is the conclusion of one *modus ponens* step and which then serves as the premise of the next must, if judged true (false) on the first occasion be judged true (false) on the second. That assumption is false. Any one of a great variety of factors can cause a person to reject a proposition previously accepted as true, especially in 'borderline cases'. That is the hallmark of vague predicates.

This suggestion towards a solution of the Sorites is that the paradox-reasoning can be deflated simply by acknowledging that people are sometimes inconsistent in their perceptual judgments. But this suggestion arose from a consideration of one special version of the paradox involving an experiment with a large number of trials, run over two days. Are other versions susceptible to a similar treatment?

The color-gradation version, which has been much discussed in recent years, is fairly similar to the ML case. Experiments have been conducted in which the color of paint is altered in minute steps by the addition, smidgen by smidgen, of yellow to a pot of red. An observer cannot distinguish the color of the paint in one pot from that of the mixture in the next which contains an extra drop of yellow, stirred well in. So the usual Sorites reasoning tells us that, after five hundred steps, the observer is committed to saying that the color of the mixture (which by now contains more yellow than red) is the same as that of the original red. But real observers don't behave like that. Adjacent shades (shades which, when placed together, cannot be told apart) are judged red by some, yellow by others, and one red, one yellow by some who see them spatially or temporally separated. What leads one to the incorrect view that the succession of steps in the reasoning commits one to a conclusion that is at odds with the evidence of one's eyes is only the incorrect thought that observational judgments are irrevocable.

An objection might be raised that there is a crucial disanalogy between the case we are considering here and the *Mona Lisa* version. After all, so the objection goes, it is quite plausible to suppose that one's estimate of the beauty of a painting changes in the course of a day but, in the absence of time-lag and of any distractions, one is bound to be constant in one's judgment about the color of a pot of paint. The reply is that this just is not so. What seems, at one instant, to be a bird at the next instant appears to be a plane; one's judgment about which is the leading edge of the Necker cube flip-flops. In each case there is a sudden revision of judgment, with no change in the object.

Another version of the Sorites is known as Wang's paradox. The predicate involved in this version is 'large'. We say of a particular number (say, 10 million) that it is large; the number one less than that is large too, as is the next number down . . . and so on, right down to 1 and 0. But surely 1 and 0 aren't large. Now, in line with the suggestion tentatively proposed for the other versions, one would have to say, in this case, that we sometimes change our minds about whether a number is large. Yet it is hard to see what could cause one to revise one's ascription of 'large' to a number. Certainly, different people differ in what numbers they call 'large' (compare a child who is just beginning to count and a number theorist doing computer work on paired primes), but surely for each we can find a number that that person would unhesitatingly term 'large' and equally unhesitatingly term the number one less than that 'large' too. So wouldn't that person be on the slippery slope towards the conclusion that 1 and 0 are large numbers?

Imagine, however, that we spoke to the mathematician immediately after a computer session, and asked whether the number 37 should be described as large. The condescending reply might be that that number is extremely small, as is 38, 39, 40. . . . But suppose next day, cycling to work, the same mathematician read a signpost indicating another 40 miles further to ride. The number 40 might now appear to be large. In mathematics a judgment about the largeness or smallness of a number can be made only relative to a context: there is no large or small *simpliciter*.

This context-dependency of the applicability conditions of 'small' and 'large' has been noted by a number of other authors. It has been pointed out, for example, that 2,000 is a small number if that is the number of students in a big university who are dissatisfied with their courses, but a large number if this is the number of students at the same university who are ex-convicts. Without a specification of the context it makes no sense to give a verdict on whether some number is large or small. In some cases, the applicability of 'large' or 'small' may be an objective matter. Perhaps there are, on average, 3 ex-convicts per 1,000 students in the United States. Then, for a particular campus of 30,000 students, a population of 89 ex-convicts would be small (below average), and 91 large. The range of application of these predicates is clear in this situation, and no contradictions ensue. But, in cases where no borderline is specified, a normal Sorites-like situation arises in which, as I argued, irresolvably conflicting judgments abound. If we are talking about the number of miles left to cycle to work, 100 is certainly a large number. But is 17? That depends on whether I am using the boneshaker I bought from the butcher or am riding my sleek racing machine; on whether I have taken the hilly route or am on the flat with a following wind; on whether the sun is gently caressing my body or the rain is bucketing down, and so on. Obviously, in a context where one has to make judgments of largeness or smallness concerning the number of miles to be cycled, there are numbers about which one's judgments will be eminently revisable and highly unstable. It does not follow that, in that context, one cannot say of any numbers that they are large or small. The numbers about which we can make clear judgments as to their largeness or smallness are simply those that, for that particular context, lie outside the murky boundaries of a murky zone.

There is, I think, a difference between Wang's paradox and the other versions of the Sorites we have mentioned. Whereas there are clear cases of heaps and clear cases of red, it is not so certain that there are clear cases of large numbers. After all, 10 million is small if we are comparing it with the number of atoms in the universe. Yet, if we are discoursing on probability measures, then the number one is large. So numbers are small or large only relative to the particular mathematical context. In some contexts, we can define a number as large if it exceeds a certain number. Such contexts do not give rise to Sorites paradoxes. But, in other contexts where the ascription of largeness is a matter of judgment, then there will be a tendency to be inconsistent in judgment. This just means that the undefined 'large' is of little use in mathematics.

Notes

An argument for the claim that terms learned by ordinary observation of the world are necessarily vague is provided in C. Wright, 'Language mastery and the Sorites paradox' in G. Evans and J. McDowell (eds), *Truth and Meaning* (New York: Oxford University Press, 1976), pp. 223-47. The rich complexity of paradoxes in the Sorites family is brought out in a paper by the same author in which he substantially modifies his earlier position: C. Wright, 'Further reflections on the Sorites paradox', *Philosophical Topics* 15 (1987), 227-90.

The experiment of producing orange from red in imperceptible stages is described in R. Parikh, 'The problem of vague predicates' in R. S. Cohen and M. Wartofsky (eds), *Language, Logic and Method – Boston Studies in the Philosophy of Science*, vol. 31 (Dordrecht: Reidel, 1983), pp. 241-61. There are a number of interesting points made in this paper, but Parikh ends up by offering a most odd solution to the Sorites – that

The Sorites paradox: vagueness and slippery slopes

the logical principle *modus ponens* is acceptable only if used *sparingly*.

A great number of articles have been written on this paradox, and a wide range of 'solutions' have been proposed. One rather striking 'solution' is to accept that natural languages are incoherent. See M. Dummett, 'Wang's paradox', *Synthese* 30 (1975), 301-24, reprinted in Dummett, *Truth and Other Enigmas* (London: Duckworth, 1978), pp. 248-68.

I mentioned the context-dependency of the ascription of vague predicates. On this matter, you might usefully consult P. Bosch, ' "Vagueness" is context-dependent. A solution to the Sorites paradox', in T. T. Ballmer and M. Pinkal (eds), *Approaching Vagueness* (Amsterdam: Elsevier Science Publishers B.V., 1983), pp.189-210.

Questions

1   Could vague terms be eliminated from natural language in favor of a more precise vocabulary? Would human beings be able to *learn* the new language?

2   If the cells of my body were removed a few at a time, then, after a time, there would be no me. Yet in the normal course of life, we lose thousands of cells each day, many of which are not replaced. Yet we preserve our identities. How can this be? Compare the case of the Ship of Theseus, discussed by Thomas Hobbes in *De Corpore*, Part II, Chapter 11. The ship was preserved by replacing planks as needed until, after a time, none of the original planks remained. But the discarded planks were collected by a man who, putting them together in their original order, reconstructed the ship.

Two difficult, but worthwhile books that address these issues about identity are D. Wiggins, *Sameness and Substance* (Oxford: Blackwell, 1980) and D. Parfit, *Reasons and Persons* (Oxford, Clarendon Press, 1984). The Hobbes discussion is reprinted in R. S. Peters (ed.), *Body, Man and Citizen* (New York: Macmillan, 1967), pp. 125-9.

3   Resolve the following 'Tachometer paradox', taken from C. Wright, 'Further Reflections on the Sorites paradox' cited (1987) in the notes, p. 84. 'A digital tachometer on a car . . . is designed to respond to . . . variations in electronic impulses. There will be limitations to its sensitivity – so sufficiently slight variations in the incoming impulse will not, presumably, provoke any variation in the reading. And now, provided we are careful at each stage not to vary the impulse too greatly, the reading will *never* vary over a series of steps, no matter how many.' This is paradoxical because the conclusion is false. Tachometers work.

Chapter nine

Logic and reasoning

One reason why formal logic is normally taught as an element in the philosophy curriculum is that it is supposed that there is an intimate connection between logic and *reasoning*. Reasoning is what good philosophers do well, and good philosophical reasoning is logical. Hence an introduction to the principles of formal logic is an indispensable constituent of a sound training in philosophy. Until very recently, this sort of argument was generally accepted without question. However, there clearly is an empirical question worth investigating : 'Does a training in formal logic improve a person's reasoning ability?' Some recent (admittedly rather crude) experiments by psychologists indicate that the answer is 'No'. But even if improving one's grasp of logic does not improve one's power of reasoning, it might still be claimed that the principles of logic *are* the principles of reasoning (for *learning about* these principles – acquiring theoretical knowledge of them – may be of no help in the practical art of *using* them effectively). More modestly, it is surely plausible to suppose that logic is not *irrelevant* to reasoning.

Deductive logic is concerned with *entailment*. If one set of propositions entails a proposition (or, correlatively, if that proposition *follows from* the set), then, if all the propositions in the set are true, the other proposition cannot be false. The rules of logic are usually stated with the aid of symbols. Thus, the rule known as *modus ponens* (an instance of which we encountered in the preceding chapter) can be formulated as follows:

p and *If p then q* entail q

The letters 'p' and 'q' may be thought of as marking positions where *any* propositions may be inserted. So, if for 'p' we substitute 'It is sunny' and for 'q' we substitute 'We shall go to the beach', then we obtain, as a trite instance of *modus ponens*, that the pair of propositions 'It is sunny' and 'If it is sunny, we shall go to the beach' together entail 'We shall go to the beach'. By the use of some simple logical rules we can derive some very complex and interesting conclusions, just as we can derive difficult and fascinating theorems from Euclid's simple postulates.

Most modern writers regard logic as a calculus – a language with a vocabulary consisting of different sorts of symbols, a precisely defined syntax specifying which combinations of symbols are permissible, and a set of rules (*modus ponens* is an example of one such rule) for deriving permissible strings of symbols (usually called 'well-formed formulae') from other well-formed formulae. *First-order logic* (which is what most writers mean by 'logic') is one such calculus with an intended interpretation of the symbols under which well-formed formulae are read as propositions which must be either true or false. Hence the claim made in the first paragraph that logic is concerned with entailment between propositions. In what is called a *deductively valid argument*, the propositions doing the entailing are called the *premises*, and the proposition entailed is called the *conclusion*.

Gilbert Harman has pointed out that there is a tendency to identify reasoning with proof or argument in accordance with rules of logic. But Harman argues that this identification is mistaken and, indeed, that logic is irrelevant to reasoning. I shall try to summarize what I take to be the central thrust of Harman's argument.

Reasoning is a procedure for revising one's beliefs, for changing one's view, for modifying one's intentions and plans. This must not be confused with obtaining a logical proof of a conclusion, which is a matter of proceeding from premises via a series of intermediate steps. In fact Harman thinks that there is a category difference between *reasoning* (reasoned change in view) and *proof*. A rule such as *modus ponens* tells us nothing about when it is reasonable to modify our beliefs.

The rules of logic are permissive rules licensing the deduction of propositions. By applying such rules, we can generate more and more logical consequences from an initial set. Now in reasoning, Harman points out, we not only add to our beliefs but sometimes subtract from the beliefs held in store and this, he claims, illustrates one vital difference between logical proof and reasoning. Another difference, he suggests, is that, unlike logical principles, principles of belief-revision are defeasible – they don't hold in all instances. Consider, for example the following principle of belief-revision: 'If one believes *p* and also believes *if p then q*, then one can infer *q*'. Unlike *modus ponens*, this principle does not always hold. Harman constructs a counter-instance:

> Mary believes that if she looks in the cupboard, she will see a box of Cheerios. She comes to believe that she is looking in the cupboard and that she does not see a box of Cheerios. At this point, Mary's beliefs are jointly inconsistent and therefore imply any proposition whatsoever. This does not authorize Mary to infer any proposition whatsoever. Nor does Mary infer whatever she might wish to infer. Instead she abandons her first belief, concluding that it is false after all. (p. 5)

In other words, if a logical consequence of some of the propositions we believe is absurd or otherwise unacceptable, then the thing to do is to revise or relinquish some of our beliefs, rather than to accept that logical consequence.

Again, principles of logic permit the drawing of an infinite number of conclusions from a set of premises. The premises *p* and *q* imply *p and q, (p and p) and q, (p or q) and q and q*, and so on. But it can hardly be a principle of reasoning that we should accept (i.e. explicitly embrace) a vast number of useless consequences of our beliefs, for that would be to clutter the mind with useless trivialities. Harman makes much of this point, and advocates a Principle of Clutter Avoidance which is 'a meta-principle that constrains the actual principles of revision. The principles of revision must be such that they discourage a person from cluttering up either long-term memory or short-term processing capacities with trivialities' (p. 15). For Harman, to have an explicit belief is to have a representation in the brain (we discussed this view in chapter 3), so clutter-avoidance is a serious matter of preventing the brain bursting.

Harman has certainly raised a challenging problem. If he is right that logic has no special relevance to reasoning, then there would be no special reason to include courses in logic on philosophy curricula. Harman's challenge forces us to take a close look at what logic is.

Modern logic was developed by mathematicians such as G. Boole, G. Frege, G. Peano, B. Russell, and A. N. Whitehead. By the end of the nineteenth century the project engaging the attention of logicians was that of using logic to support, or provide a foundation for, mathematics. This enterprise, known as *logicism*, consisted of (a) defining all mathematical concepts in logical terms, such as *negation, conjunction, disjunction*, and *set membership*; (b) deriving all the theorems of mathematics from purely logical axioms.

A great variety of logical systems were investigated and logicians became concerned with problems such as 'Can this system generate theorems that contradict each other (or can we prove that it can't)? and 'Can one prove within this system all that one can prove within that one?' Logical systems thus came to be regarded as calculating devices – mechanisms for the proving of theorems – and the properties of these devices became a central object of logical study.

It is now widely acknowledged that the aims of logicism were not achieved, but, despite this apparent failure, it is a fact that the logicist conception of logic as calculus became (what Thomas Kuhn, in *The Structure of Scientific Revolutions*, calls) the *paradigm*, and still survives even though logicism has been widely thought to be moribund. Providing an explanation of this fact is an interesting task that I shall not here undertake. The only point I wish to make is that the traditional idea of logic as a codification of the principles of good reasoning fell into neglect under the influence of logicism. Concern with reasoning in ordinary language faded, and was replaced by formal investigations of the properties of deductive systems.

One symptom of the neglect of the study of ordinary reasoning in ordinary languages was that the meanings of symbols in the interpreted artificial languages of formal logicians did not closely match that of their natural language counterparts and the derivations permitted in logical systems did not accurately reflect the inferences deemed permissible in ordinary argumentation. This did not particularly worry those many logicians in the early part of this century who, like B. Russell, regarded natural language as vague, ambiguous, inefficient, and (after A. Tarski) inconsistent – a medium quite unsuited for the needs of the exact sciences.

In stark contrast to the logicist conception of logic is a view known as *psychologism*, which was defended in one form or other by many nineteenth-century writers including John Stuart Mill and Charles Sanders Peirce. Mill, following Archbishop Whateley, takes logic to be 'the analysis of the mental processes that take place whenever we reason' (*System of Logic*, Intro., section 2). Logic, in Peirce's words, 'rests upon observation of real fact about mental products' (quoted in C. Eisele). That is, it is the empirical study of what is produced by our acts of reasoning. Yet logic can hardly be an empirical generalization over people's actual reasonings, for otherwise all the laws of logic would be false – since most of us reason incorrectly at least some of the time. Is logic, then, prescriptive: does it tell us not how we do reason, but how we *ought* to? But what could be the source of such prescriptions? Were they handed down from heaven on a stone tablet? Presumably the laws of logic are not the kind of thing that we lay down, as we lay down the rules of chess.

Whereas it might plausibly be claimed that numbers are abstract entities existing independently of the human mind, so that the mathematical rules governing the relationships between numbers are 'out there', waiting to be discovered, the same does not seem to be true of the rules of logic. The reason for this is that logical principles involve concepts, or the meanings of words, and these seem to be very much a product of the human mind. Consider, for example, the logical connective 'if . . . then'. Suppose it were discovered experimentally that 90 per cent of people accepted as valid the following kind of inference:

If p then q; q; therefore *p.*

(A not outrageous supposition – experiments have shown that many people do accept such an inference.) One could, presumably, say that each person in the 90 per cent group was reasoning incorrectly – committing the fallacy of *affirming the consequent.* But is it not an equally good hypothesis that what those people *mean* by 'if . . . then' is 'only if' (for if we substituted '*p* only if *q*' for 'if *p* then *q*' in the above argument-skeleton we should obtain a valid inference form). What if it came about that *everybody* came to accept affirming the *consequent* as valid? Wouldn't that show that 'if . . . then' had come to mean the same as 'only if' (assuming that no other differences were apparent)? Here the connection between *inference* and *meaning* becomes visible.

What the logical connectives mean is a function of our inferential practices. Hence the preferability of a *naturalistic* account of logic, such as that offered by Mill, to a Platonistic account of the sort favored by Frege in which (as we could somewhat tendentiously say) meanings are seen as immutable mind-independent entities subsisting we know not how. Yet *prescriptivity* must also figure in our account, since we surely want to say sometimes that a person is not using a logical connective *correctly* – doesn't properly grasp its meaning. That suggests the existence of standards – prescriptions concerning how such words *ought* to be used.

Can't we have it both ways, by maintaining that the laws of logic are descriptive of much of our common inferential practices and also prescriptive of how we ought to reason? It is surely a plausible speculation that, as language began to evolve and convergences in the use of words emerged, so conformity to widely accepted use became a practical necessity and thence deviation came to be regarded as breaking *rules* of what is to count as correct use. If this story is right, then these rules grow out of regularities and conventions; their being rules depends on their being regarded as such. Their being (almost universally) regarded as rules is what fixes the meanings of that part of our vocabulary that we don't fix by definitions. This is why, for example, if someone candidly asserts a proposition of the form '*p* and it is not the case that *p*', or infers 'it is not the case that p' from '*p*' alone, we are right to say that that person does not understand the meanings of at least some of the words being used.

As we saw, Harman noted that jointly inconsistent propositions imply any proposition whatsoever. Now this is certainly true if our criterion of implication is that a set of propositions implies a conclusion if and only if there are no circumstances under which the set of propositions could be true when the conclusion is false. For, if the set of propositions is an inconsistent pair, then there are no circumstances under which the set (i.e. one proposition and its negation) could be true. This criterion for implication or entailment is accepted by most modern logic texts. But we have been arguing that logic should be the enterprise of attempting to descry the laws of good reasoning. It is not our practice to infer any proposition from a contradiction, nor would such a practice have anything to commend it. That is why some logicians, in recent years, have been advocating that we abandon the very weak, or liberal, criterion of implication mentioned above in favor of a more stringent criterion that more accurately reflects what, in ordinary reasoning, we count as a conclusion following from a set of premises.

In good reasoning, as Harman points out, we sometimes abandon beliefs, so we should expect a logic that accurately reflects our inferential behavior to possess the means for reducing as well as accumulating results. The rule of *reductio ad absurdum*, properly understood, is one such rule, and, in artificial intelligence research, various logics have been proposed which allow for subtraction when a program's 'beliefs' are in conflict.

We should expect our logic not to accredit arguments that are obviously invalid. Systems of classical first-order logic manifestly fail in this respect. For example, the following three arguments, when translated into their symbolic counterparts, are reckoned valid by classical logic:

If you strike this match, it will light.
Therefore, if you wet this match and strike it, it will light.

Logic is not confusing.
Therefore logic is confusing only if it isn't.

If it is seven o'clock you can hear the news report, and if you can hear the news report you have ears.
Therefore if it is seven o'clock you have ears.

Clearly these arguments are invalid, which shows that the logical behavior of 'if . . . then' is not captured by its artificial counterpart, material implication (which, as you'll see from logic texts, is written as a right-pointing arrow or as a horseshoe). (A material conditional of the form 'A ⊃ B' is true except when A is true and B is false). But what are the rules for the use of 'if . . . then'? Must the antecedent of a true 'if . . then' conditional be relevant to the consequent? If the antecedent is false, does the conditional have a truth-value at all? Is this conditional transitive or does the third argument cited above demonstrate that it is not?

Questions such as all of those raised in the preceding paragraph are surely questions for the logician to answer. They are questions about how we reason, or how we ought to. Insight into the human ability to reason is to be gained by constructing logical systems with deductive characteristics matching generally accepted inferential procedures. When this has been achieved (and we are not remotely near achieving it) then we shall be in a position to formulate prescriptions for improving those procedures. If this enterprise is logic, then the answer to Harman's doubt about whether there is any special connection between logic and reasoning is that there is. Logic identifies the principles of good reasoning. These are not principles to which we (normally) explicitly appeal when reasoning, but are principles to which, as a matter of psychological fact, we conform when reasoning correctly.

Notes

A very fine history of logic (which is also, therefore, a history of the changing conception of what logic is) is W. and M. Kneale, *The Development of Logic* (Oxford: Clarendon Press, 1962), esp. pp. 1-22.

The problem to which this chapter is addressed was set forth in G. Harman, *Change in View* (Cambridge Mass.: MIT Press, 1986).

A shorter work on the same theme, which touches also on matters discussed in chapters 3 and 4, is K. Bach, 'Default reasoning: jumping to conclusions and knowing when to think twice', *Pacific Philosophical Quarterly* 65 (1984), pp. 37-58.

Gottlob Frege is often referred to as the father of modern logic. His first child, quantification theory (which we mentioned in chapter 5), is exhibited in G. Frege, *Begriffsschrift, a Formula Language, Modeled upon that of Arithmetic, for Pure Thought*, in J. van Heijenoort (ed.), *From Frege to Godel* (Cambridge, Mass.: Harvard University Press, 1967), pp. 5-82.

Frege's attempt to derive the whole of arithmetic from logic, in G. Frege, *The Basic Laws of Arithmetic*, translated and edited by M. Furth (Berkeley: University of California Press, 1964) was shown to be unsuccessful by B. Russell in a famous letter reprinted (with Frege's reply) in J. van Heijenoort (ed.), *From Frege to Godel*, pp. 124-8.

For the doctrine of *psychologism*, I drew on J. S. Mill, *A System of Logic*, people's edn (London: Longmans, Green and Co., 1898 (1st edn, 1843) esp. Introduction, Sections 2, 7, and the concluding footnote. The Peirce quotation is from C. Eisele (ed.), *The New Elements of Mathematics*, vol. 4 (The Hague: Mouton, 1976), p. 267.

Gordon Baker terms Mill's position on the nature of logic 'inductivism'. For a thorough historical discussion of the views of Mill, Wittgenstein and other leading players, see Baker, *Wittgenstein, Frege and the Vienna Circle* (Oxford: Blackwell, 1988).

Experimental studies by psychologists on reasoning are discussed in P. Johnson-Laird, *Mental Models: Towards a Cognitive Science of Language, Inference and Consciousness* (Cambridge, Mass.: Harvard University Press, 1983).

The examples of intuitively invalid arguments reckoned valid by classical propositional logic all come from C. L. Stevenson, 'If-iculties', *Philosophy of Science* 37 (1970), 27-49. There are many discussions about the differences between the material conditional and ordinary 'if . . . then'. A recent interesting, but difficult, one is P. F. Strawson, '"If" and "⊃"' in R. Grandy and R. Warner (eds), *Philosophical Grounds of Rationality* (Oxford: Oxford University Press, 1986), pp. 229–42.

Questions

1 I mentioned that, in classical logic, it is accepted that a contradiction entails everything. Here is a proof:

(1) *p* and not-*p*   A contradiction
(2) *p*   Follows from (1)
(3) *p* or *q*   Follows from (2); *q* is any proposition
(4) not-*p*   Follows from (1)
(5) *q*   Follows from (3) and (4).

What, if anything, is wrong with this proof?

2 What are the criteria for *entailment*, that is, under what circumstances is it correct to say that one proposition logically follows from another? The informal discussion in A. R. Anderson and N. D. Belnap, *Entailment* (Princeton: Princeton University Press, 1975) would make a

good starting-point, and is a useful source for further references. A clear introduction to this and some of the other issues broached in this chapter is contained in the first three chapters of S. Haack, *Philosophy of Logics* (Cambridge: Cambridge University Press, 1978).

3   Does logic describe how we reason, or prescribe how we should? Again, S. Haack, *Philosophy of Logics*, esp. chap 12, offers a useful introduction to this question.

Part three

Epistemology

Introduction: What do we know, and how do we know it?

Epistemology, otherwise known as the theory of knowledge, is a subject that is concerned with such questions as what knowledge is, what knowledge, if any, we have and how it is acquired. I say 'if any' because, of course, many people take the skeptical view that we know nothing, and that none of our beliefs can be supported by adequate evidence. Socrates, in his speech to the Athenians reported in Plato's *Apology*, said that he knew one thing – namely that he knew nothing. Pyrrho of Elis (*c.* 365–275 BC), probably the first systematic skeptic, advocated a total suspension of judgment. René Descartes, in a similar vein, argued that we had reason to doubt virtually everything, and he essayed in his *Meditations* to see what could be salvaged once we took these doubts seriously. Skepticism has taken many forms over the course of history. One modern version, discussed by Hilary Putnam, challenges us to prove that we are all not just brains in vats. After all, a brain in a vat could be supplied with the same neural inputs as your brain receives, and so enjoy the same sensations, beliefs, emotions, etc. Its experiences would be indistinguishable from yours. So can we find evidence, or produce an argument to show that we are real embodied humans, and not just brains suspended in nutrient baths? (Putnam thinks we can, but whether this Putnam is anything more than a set of inputs to my brain, I'm not sure.)

Philosophical discussions of knowledge are usually concerned with *propositional* knowledge, that is, knowledge that such and such is the case. But there is a quite different kind of knowledge – knowledge *how*. A person may possess all the theoretical knowledge available about (say) swimming without knowing how to swim, and conversely, someone who knows how to swim may know no theory – may be acquainted with not a single true proposition about swimming. Knowledge of the propositional kind tends to be the more highly valued, although the nature and status of such knowledge has been put under scrutiny in recent years by sociologists, literary critics, and others, and there is increasing pressure, in many educational systems, to devote more school time to the inculcation of knowledge-how. A question that perhaps deserves to be more discussed than it has been is whether these categories of knowledge are exhaustive. Is knowledge of language, for example, happily classified as knowledge-how or knowledge-that?

If we confine our attention to propositional knowledge, we may ask what kinds of propositions are candidates as the objects of knowledge? In his *Monadology*, Gottfried Wilhelm Leibniz (1646–1716) wrote

> There are also two kinds of truths: those of reasoning and those of fact. The truths of reasoning are necessary, and their opposite is impossible. Those of fact, however, are contingent, and their opposite is possible. When a truth is necessary, we can find the reason by analysis, resolving the truth into simpler ideas and simpler truths until we reach those that are primary
>
> (cited in M. Morris, *Leibniz*, p. 9)

Leibniz, like Descartes and Benedictus de Spinoza, (1632–77) was a *rationalist*. That is to say, he believed that truths about the nature of things can be achieved *by reason alone*. Rationalism is usually contrasted with *empiricism*, the doctrine that all knowledge (except that which can be derived from the analysis of concepts) is based upon experience. The foundations of empiricism were historically laid by a group of British writers including Francis Bacon (1561–1626), Thomas Hobbes (1588–1679), John Locke (1632–1704), George Berkeley (1685–1753), and David Hume (1711–76).

Empiricism is the doctrine that is more likely to appeal to common sense, yet there are some notorious problems. For example, suppose that there is at present in my visual field a pillar to the right of a post. According to standard empiricist doctrine I gain, through perceptual experience, an impression of a pillar and of a post. But how, through perception, can I gain an impression of a 'to the right of'? So how do I gain the belief or the knowledge that the pillar is to the right of the post? You might reply that there is no such thing as a 'to the right of' for me to get an impression *of*. True (I'd say) – but then just how can we account for the fact that we do distinguish perceptually a situation in which a pillar is to the right of a post from one in which the pillar is to the left of the post? It seems that we must broaden our theory so that it can accommodate not only perceptions of objects but also perceptions that objects stand in certain relations to one another. This may be a step in the right direction, but it is a step away from the standard empiricist doctrine retailed above. An impression *of* something is vastly different from knowledge *that* such and such is the case.

Again, I see the bus hit the pedestrian, and the pedestrian fall to the ground. If asked, I should have no hesitation in saying that what caused the pedestrian to fall was the impact of the bus. Yet all that I actually saw was a sequence of events; I didn't perceive a *cause*. How, on empiricist principles, can I account for all the knowledge about causes that I undoubtedly possess?

A solution to these difficulties was provided by Immanuel Kant, whose *Critique of Pure Reason* (1781) might be described, in very general terms, as bringing together the rationalist and empiricist traditions. It is a beautiful and intricate text, arguably the most difficult single work in the whole of philosophy. In his guide to the *Critique*, called *Prolegomena to any Future Metaphysics*, Kant says that 'the proper problem, on which everything depends, is . . . *How are synthetic propositions a priori possible?*' A proposition such as 'All bachelors are unmarried' is one that we can tell is true just by analyzing the meanings of the constituent words, and is hence called an *analytic* truth. Such propositions don't contain much meat. Synthetic propositions, by contrast, are non-analytic; they are informative. Kant set himself the task of showing that there are synthetic propositions knowledge of whose truth is a priori, that is, independent of experience. Two examples of *synthetic priori* propositions cited by Kant are '7 + 5 = 12' and 'every event has a cause'. Note the difference between discovering *what* cause a particular event has (this might be the subject of a scientific experiment) and showing that every event *must* have some cause or other – which is something that cannot be determined by experimental means. Kant believed that showing synthetic propositions to be a priori possible was a necessary step not only to establishing metaphysics as a science but to establishing the very possibility of mathematical and scientific knowledge. At the beginning of the *Critique*, Kant accepts that the raw data we receive through the five senses *contributes* to our acquisition of knowledge, but he subsequently tries to demonstrate that, within the mind itself and prior to any experience, there exists the means for organizing such data. We see the world as we do partly because of the order imposed by the mind. (This is an extremely crude – even boorish – summary of Kant's position.)

We have been looking at the question of how empirical knowledge is acquired. A consuming interest of modern epistemologists is the question of how such knowledge is *justified* or, better, how *claims* to empirical knowledge can be justified. There are those who argue that in justifying a belief one adduces futher beliefs so that if knowledge-claims are to be properly supported, there must be a solid foundation of beliefs that do not require justification – beliefs that are not inferred from other beliefs. Views of this kind, collectively known as 'foundationalism', have been subject to some very damaging criticism, and a number of alternatives have emerged. One of the most interesting is W. V. Quine's proposal to *naturalize* epistemology. The idea is that to understand knowledge is to understand the thinking of those (us) who do the knowing. Quine writes:

> The stimulation of his sensory receptors is all the evidence anybody has had to go on, ultimately, in arriving at his picture of the world. Why not just see how this construction really proceeds? Why not settle for psychology?
>
> ('Epistemology naturalized', p. 75)

It may seem odd, unsatisfactory, circular, to justify knowledge by appeal to particular kinds of knowledge (psychology and the neurosciences). Is this, as Quine supposes, the best we can do?

References

Berkeley, G. *Treatise Concerning the Principles of Human Knowledge*, edited by G. J. Warnock (1962), London: Collins. Originally published 1710.

Descartes, R. 'Meditations on first philosophy' in E. Anscombe and P. T. Geach (eds) (1969) *Descartes: Philosophical Writings*, London: Nelson.

Hume, D. *Treatise of Human Nature*, edited by L. A. Selby-Bigge (1888), Oxford: Oxford University Press. Originally published 1739-40.

Kant, I. *Critique of Pure Reason*, edited by N. Kemp Smith (1929), London: Macmillan. Originally published 1781.

Kant, I. *Prolegomena to any Future Metaphysics that will be able to present itself as a Science*, edited by P. G. Lucas (1953); Manchester: Manchester University Press.

Leibniz, G. W. 'Monadology', in M. Morris (trans.) (1968) *Leibniz: Philosophical Writings*, New York: Dutton, section 33.

Locke, J. *Essay Concerning Human Understanding*, edited by P. H. Nidditch (1975), Oxford: Oxford University Press. Originally published 1690.

Plato, 'Cratylus', in B. Jowett (ed.) (1892), *The Dialogues of Plato*, New York: Random House.

Putnam, H. (1981) *Reason, Truth and History*, Cambridge: Cambridge University Press.

Quine, W. V. (1969) 'Epistemology naturalized' in Quine, *Ontological Relativity and Other Essays*, New York: Columbia University Press, pp. 68-90.

Stroud, B. (1984) *The Significance of Philosophical Scepticism*, Oxford: Oxford University Press.

Introductory texts

Armstrong, D. M. (1973) *Belief, Truth and Knowledge*, Cambridge: Cambridge University Press.

Bennett, J. (1971) *Locke, Berkeley, Hume: Central Themes*, Oxford: Oxford University Press.

Bonjour, L. (1985) *The Structure of Empirical Knowledge*, Cambridge, Mass.: Harvard University Press.

Carr, B. and O'Connor, D. J. (1982) *Introduction to the Theory of Knowledge*, Brighton: Harvester.

Chisholm, R. M. (1989) *Theory of Knowledge*, 3rd edn, Englewood Cliffs: Prentice Hall.

Goldman, A. I. (1986) *Epistemology and Cognition*, Cambridge, Mass.: Harvard University Press.

Hamlyn, D. W. (1971) *The Theory of Knowledge*, Garden City NY: Doubleday.

Kornblith, H. (ed.) (1985) *Naturalizing Epistemology*, Cambridge, Mass.: MIT Press.

Lehrer, K. (1974) *Knowledge*, Oxford: Clarendon Press.

Moser, P. K. (ed.) (1986) *Empirical Knowledge: Readings in Contemporary Epistemology*, Totowa NJ: Rowman & Littlefield.

Parkinson, G. H. R. (ed.) (1988) *An Encyclopaedia of Philosophy*, London: Routledge, pp. 123-248.

Pollock, J. (1974) *Knowledge and Justification*, Princeton: Princeton University Press.

Scruton, R. (1984) *A Short History of Modern Philosophy from Descartes to Wittgenstein*, London: Ark Paperbacks.

Shope, R. (1983) *The Analysis of Knowing*, Princeton: Princeton University Press.

Wolgast, E. (1977) *Paradoxes of Knowledge*, Cornell: Cornell University Press.

Chapter ten

The surprise examination

The logico-semantical paradoxes we encountered in chapters 7 and 8 have been around for over two thousand years, and are unsolved to this day. But the paradox I am now going to discuss is a paradox about *knowledge* and is less than fifty years old. My feeling is that there has been some very effective recent work on this problem, and I very much doubt that it will still be considered paradoxical two thousand years hence. The paradox is frequently recounted as a story about a prisoner due to be hanged, but since a violent variant of my own appears a little later, I'll start with another common version, one in which a class of students is due to be given a test.

A teacher says to his class, 'I'm going to give you a surprise examination one day next week.' 'On what day will that exam take place?' asks one of the students. The teacher replies, 'One day in the next school week, I am going to give you an examination, but before then you won't know just which is the day for the examination.' The students don't much like the idea of a surprise examination, so they get together to discuss it with a view to trying to predict the day on which the examination will be held. One point they all agree on very quickly is that the examination cannot be held on Friday, since that's the last day of the school week, and if the examination had not taken place before then, that would be the only day available for the examination, so it couldn't be a surprise. In other words, on Thursday night they would know that the examination had to take place on Friday, so it couldn't be a surprise examination in the sense specified by the teacher. Friday is definitely ruled out as the examination day.

But then one of the students says 'Suppose we get through to Wednesday without having the examination. Since, as we have already agreed, Friday is definitely ruled out as a possibility for examination day, then by Wednesday night, Thursday would be the only possible day remaining for the examination. But since the examination would then have to take place on Thursday, it would not be a surprise examination, so we can also definitely rule out Thursday as the day for the teacher's surprise examination.'

The students accept this point, and, before long, another one of them sees that, since Thursday and Friday have been eliminated as possible days for the surprise examination, then, by Tuesday night, assuming the examination had not already taken place, it would be clear that Wednesday was the only available day, so that no surprise examination could take place on Wednesday either. By now, all the students realize that, by arguing in a similar way, it can be shown that Tuesday cannot be the day for the surprise examination, and nor can Monday. So by a quite simple argument they have shown that a surprise examination cannot be held any day next week. They are relieved – no examination – and proceed to enjoy the weekend.

However . . . one day in the following week, the teacher walks into the class, announces 'Here is the examination I promised', and distributes the question papers. Now, the students did not know, the night before, that the examination would take place on that day (and they thought they had proved that no surprise examination could be given). So this was a surprise examination, just as the teacher had promised.

But the students had previously worked out an apparently perfect argument that no such examination was possible. There must, then, be something wrong with their argument, yet that argument seems absolutely secure. So here we have a paradox.

What is the solution? Most people agree that Friday can be definitely eliminated as a possible day for the surprise examination, but some think that Thursday can be ruled out only on Wednesday evening, if no examination has taken place earlier in the week. This is a mistake. As soon as the teacher makes his announcement, the students can see that Friday must be eliminated as a possible day for the examination, so they can tell, there and then, that if by Wednesday evening no examination had been given, the teacher could not fulfill his promise of giving a surprise examination, since Thursday would be the only available day. They know that the teacher must give the examination before Wednesday evening if he is to fulfill his promise. And the next step of the argument shows that the examination must be given before Tuesday evening, etc.

I believe that a good way to approach a correct solution is to consider paradoxes similar to this one that are either simpler or are variations that seem to depend on similar kinds of reasoning. For example, instead of the teacher saying that the surprise examination will be held on one of the five days next week, imagine a teacher saying, on Wednesday, 'A surprise examination will be held on one of the days remaining in this week.' Or imagine a teacher saying 'A surprise examination will be held tomorrow.' The reasoning is similar in these cases, but some inessential details have been stripped away, leaving the problem in a somewhat sharper form.

Again, consider what we might call the 'Deerhunter' version of this paradox (after the film of that name). Here an American soldier is captured, and is seated at a table surrounded by enemy soldiers. Out of sight of the prisoner, one of his captors places a bullet in one of the six chambers of a revolver. The gun is then handed to the American who is commanded to point it at his head and to keep squeezing the trigger. He is told 'On one squeeze of the trigger, you will blow your brains out, but you will not know which squeeze of the trigger is the fatal one.'

The American reasons: 'If, after five clicks of the trigger, I have not blown my brains out, only one chamber would remain for the bullet to be in, so I would know, at that stage, that the bullet is in the final (sixth) chamber. Therefore I know even now that the bullet cannot be there, since my captors have assured me that I will not know which is to be the fatal squeeze, and if there were only one chamber left, with one bullet in it, I should know just that. But, then I also know that after the fourth uneventful click I would know that the bullet must be in the fifth chamber (the sixth having just been ruled out as a possibility), so it can't be there either.' By reasoning similar to that of the students in the 'surprise examination' case, the American concludes that the bullet cannot be in any chamber, and so is greatly surprised when, on the third squeeze of the trigger, he blows his brains out.

What difference does it make to the reasoning if, in this example, neither the American nor his captors know the location of the bullet after the barrel is spun? Another point to ponder is that the captive, while probably dismayed at his captors' brutality, does not question their integrity.

A further example, one of a series constructed by Roy Sorensen: Here is a game in which you are blindfolded and put on a grid, as shown in the diagram, where the outer edges are walls. You are allowed to move only Up, Down, Left or Right, each move being one pace which takes you the distance of one square, unless you bump into a wall. You are allowed only two moves to discover your position. Now, it seems possible to put someone on the grid in such a position that he would not be able to discover where he was in any two moves. For example, if I put you in position 4 and you make the two-move sequence L (bump into a wall), U, then you could not know that you are in position 4, since you might equally well be in position 7. Likewise, if you make the moves U, U (bump) you would not know whether you are in position 4 or 5 or 6.

1	2	3
4	5	6
7	8	9

Suppose, then, that I put you, blindfolded, on the grid and tell you that you have been put in a position not discoverable in two moves. You disagree, and give the following reason: 'I cannot be in any of the corner squares, since there are two-move sequences that would tell me which corner square I am in. (For example, L (bump), D (bump) would be sufficient to tell me that I could only be in position 7.) But, having eliminated the corner squares, I can now eliminate the possibility that I am in positions 2, 4, 6, or 8. (For example, U (bump) would tell me that I am in position 2 – since positions 1 and 3 have already been eliminated). Therefore I must be in position 5.'

However, you are wrong, since I actually put you in position 4. So what is wrong with your reasoning? Something must be wrong, because you could equally have reasoned this way: 'I cannot be in the corner squares. Nor can I be in positions 2, 4, or 8. Nor can I be in position 5 since, with positions 2 and 8 now eliminated, I could discover that I am in position 5 by the sequence R, R (bump). Therefore I must be in position 6.'

A final paradox, which seems to be related to those just discussed, occurred to me when I was searching for a house to buy. Imagine thay you were offered the most magnificent house in the world. Under normal circumstances the price would be equivalent to what it would take you many lifetimes to earn, but the site has just been scheduled for a nuclear power station, and must be vacated in ten years' time, when the bulldozers are due to move in. All that this extravagantly beautiful property will now cost you is your total savings plus the maximum amount you could borrow on a twenty-year mortgage. The only condition attached to the sale is that, whenever the house subsequently changes hands, the sale price must remain the same.

Should you buy? The answer seems to be 'Yes', since although if you kept the house for ten years you would have nothing except a huge debt, the sensible thing to do would surely be to enjoy the house for a while, and sell it long before the demolition date. You would get back exactly what you paid and, after all, the house is truly magnificent, would still be an amazing bargain, and you would have had great pleasure living in it.

You would be crazy not to buy this dream house and yet (here's the paradox) you would be crazy to buy it. For consider: Assuming that the legal transaction of transfer of ownership takes a minimum of one day to complete, then nobody in their right mind would buy the house one day before it is due to be demolished, for they would not be able to sell it and would have wasted a huge sum of money on a house that they no longer owned after one day. Now, equally, no rational person would buy the house two days before expiry of the lease because anybody could reason, as we have just reasoned, that no sane person would subsequently buy what, after the transaction, would be a house due to be razed the next day. But then, if reason tells us that nobody would buy the house two days before the expiry date, that same reason would deter anyone from buying the house three days before that date, since that person would know that it would be impossible to find a new buyer. By similar reasoning, nobody would buy the house four days before expiry, nor five days, nor six, nor a week . . . nor ten years. So will you turn down this offer-of-a-lifetime?

Notes

Some ten years after the first appearance of the 'surprise examination' paradox, one of the most eminent philosophers of this century, W. V. Quine, declared it solved. See W. V. Quine, 'On a supposed antinomy', reprinted in his *The Ways of Paradox and Other Essays*, enlarged edn (Cambridge, Mass.: Harvard University Press, 1976). Although many subsequent writers have found Quine's solution wanting, in his autobiography *The Time of My Life* (Cambridge, Mass.: MIT Press, 1985) Quine declares his continued allegiance to it. My preferred discussion is F. Jackson, 'The easy examination paradox' – chapter 7 of his *Conditionals* (Oxford: Blackwell, 1987).

The 'grid' version, the paradox of the silent virgin and others are laid out in Roy A. Sorensen, 'Recalcitrant versions of the prediction paradox', *Australasian Journal of Philosophy* 60 (1982), 355-62.

After trying to discover your own solution to these, you may be in a good position to assess the answers given in Doris Olin, 'The prediction paradox: resolving recalcitrant variations', *Australasian Journal of Philosophy* 64 (1986), 181-9.

My example of the magnificent but condemned house is identical in shape to the paradox in R. Sharvy, 'The bottle imp', *Philosophia* 12 (1983), 401.

Replies to Sharvy (by Roy Sorensen, Saul Traiger, and Michael Wreen) are presented in *Philosophia* 15 (1986), 421-44, and there is a further contribution by Sorensen in *Philosophia* 17 (1987), 351-4.

An interesting problem that seems to possess an underlying similarity to that of the surprise examination is presented in M. Hollis, 'A paradoxical train of thought', *Analysis* 44 (1984), 205-6. Replies to Hollis (by Doris Olin and Michael Kinghan) are contained in *Analysis* 46 (1986), 18-24, with a rejoinder from M. Hollis, 'More paradoxical epistemics', *Analysis* 46 (1986), 217-18, and rejoinders to the rejoinder.

Questions

1 Solve the following problem: An eccentric billionaire presents you with a vial of toxin that, if you drink it, will make you painfully ill for a day, but will not threaten your life or have any lasting effects. He offers you one million dollars if, at midnight tonight, you intend to drink the toxin tomorrow afternoon. You will be paid the money *just for having that intention*. If, after midnight, you change your mind, and decide not to drink the stuff, you'll still get the million dollars. Since you know this is the deal, you know that you won't drink it after having succeeded in forming the intention at midnight which qualifies you for the million. But how can you *intend* to do something that you know you will not do? (Reference: G. Kavka, 'The toxin puzzle', *Analysis* 43 (1983), 507.) Roy Sorensen, in 'A strengthened prediction paradox', *Philosophical Quarterly* 36 (1986), 505–13, argues for a family connection between Kavka's puzzle and the surprise examination; see also his *Blindspots* (Oxford: Clarendon Press, 1988).

2 The problem of the magnificent but condemned house can be seen as a question about *rationality*: Would it be reasonable for you to buy the house? By buying it you create a case of someone (the previous owner) having sold the place successfully and this knowledge might encourage a purchaser to buy from you. It seems, similarly, that there is at least some

reasonable chance of the purchaser being able, in turn, to sell the property. Contrast this with the competition for accession to the priesthood at the ancient shrine of Nemi, described in J. G. Frazer's famous work *The Golden Bough: A Study in Magic and Religion* (London: Macmillan, 1932–6); abridged edn edited by M. Douglas (London: Macmillan, 1978). The rule was that one acceded to the priesthood only by slaying one's predecessor. So success would guarantee one's own slaying.

Chapter eleven

How are knowledge and belief related?

Knowledge is precious, belief is cheap. Anyone can have beliefs or opinions about all manner of subjects, but we tend to regard knowledge as a rare and precious commodity. People study long and hard to acquire knowledge and, in our society, those who have knowledge are highly regarded.

Many of our beliefs turn out to be *false*. If you discover evidence against one of your beliefs, then, if you are a rational person, you will discard that belief, or view it with suspicion. But suppose one keeps finding evidence that seems to support a belief that one holds. One's belief will grow stronger until, perhaps, one cannot doubt its truth, and one may say, 'I now *know* to be true what I used to merely believe.' Such ways of talking reflect the supposition that there is a scale with 'mere opinion' at one end, and 'knowledge' at the other, and that with diligent effort we can progress from belief to knowledge. A person who knows that a proposition is true is in a superior state to someone who only believes that proposition. The conception of knowledge as a possession of the superior person seems to have been prevalent in the ancient world. It may be interesting, then, to try to discover exactly how knowledge differs from belief.

At first sight, the difference may seem fairly obvious. We have said that knowledge is 'stronger' than belief – if you believe something, you don't necessarily know it, but if you know something, you must at least believe it. Also, while beliefs may be false, a proposition cannot be known unless it is true. You may think you know something, but if what you think you know is false then you do not know it. Is knowledge, then, just true belief? The answer must be 'no'. A person's evidence for a belief may be quite insubstantial, but that belief may turn out to be true. If one is not justified in believing a proposition, one cannot be said to know that it is true – one's belief might be just a lucky guess. So if a belief is to count as knowledge, it must be a justified belief. We therefore arrive at the equation 'Knowledge is justified true belief'.

Let us now use the logical shorthand we introduced in chapter 9. To remind you: Just as, in algebra, we may let the variable x stand in place of any number, so here we shall use the letter 'p' to stand in place of an arbitrary proposition. We may now state the conditions arrived at in the previous paragraph in the following way: A person knows that p if, and only if (i) the person believes p, (ii) the person is justified in believing p, and (iii) p is true.

That was all quite simple. We seem to have set down all the conditions necessary and sufficient for knowledge, and, in so doing, to have explained the difference between knowledge and belief. However, I shall now adapt two examples from a famous article by Edmund Gettier ('Is justified true belief knowledge?' *Analysis* 23 (1963), 121-3) which show that the three conditions we have stated are quite insufficient.

Suppose that you and Ronald have applied for a job in a bank. Ronald goes in first for his interview with the president of the bank, but the glass door to the president's office is not soundproof and you, waiting outside, see and hear everything that happens. In order to test his awareness of money matters, Ronald is asked if he knows how many coins he has in his pocket. He replies 'Ten'. You then see him empty the content of his pocket on the table, and there are indeed ten coins. The interview proceeds well, and you distinctly hear the president assure Ronald that he will get the job. You therefore have strong evidence for the proposition

(a) Ronald has ten coins in his pocket, and Ronald will get the job.

So you are justified in believing

(b) The person who will get the job has ten coins in his pocket

since you realize that (a) entails (b).

Now, (b) turns out to be a true belief, but not because Ronald will get the job. Unknown to you, it is you who will get the job and also, unknown to you, you have ten coins in your pocket. Proposition (b) is true because of the number of coins in your pocket, but, since you don't know the number of coins in your pocket, you can hardly be said to know that (b) is true. But, as we have seen, you are justified in believing the true proposition (b). Therefore knowledge is not justified true belief.

Another example: Your friend Tina has, for all the time you have known her, owned a car. In fact, every car she has owned has been a Toyota and she frequently tells you that she considers these by far the best make of car. Today you see her driving a Toyota, so you have ample evidence for the proposition

(c) Tina owns a Toyota.

You have another friend, Jerry, but you have no idea where he is at the moment. Nevertheless, you construct the following propositions, each of which, as you realize, is entailed by (c) – so you are justified in believing all of them:

(d) Either Tina owns a Toyota or Jerry is in Jersey.
(e) Either Tina owns a Toyota or Jerry is in Jaiphur.
(f) Either Tina owns a Toyota or Jerry is in Java.

We needn't worry about why you bothered to construct these propositions. All that matters is that, as you realize, each of them is entailed by (c).

Suppose, however that Tina no longer owns a car, but is today driving a rented Toyota. Suppose also that quite by chance, and completely unknown to you, your friend Jerry is in Java. This means that proposition (f) which, as we have already seen, you are justified in believing, is also true. Nevertheless, it could hardly be said that you *know* that (f) is true, since your belief that Tina owns a Toyota is false, and you know nothing about the location of Jerry. Again, we must conclude that knowledge is not justified true belief.

Is there anything wrong with the reasoning we have used in these two examples? In both of them we relied on certain unstated principles, for example, the principle that if a proposition *p* is true, then the proposition 'Either *p* or *q* must be true' (to put this another way, that *p* entails 'Either *p* or *q*'). We also made use of the principle that if a person is justified in believing a proposition, and realizes that this proposition entails another proposition, then that person is justified in believing the latter proposition. These are rather fundamental principles, so a great virtue of the Gettier puzzles is that they force us to examine whether some of the basic principles we rely on in reasoning are in fact valid.

Nevertheless, both of the principles I cited seem, on reflection, to be acceptable – I certainly can't see any way of showing that either is not. So we appear to have proved that the intuitively plausible equation of knowledge with justified true belief is erroneous.

But let us take a closer look at what the justification of a belief is. When we write out a proof in geometry, each line in the proof is justified by one or more preceding lines. In general, what justifies a proposition is one or more other propositions. Now, one could argue that if a person knows that a proposition is true, then that person must also know that the justifying propositions are true. Yet, in each of the above examples from Gettier, the justifying propositions are false (and so, obviously, cannot be known to be true). You might be inclined to say, then, that this is the flaw in Gettier's reasoning: He wrongly assumed that a proposition which is known to be true can be justified by other propositions, some of which are not known to be true. You may wish to insist, against Gettier, that something can count as a piece of knowledge only if it is justified by propositions known to be true.

One problem with this line of objection is that it lays down a very stringent (and, perhaps a too stringent) condition. The condition is that if a person knows that a proposition is true, that person must know that the justifying propositions are true. But then, if someone knows that the justifying propositions are true then, so the stringent condition demands, that person must know that the propositions justifying *them* are true. And so on. In order to know that a proposition is true it seems necessary for us to know a whole chain of propositions, and this chain will be endless, unless there are some propositions that can be known directly – propositions that do not require any justification. Are there any such propositions? Some candidates that have been proposed are 'I am thinking', 'Everything is identical to itself', 'I appear to be seeing a red patch', 'Either *p* is the case or it is not the case' and 'I am in pain'. But, even if there is such a set of self-justifying propositions, it is hard to believe that from this set we can generate the whole of our knowledge.

Notes

E. Gettier, 'Is justified true belief knowledge?', *Analysis* 23 (1963) 121-3, reprinted in A. Phillips Griffiths (ed.), *Knowledge and Belief* (Oxford: Oxford University Press, 1967).

The number of published discussions of Gettier's puzzle must now run into the hundreds. One which is clear and which locates the problem in a wider setting is D. M. Armstrong, *Belief, Truth and Knowledge* (Cambridge: Cambridge University Press, 1973), pp. 152ff. For a book-length assault on the problem; see K. Lehrer, *Knowledge* (Oxford: Oxford University Press, 1974).

The classical source of philosophical enquiry into knowledge and belief are the dialogues of Plato. See especially *Meno*, 86,98; *Theaetetus*, *passim.*; both in B. Jowett (ed.), *The Dialogues of Plato* (New York: Random House, 1892).

Questions

1 In this chapter, we made use of the principle that from a proposition *p* one may infer *p or q*. And indeed the latter does seem to follow from the former, for if *p* is true, then *p or q* cannot be false. The principle is well known in classical logic, and is called the Rule of Addition, or the Principle of Dilution. Yet the use of this principle led us to Gettier's puzzling conclusions, and as you may remember from one of the questions in chapter 9, the principle was also used in the proof that anything follows from a contradiction. This may cause us to be a bit suspicious of the principle. Is it really as innocuous as it looks?

2 It may be perfectly sensible, on some occasion, to say 'Canberra is the capital of Australia, but Bruce doesn't believe it', or, indeed, to utter any proposition of the form '*p*, but he doesn't believe it'. However, for me to utter any proposition of the form '*p*, but *I* don't believe it' would be absurd. Why, exactly? This problem is known as 'Moore's paradox', after G. E. Moore (1873–1958), who presented it at a meeting of the Moral Sciences Club, Cambridge, October 1944. For discussion, see J. Hintikka, *Knowledge and Belief* (Ithaca: Cornell University Press, 1962); J. N. Williams, 'The absurdities of Moore's paradoxes', *Theoria* 48 (1982), 38-46; L. Goldstein, 'Wittgenstein's late views on belief, paradox and contradiction', *Philosophical Investigations* 11 (1988), 49-73.

3 If knowledge is not justified true belief, what is it?

4 In justifying our beliefs, we show how they may be inferred from other propositions. Does this imply that there are certain beliefs that do not stand in need of any justification, which provide the 'foundations' of our knowledge. A sustained argument against such foundationalism is to be found in L. Bonjour, *The Structure of Empirical Knowledge* (Cambridge, Mass.: Harvard University Press, 1985).

5 The person reading this sentence does not believe it to be true. True or false?

Chapter twelve

Why are we taught what we are taught?

What education we receive is of vital importance to us since, however much we pick up on our own or from parents or friends, a major source of what most of us know is our schooling, and what a person learns is a major determinant of what that person is. At school a variety of subjects are on offer, and it is interesting to consider why just those subjects figure in the curriculum and what determines which parts of a subject are taught. It might be thought that the explanation is fairly straightforward and could be stated as follows: Education serves to provide people with the knowledge and skills they need to make their way in the world. There are different kinds of knowledge – the concerns and methodology of a mathematican are, for example, different from those of a historian – so there are natural subject areas. The school curriculum is designed both to cater for the particular strengths and interests of individuals who may specialize in a small range of subjects and, at elementary level, to ensure that all students have the opportunity to acquire those basic skills, such as reading, writing, and simple arithmetic, without which much other knowledge-acquisition would be impossible.

Unfortunately, this explanation of the content of the school curriculum is a drastic oversimplification, and finding out why will bring us to the heart of important issues in the philosophy and sociology of education. We might begin by questioning the claim that there are natural subject-areas, that is, natural subdivisions of knowledge. It is all too easy to suppose that there are such subdivisions, since the curriculum traditionally includes, as distinct fields of study, physics, chemistry, geography, history, art, mathematics, etc., which are separately taught and separately tested. Yet, first, although the separation of these disciplines is now well entrenched, it has not existed all that long, originating, in fact, in the nineteenth century. Second, that a subject area is traditional does not, of course, make it natural – perhaps the way that the field of learning is divided up is a matter just of convention or convenience, or a reflection of the power of subject-based interest groups, or a measure of how a society distinguishes between high- and low-status knowledge. Third, even if knowledge is naturally partitioned in some way or other, it does not follow that the curriculum reflects, or ought to reflect, this partitioning.

The thesis that there are, as he calls them, different forms of knowledge was stated and ably defended by Paul Hirst. Hirst was concerned to give a philosophically respectable defense of 'an education based fairly and squarely on the nature of knowledge itself' (*Knowledge and the Curriculum*, p. 30). For Hirst, education is a matter of promoting the development of the mind, and such development of the mind is a matter of acquiring knowledge. Knowledge, so far as he is concerned, is primarily knowledge of true propositions. Hirst argues that there are different types of proposition and, correlatively, different kinds of knowledge. For example, mathematical discourse includes a distinctive range of central concepts which is quite different from the range of central concepts used, say, in religious discourse. In a mathematics text, for example, one doesn't come across the notions of *God*, *sin*, and *prayer*. Scientific discourse employs different criteria of truth and validity than, say, the language of aesthetic evaluation, and, again, the methods used for testing the truth of scientific propositions (e.g. observation and experiment) are quite different from those used for testing mathematical propositions. One learns to appreciate literature in a way that is quite different from the way one learns to solve simultaneous equations or to extract the square root and both of these ways of knowing are different from the way one learns about historical events. Hirst suggests that the following 'forms of knowledge' are distinct and irreducible: mathematics, literature and the fine arts, religion, moral knowledge, philosophy, history and the human sciences. He suggests that all of these be included as subjects on a 'liberal' curriculum.

The 'forms of knowledge' thesis has, I think, a certain plausibility, but it has attracted various kinds of criticism. One might question whether Hirst's conception of knowledge is sufficiently *generous* – he is concerned principally with propositional knowledge (knowledge that can be expressed in statements) and is insufficiently concerned with the skills or 'know-how', so strongly emphasized by J. Dewey, that a well-rounded education ought to instill. For example, the learning of foreign languages seems to be something that a liberal education might reasonably foster, yet skill in languages does not fall within any of Hirst's forms. In recent years, a more extreme kind of criticism has been gaining momentum, particularly in the USA. These critics complain that the dominant approach to education is 'left-brained' (by which they mean that it concentrates on rational thought processes) and they urge that the nourishing of the right brain through techniques such as relaxation training, hypnosis, meditation, biofeedback, and body-therapy should form an essential part of schooling. Whether this is a *sound* criticism of Hirst depends, of course, on establishing that such techniques confer real educational benefit.

One might also question whether the distinctions between the various forms of knowledge are as sharp as Hirst thinks they are. As subject areas develop, they tend to employ richer arrays of concepts and to embrace larger ranges of techniques and procedures, so one might expect increasing overlap between the different forms. Hirst seems to recognize this, for he insists that the categories of understanding that he isolates do *not* constitute an unchanging structure that is implicit in all rational thought in all times and places. He adds, 'That there exist any elements in thought that can be known to be immune to change, making transcendental demands on us, I do not accept' (*Knowledge and the Curriculum*, p. 76).

Since Hirst is here stressing the difference between his procedure and a Kantian investigation of the necessary a priori conditions of all human experience, then one might wonder, as John Wilson wonders, whether Hirst is conducting a conceptual enquiry or a sociological one. As Wilson sees it, there are two possibilities: (i) Hirst's distinctions are empirical; they are culture-relative so we should have no valid reason for recommending them for curricular purposes; (ii) the distinctions are logical, timeless, and culture-independent. In Wilson's view, it must be by such logical criteria that 'forms of thought' are identified. We must, he thinks, have some culture-free criterion for determining whether a proposed categorial partitioning of knowledge is 'real' or not and, he adds, this criterion must presumably be found somewhere in the realm of logic or conceptual necessity. He writes: '[W]e have to show, by conceptual rather than empirical argument, that certain basic types of experience giving rise to certain structures of thought and language are inevitable for any rational creatures living in a space-time continuum' (p. 92).

Wilson is what philosophers call a Realist: he holds that the world (of knowledge) is subdivided *naturally*, or *objectively* (i.e., in a mind-independent fashion) and that our analytical task is to discover where the natural boundaries lie – we must learn to read the map of knowledge. According to Wilson, Hirst and other philosophers have *misread* the map; they go astray by paying too little attention to those experiences and structures which have more to do with emotion than with perception.

What Wilson is saying is that cognition and conation are not unrelated, and this point, if it is correct (as I believe it is) is obviously of deep significance for research in artificial intelligence, and may have serious consequences for educational theory. However, as an objection to Hirst, Wilson's assault is less than devastating. We can, perhaps, agree that there may be certain 'emotional universals', the delineation of which might have significant implications for curricular design, but that is only to say that Hirst should have been more *circumspect*. Wilson intends his critique to cut deeper. He thinks that empirical and a priori enquiries are *toto mundo* distinct, and that Hirst's enterprise, by floundering between the two, founders.

A complicated answer to Wilson would involve scrutiny of the debate, initiated by a famous paper of Quine's, on the *illusoriness* of a sharp distinction between the empirical and the a priori. But, for a briefer reply, we can turn back to Kant himself. Kant stressed that his transcendental enquiry into the necessary conditions of experience concerned only *human* cognition, not the cognitive powers of other animals. Kant essays to deduce non-experimentally what fundamental concepts *we* must possess in order to have experience of objects. His datum is empirical facts about human cognition. Similarly, Hirst's datum is empirical facts about human knowledge as it is here-now, and he wishes to lay bare, by conceptual analysis, the fundamental categories into which this knowledge divides. There is nothing methodologically unsavoury about that; it seems an entirely respectable ambition.

Hirst's strategy seems to survive the various criticisms we have retailed, and the essentials of his theory remain untouched: there does seem something correct in the claim that (for example) the body of mathematical truths is independent of the propositions that God exists or that water consists of hydrogen and oxygen and it does seem true, and well worth pointing out, that the teaching of mathematics, religion, or chemistry involves introducing the student to very different fields of enquiry. Yet, even if Hirst is right about all this, there appears to be an enormous gap (as he himself later recognized) between his philosophical analysis of the forms of knowledge, and the practical task of designing school curricula.

From the fact that X and Y are different forms of knowledge it does not follow straightforwardly that X and Y ought to be taught separately. If, to put it crudely, the same mental skills are employed in the learning of X and Y, there might be a case for not treating them as separate teaching areas. If, on the other hand, the mental skills required for acquiring X are quite different from those required for acquiring Y, that would have profound implications for the ways in which these subjects should be taught. Are there discrete kinds of mental skill, distinct mental faculties subserved, perhaps, by distinct portions of the brain? A purely philosophical analysis of the nature of knowledge, such as Hirst provides, cannot possibly issue in any hard empirical conclusions about the nature of different mental faculties or skills. What is required is empirical research, for example, on brain-damaged subjects and on idiot-savants, for it is by such means that interesting facts about the modularity of the mind are revealed. Research of just this sort is reported in Howard Gardner's book *Frames of Mind*, and Gardner does assemble some impressive evidence that mental abilities do fall into discrete categories. But there does not appear to be any neat mapping of Hirst's different forms of knowledge onto these different 'frames of mind'.

In a popular work called *Multimind*, the psychologist Robert Ornstein proposes a categorization of abilities (or 'talents', as he calls them) quite different from Gardner's. Ornstein's provisional list of modules for which, he claims, 'there are either reasonably well identified areas of the brain . . . or . . . are clearly overall functions of the brain' (pp. 54-5) comprises the following eleven: *activating, informing, smelling, feeling, hearing, moving, locating/ identifying, calculating, talking, knowing,* and *governing*. By contrast, the multi-talented Jerry Fodor argues (much more cogently) that, while human *input systems* are modular, the central systems are not. Whatever the truth turns out to be about the diversity of our mental skills, it is highly unlikely that the diagnostic route taken by Hirst will lead to the same place as that to which psychological and neuroscientific investigation is destined to lead. And surely the question of how best to train these skills – a matter of teaching method and curricular design – will not take care of itself once the basic forms of knowledge or the multiplicity of distinct intelligences or talents have been identified.

Even if it were demonstrated that there are a number of

subject-areas essentially different in the mental skills they draw upon, and each demanding its own particular teaching techniques, there would be no immediate conclusion as to the accommodation of these subject-areas in the curriculum. For it might be argued that not all forms of knowledge are *worth* acquiring, or, at least, that no useful purpose is served by teaching them all. What shapes a curriculum is not simply a matter of what learnable subjects can be identified, but is importantly influenced by what policy-makers take to be the *purpose* of education.

Many people assume that the purpose of education is to provide a training which suitably prepares a person for working life. This conception is clearly quite different from that of Hirst, who sees the purpose of education as promoting the development of a person's capacity for all kinds of rational activity, whether these be work-related or not. Another view might be that education should primarily be a process of socialization – inculcating in a child the habits, attitudes and, hopefully, virtues of the society of which that child is in the process of becoming a fully-fledged member. Yet another position might be that all of these conceptions of the purpose of education are wrong, since they falsely assume that educators have the right to dictate certain educational objectives for the learner. Some interpretations of the so-called 'child-centered' approach hold that it is for learners themselves to determine which directions their enquiries should take. In the preface to their book *Education and Social Control*, R. Sharp and A. Green write:

> The child centred teacher sees him, or herself as engaging in a radical critique of authoritarian-elitist assumptions of the more formal, traditional approaches to education. He does not wish to subordinate the child's individuality to some predefined social requirements or impose 'high culture' upon the child in an arbitrary fashion because these would frustrate the realization of the child's inner potential. (p. vii)

The purpose of education, on this view, is to provide an environment conducive to the child's development. Presumably to an advocate of the pure child-centered approach, the very idea of a prescribed curriculum is anathema. A still more extreme view regards as anathema the very idea of a prescribed education.

Evidently, then, one of the forces that shapes educational policy is the prevailing doctrine about the purpose of education. If so, then part of the explanation of why we are taught what we are taught must involve an explanation of why the prevailing doctrine prevails. It would be nice to think that the deliberations of philosophers and educationalists were the fountain of these policy-guiding principles, but this turns out not to be the case. More powerful forces are at work. For example, political pressures frequently exert a decisive influence. There are many cases where governments that see education as a means of producing citizens loyal and obedient to the state or to a specific political ideology take firm control of educational policy-making. An authoritarian regime may, for its own political ends, ensure that all major decisions on education are taken by central government, thus denying any effective control to groups more knowledgeable about, and more intimately involved in, the business of teaching. Conversely, a government ideologically opposed to state paternalism may, in effect, hand over major decisions to parents.

Popular prejudices about the function of education may also exert a decisive (usually conservative) influence on educational policy, especially when a government is anxious to respond to public opinion. Resistance to educational innovations often has its seeds in the attitudes of parents or employers who are suspicious of new ideas, the benefits of which they do not comprehend. This was what determined the fate of the short-lived Austrian school reform movement which flourished in the early part of this century and numbered amongst its supporters such intellectuals as Rainer Maria Rilke, K. Popper, and L. Wittgenstein. The movement sought to replace the old 'drill schools' of the Habsburg empire with a child-centered program of 'self-activity' and active participation by students in the learning process. But the peasantry regarded the idea of teaching a child to be independent and thoughtful as threatening the traditional way of life and social structure on which its livelihood depended, and would not tolerate the new system.

Another influence on the school curriculum is activity at the cutting edge of research, especially when the knowledge developed is seen to relate to technological advances and to have vocational implications (e.g. computer studies). New discoveries and whole new disciplines come into being, with the consequence that schools may need to provide preparatory training. Perhaps, curiously, the emergence of new disciplines sometimes results from social and financial pressures rather than from any real academic need of a special subject-area in which to accommodate a body of new discoveries and techniques. A classic example of this is psychology, which was invented so as to give better career opportunities to those working in a discipline (physiology) where the number of available positions was stable or declining, and where those at the top were not liable to be dislodged. Social forces of this kind have been largely responsible for the recent proliferation of scientific disciplines, and clearly it is social forces that have created new academic areas such as women's studies and ecology.

Of course, once a new academic discipline is created, consequential changes occur all down the line: the new subject infects school curricula, people are hired to teach it, textbooks are written, resources are allocated. One worrying thing about this process is that it is not easily reversible. When so much has been invested in it, how can a new discipline be scrapped even if it turns out to be a dud? Other worries about the proliferation of disciplines are that it leads to greater fragmentation of the curriculum, to narrower specialization by students, and to an increase in the number of mutually unintelligible jargons.

I have by no means given an exhaustive account of all the influences on what is taught within an educational system. One might have discussed the role of interest groups, such as publishers and large sponsoring companies, which exert powerful financial control, the effects of conferences and research papers, and many other factors. But to have done so would have demanded a long excursion into sociology which I am unable to conduct. My aim has merely been to illustrate some of the theoretical problems that beset any serious attempt to design a good curriculum, and to note some of the practical difficulties that might be met in attempting to resist the many social and political pressures that are liable to hinder the implementation of such a design.

Notes

P. Hirst's position is set out in P. J. Hirst and R. Peters, *The Logic of Education* (London: Routledge & Kegan Paul, London, 1970); P. J. Hirst, *Knowledge and the Curriculum: A Collection of Philosophical Papers* (London: Routledge & Kegan Paul, 1974), esp. pp. 30ff. P. J. Hirst, 'Educational theory', in Hirst (ed.), *Educational Theory and its Foundation Disciplines* (London: Routledge & Kegan Paul, 1983).

Hirst's views have sparked a great deal of controversy. For a useful survey of objections, see M. Schilling, 'Knowledge and liberal education: a critique of Paul Hirst', *Journal of Curriculum Studies* 18.1 (1986), 1-16.

Hirst's thesis is explained and defended in J. Mackenzie, 'Evers and Walker and forms of knowledge', *Journal of Philosophy of Education* 19

(1985) 199-209, which contains several clarificatory points, although the paper is difficult and somewhat meandering.

J. Wilson's criticisms are contained in J. Wilson, *What Philosophy Can Do* (London: Macmillan, 1986).

The 'famous paper of Quine's' that I mentioned is W. V. Quine, 'Two dogmas of empiricism', in Quine, *From a Logical Point of View* (New York: Harper, 1953).

J. Dewey's influential work is J. Dewey, *Democracy and Education* (New York: Macmillan, 1978).

On the theory of discrete mental faculties, see H. Gardner, *Frames of Mind* (Cambridge, Mass.: Harvard University Press, 1984); R. Ornstein, *Multimind* (London: Macmillan, 1986); J. Fodor, *The Modularity of Mind: An Essay on Faculty Psychology* (Cambridge, Mass.: MIT Press, 1983).

For a critique of utilitarian evaluations of educational practices, see R. S. Peters, 'Education as initiation', in R. D. Archambault (ed.), *Philosophical Analysis and Education* (London: Routledge & Kegan Paul, 1965).

On the child-centered approach, I mentioned R. Sharp and A. Green, *Education and Social Control* (London; Routledge & Kegan Paul, 1975).

The argument against the state prescribing a uniform curriculum is propounded in uplifting prose, by J. S. Mill, 'On liberty' (1859), in M. Warnock (ed.), *Utilitarianism* (London: Collins, 1962).

Many members of Austria's intelligentsia were actively involved in that country's school reform movement. An attempt to explain why Wittgenstein forsook the possibility of a glittering academic career in favor of the life of a humble schoolmaster in rural Lower Austria, and to explain how his involvement with school reform influenced his later philosophy, is offered in W. W. Bartley III, *Wittgenstein* (London: Quartet Books, 1974).

The classical study of the emergence of psychology as an academic discipline is J. Ben David and R. Collins, 'Social factors in the origins of a new science: the case of psychology', *American Sociological Review* 31 (1966), 451-65.

A detailed account of how social forces operate to produce new disciplines within science is given in W. Hagstrom, *The Scientific Community* (New York: Basic Books, 1965), esp. pp. 208-22.

Questions

1 What is the purpose of education?

2 Should a state seek to ensure that a uniform education is had by all (young) children, or should stress be placed on diversity and choice? Mill, in 'On liberty', in G. Warnock (ed.), *Utilitarianism (1962)* strongly advocates the latter. For a useful discussion of this question in relation to

the implications for educational practice in a multiracial society, see J. Wilson, 'Race, culture and education: some conceptual problems', *Oxford Review of Education* 12 (1986), 3-16.

3   Is a general 'liberal curriculum' appropriate for our present needs?

Part four

Ethical and social issues

Introduction: ethical theories

In his introductory text, *The Philosophy of Right and Wrong*, Bernard Mayo usefully divides moral questions into three types. The first type are questions about what a person ought to do in particular situations. For example. 'Should I give some money to this beggar?' 'Is it right for me to try to stop my young daughter cursing and swearing?' 'Would it be quite wrong for me to write a glowing recommendation for a not-so-glowing student knowing, as I do, that most references are rather over-complimentary?' The second type consists of what Mayo calls 'questions about *major general* issues' (p. 15), such as the rights and wrongs of abortion, eating animals, euthanasia, obscenity, pornography, discrimination against or in favor of certain groups of people, punishment of criminals, and warfare. The third type consists of questions at a higher level of abstraction, and would include, for example, 'Is the right course of action the one that brings about the greatest happiness?' 'Are moral judgments subjective or objective?' 'What reasons do we have for acting morally?'

Questions of the first type confront us more or less every day, and call for practical decisions. Such decisions are likely to be judicious, thoughtful ones if we have spent time reflecting deeply on questions of the second sort. In thus reflecting we are doing what has come to be known as *applied ethics*. This title may strike you as pleonastic – surely ethics is, above all else, a practical subject – until you consider questions of the third type, which are surely also central to ethical reasoning, yet which are evidently not immediately applicable to issues 'on the ground'. Questions of the third sort have to do with the meanings of moral terms and with the nature of moral judgments. There is some sense in regarding questions of the third kind as fundamental. After all, if we are not clear about what moral terms such as 'good', 'ought' and 'right' *mean*, then our moral discussions about substantive issues are liable to be nebulous and inconclusive; and if we are not clear about what moral judgments are – what differentiates them from other kinds of judgment – then we don't have a subject.

But why is there a particular problem about the meanings of moral terms? Surely we can look them up in a dictionary. The answer to this is that, in the case of moral expressions, dictionaries are *not* authoritative. When, for example, I look up 'good' in my dictionary, I find 'having such qualities as are useful, proper and satisfactory'. This definition commits what G. E. Moore, in his *Principia Ethica* (1903) calls the 'naturalistic fallacy'. Moore's point is that every good thing may *also* have such other qualities, but it is a mistake to infer that, in calling something 'good', we are denoting those qualities. Moore goes on to argue that 'good', like 'yellow', is *indefinable*, so that goodness is a simple quality, not an amalgam of other qualities, and should not be confused (as it is often confused) with some property of natural objects. David Hume, in the eighteenth century, had made a rather similar point concerning the moral word 'ought': a certain action that I am thinking of performing may give pleasure to lots of people, it may prolong my life, it may save the whale or save the world; but that a proposed action has such properties does not entail that it ought to be performed. In other words, 'ought' cannot be defined naturalistically.

If Moore is right that the quality of goodness is not a quality that can be perceived by the senses, it follows that our judgment that something is good must be achieved by some other means – by a 'moral intuition'. For this reason, Moore's view is often termed 'intuitionism'. From this very brief summary of his position, it can be seen that Moore rejects the view presupposed by my dictionary – that 'good' can be defined – but agrees with the dictionary to the extent of holding that 'good' denotes a quality. By the mid 1930s a more radical proposal had established itself in the ethical marketplace. According to this theory, which is known as 'emotivism', the word 'good' denotes no quality at all. The idea is an interesting one, because 'good' is certainly a predicate, and the role of predicates is normally thought to be that of denoting qualities.

Why should emotivists deny that moral expressions denote qualities, and what role do they think that such expressions play? Well, there's obviously something disturbingly unsatisfying about the intuitionist's idea that there are objective qualities that cannot be detected by any of the usual means of verification, but can only be apprehended by this peculiar 'sixth sense' of moral intuition. Occult properties and extra-sensory perception of them have a place in science fiction, but morality is concerned, at bottom, with the serious, hard issues of practical life, and these won't be solved by a retreat to mysticism. Both of these problems (the strange properties and the means of accessing them) are bypassed if, like the emotivist, we deny that moral utterances are factual statements in which things, or actions, are ascribed properties. The emotivist says that moral utterances are not statements of fact, but are *expressions of emotion or feeling*. So, for an emotivist, someone who says 'It was right to drop the atomic bomb on Hiroshima' is doing something like giving a cheer for President Truman; someone who replies by saying 'Dropping the bomb was an evil act' is expressing disgust: neither person is making a statement; they are just evincing their feelings.

It may have occurred to you that, if moral utterances are like outbursts of 'Hooray!' or 'Ugh!', or like gasps of pleasure or cries of pain, then there can be no such thing as genuine moral debate. A. J. Ayer, perhaps the most uncompromising exponent of emotivism, readily accepts this consequence. He points out, in his iconoclastic first book *Language, Truth and Logic* (1936), that expressions of emotion are neither true nor false, so no pair of moral utterances can contradict one another (pp. 107–8). Now, this would mean not only that the two people giving their views about the dropping of the atomic bomb are not making opposing statements; it also means that there would be no question of one person persuading the other that his view was true and hers false, for, as we mentioned, on the emotivist's view there is no truth or falsity in moral utterances. This does not mean that a person's moral opinions cannot change; it's just that such change cannot result from rational persuasion.

Many people are attracted (at least initially) to the emotivists' claim that one's moral views are subjective – a reflection of one's feelings or tastes. People's moral values, we know, are not easily dislodged, and if some people hold a deep moral conviction that you don't share, you may think that all there is to say is that they see things differently from you. Yet such a response may be premature and unduly pessimistic. Because if you review some of the moral convictions you hold really strongly, you are likely to conclude that your holding them is not just a matter of individual fancy, but is based on principles that you could defend.

Take promise-keeping, for example. Someone breaks a promise made to a stranger. You, who are aware of this, say to the culprit 'You ought not to break promises.' There is surely a big difference between that sentence and a sentence like 'Tom does not break promises.' The latter sentence is just about Tom; the sentence does not entail, for example, that Mary does not break promises. Yet the first sentence, although it is directed at a particular culprit, entails that *anyone* in relevantly similar circumstances ought not to break promises. 'Anyone', of course, includes oneself. Why is it that moral judgments are thus universalizable, that is, of general application? The answer that Immanuel Kant had given, in his great moral treatises written at the end of the eighteenth century, was that, by a rational analysis of the very nature of promise-keeping we can deduce that it is our moral duty not to break promises. Kant argued that there are objectively true moral judgments, and by a rational process people can work out where their moral duties lie. An important aspect of Kant's theory is that people should figure out *for themselves* what their moral obligations are. People who only act on orders (even if they think they are the orders of God) are not acting morally, for they are shirking the responsibility of freely deciding which actions are right and which are wrong. Whereas a utilitarian philosopher would say that an action is right if it leads to the greatest happiness of the people affected, Kant would claim that a consideration of such consequences is quite irrelevant to determining whether an action is right or wrong; we need to look into the intrinsic nature of killing, lying, stealing, promising, etc. in order to discover our moral obligations and to form our moral judgments. It is not simply a matter of adding up costs and benefits, and it is emphatically not 'all a matter of taste'.

The moral theory that has been most influential in the second half of the twentieth century is one that draws upon Kant, welding elements of his thought to aspects of emotivism and utilitarianism. The theory is known as *prescriptivism*, and its main champion has been R. M. Hare. Like the emotivists, Hare does not believe that moral utterances describe facts. He maintains that they guide conduct, that is, that they *prescribe* certain kinds of behavior (and proscribe others). On the basis of what do we make such prescriptions? Like Kant, Hare argues that universalizability is one criterion: our moral judgments should apply to the conduct of ourselves and to that of all other people, and the aim of so shaping conduct is to increase welfare (in this respect, Hare's thinking is utilitarian).

All of the theories we have been considering address themselves to questions of the third type, in Bernard Mayo's classification. These are weighty, unresolved questions, and it would be foolhardy to put off dealing with practical concerns of types one and two until these deep, abstract questions have been satisfactorily answered. Nevertheless, until about twenty years ago, what was taught at colleges and universities under the heading 'moral philosophy' was almost exclusively abstract theories, with real moral concerns being alluded to merely as illustrative examples. The situation has now changed dramatically. Much, and in some cases all, of the teaching in modern philosophy departments is devoted to applied ethics. Hospitals and businesses in the U.S. are employing people trained in this area. The literature is now bulging with the fruits of research, and several journals have sprung into existence in response to this explosion of effort. The list of problems investigated is impressively vast and diverse – nuclear deterrence, homosexuality, overpopulation, masturbation, animal rights, donation of company funds to charity, special obligations to relatives, sexism, treatment of the mentally retarded, selfishness, surrogacy, environmental protection – to name a random few. Some of this work has had an impact on type three theorizing. In particular, there has been of late a revival of the conception of moral philosophy that informs the writings of Aristotle (384–322 BC). This has been provoked by the feeling that the concepts that have traditionally been the focus of moral theorizing – concepts such as *good* and *bad, right* and *wrong, duty* and *obligation* are instruments that are too insensitive for probing the moral and emotional intricacies of real (not artificially contrived) cases where we are confronting acute moral dilemmas. In Aristotle's moral writings the central concern is with what constitutes a worthwhile, flourishing life. Aristotle attempts to identify those virtues (or 'excellences') for which we should strive and to demonstrate how people growing up in a community can come to recognize those virtues as desirable. Several writers are now discussing particular moral problems within the framework of such a 'virtues-based' system of ethics. Two of the topics in the following section – the right to life and human sexual relationships – have been particularly illuminated by discussions in this mold.

References

Aristotle, *Nicomachean Ethics*, in J. A. K. Thomson (trans.) (1955) *The Ethics of Aristotle: The Nicomachean Ethics*, London: Penguin.
Ayer, A. J. (1936) *Language, Truth and Logic*, London: Victor Gollancz.

Hare, R. M. (1981) *Moral Thinking: Its Levels, Method and Point*, Oxford: Clarendon Press.

Hume, D. (1911) *A Treatise of Human Nature*, Book III, Part (i), Section 1, London: J. M. Dent & Sons.

Kant, I. 'Groundwork of the metaphysics or morals', in H. J. Paton (1948) *The Moral Law*, London: Hutchinson.

Mayo, B. (1986) *The Philosophy of Right and Wrong*, London: Routledge & Kegan Paul.

Moore, G. E. (1903) *Principia Ethica*, Cambridge: Cambridge University Press.

Introductory texts

Almond, B. (1987) *Moral Concerns*, Atlantic Highlands, NJ: Humanities Press.

Aune, B. (1979) *Kant's Theory of Morals*, Princeton: Princeton University Press.

Beauchamp, T. L. and Childress, J. F. (1983) *Principles of Biomedical Ethics*, 2nd edn, New York: Oxford University Press.

De Marco, J. P. and Fox, R. M. (eds) (1986) *New Directions in Ethics: The Challenge of Applied Ethics*, New York: Routledge & Kegan Paul.

Feinberg, J. (1986) *The Moral Limits of the Criminal Law*, vols 1-4, New York: Oxford University Press.

Foot, P. (ed.) (1967) *Theories of Ethics*, Oxford: Oxford University Press.

Lackey, D. (1989) *The Ethics of War and Peace*, New York: Prentice Hall.

Lamb, D. (1988) *Down the Slippery Slope: Arguing in Applied Ethics*, New York: Croom Helm.

Mackie, J. L. (1977) *Ethics: Inventing Right and Wrong*, Harmondsworth: Penguin.

Mayo, B. (1986) *The Philosophy of Right and Wrong*, London: Routledge & Kegan Paul.

O'Hear, A. (1985) *What Philosophy Is*, Harmondsworth: Penguin, pp. 254-99.

Perry, J. and Bratman, M. (eds) (1986) *Introduction to Philosophy*, New York: Oxford University Press, pp. 477-86.

Rachels, J. (1986) *The Elements of Moral Philosophy*, Philadelphia: Temple University Press.

Singer, P. (ed.) (1986) *Applied Ethics*, Oxford: Oxford University Press.

Smart, J. J. C. and Williams, B. (1973) *Utilitarianism for and Against*, Cambridge: Cambridge University Press.

Williams, B. (1972) *Morality: An Introduction to Ethics*, Cambridge: Cambridge University Press.

Chapter thirteen

The right to life

When is it right to kill someone? I suppose that most people would indignantly reply 'Never!', but, if you think about it a bit more you will see that this answer is not obviously correct. Suppose, for example, that you are being robbed by a man carrying a knife and there is no doubt that, having taken your money, he will kill you so as to eliminate the possibility of you identifying him to the police. Under these circumstances, if you could kill him before he killed you, wouldn't it be not only sensible, but also right to do so if there were no other means of preventing your own death?

Take another case: You are visiting a hospital, and hear the agonized cries of an old woman. She is lying in a bed helpless, and is connected to a 'life-support system' with various tubes leading into and out of her body. You discover that she has a terminal illness, has spent the last few years in dreadful pain and will spend the rest of her life in inescapable anguish. She talks rationally and begs you to switch off the life-support system so that she will be able to die swiftly and with dignity.

What should you do? The old woman has the right to go on living, so most people would say, but she no longer wishes to exercise that right. Should we force her to go on living against her will? When the question is put this way, the correct response seems to be that it is right to do as the old woman wishes, and kill her.

Not everyone would agree with this, however. They would say that when the destruction of a human life is avoidable (unlike in my first example) then it should be avoided. So they would let the old woman continue to suffer, since she is clearly a human being. But consider now a situation where this is not so clear. Imagine that we have before us a human body which is surviving in a state similar to that of a vegetable. The body is completely immobile and in a permanent coma. Even if we believe that all human beings have a right to life, we don't believe that vegetables have such a right, and this body in front of us is just a vegetable in human form.

What about a foetus which is only four or five weeks old? This does not even look like a human being and is quite incapable of independent existence. Does it have a right to life? The question is widely discussed. Many women who become pregnant do not want to give birth to a child. Do they have the right to get the foetus destroyed or don't they?

An argument often put forward by those morally opposed to abortion is this: A 5-week-old foetus has just as much a right to life as a 6-week-old foetus, and similarly a 6-week-old foetus has as much a right to life as a 7-week-old, as an 8-week-old, as a 9-week-old, . . . as a 36-week-old foetus. And surely a fully formed foetus just before birth has as much a right to life as a new-born baby. So (the argument continues) since babies have a right to life, so do 5-week old foetuses; therefore the destruction of such a foetus is morally wrong.

One way of dealing with this argument is to grab the bull by the horns, and try to show that young babies do *not* have the right to life. This is just what Michael Tooley attempts to show in *Abortion and Infanticide*. In brief, Tooley's argument is this: A creature can have the right to something only if it is capable of wanting that thing. Now, for a creature to be able to want its own existence to continue it must at least have the concepts of itself and of the future. A machine like a motor car does not possess these concepts, so it cannot be said to want to survive, and that's why we do not say that a motor car has a right to life. But an infant of less than about three months does not possess these concepts either. The child's acquisition of the relevant psychological capacities is dependent on certain developments of the brain, specifically, the ability of neurons to fire rapidly and repeatedly. This in turn depends on the axons of certain neurons becoming coated with a protein called myelin, and this process does not take place until at least three months after birth.

Before the age of three months, an infant does not have the idea of itself as a continuing subject of experiences (there is much additional experimental evidence that shows this), so it cannot be said to want its own survival; and where there is no want, there is no right. Another way of putting this might be to say that, although an infant less than three months old is, biologically, a human being, it is not yet a *person*.

Tooley concludes that abortion and infanticide (the destruction of very young infants) is not morally wrong. This may seem to you an outrageous conclusion, but it is worth remembering that infanticide has been widely practised, and regarded as morally unproblematic, in most civilizations not under the influence of the Judaeo-Christian tradition. The question we should ask, however, is 'Is Tooley's argument a good one?' One problem with it emerges if we consider the question, 'Is it right to kill normal, healthy people while they are asleep?' When people are asleep they are not conscious of themselves as continuing subjects of experience; they are not, while sleeping, desirous to live, so why would there be anything wrong with murdering them in their sleep? Presumably Tooley would reply that people have the right to live if they *possess*, even though, at a particular, time they are not *exercising*, the relevant concepts. So the answer will be that the person is not exercising the concept while asleep, but will *soon start* exercising it upon waking, especially if a life-threatening situation looms. That reply is correct. And surely a similar sort of reply could be made on behalf of the new-born baby. The only difference is that its 'waking up' period is a few months, not a few hours. But that difference cannot make a *moral* difference, can it?

If Tooley does want to insist that what does make the difference is that the sleeping person actually possesses the concepts of the *self* and *the future* but that the newborn does not, then he would be committing himself to killing on a much larger scale than he intends. For there are plenty of individuals who, through senility, no longer possess those concepts, so Tooley's argument would lead one to conclude that it would not be wrong to kill them too. Tooley does not want to be saddled with this conclusion, so he amends his definition of *possessing a right* in such a way that the possession of a particular right only requires that a person *either* has the relevant concepts or *has had* them in the past. But then, of course, an opponent of Tooley's who wishes to condemn infanticide need only seek a similar modification to the definition so that it reads, 'X has the right to life if and only if X has the relevant concepts or *will* have them in the near future.'

Another argument that Tooley uses is quite neat: If a man and a woman do not engage in sexual intercourse, then they fail to initiate a process that may result in the birth and subsequent development of a healthy child. Now abortion and infanticide are ways of intervening in such a process. But there is no morally significant difference between intervening in a process and thereby preventing its normal outcome, and deliberately failing to start such a process. Therefore, since we don't condemn the avoidance of sexual intercourse as being morally wrong, we should not say that abortion and infanticide are morally wrong either.

The argument looks persuasive until we ask just what 'process' Tooley has in mind. Where does the process *end*? One process that sexual intercourse sometimes initiates is the life of a new person whose natural death is the normal termination of that process. Surely Tooley doesn't want to say that we can 'intervene' in *that* process anywhere along the line.

In the short space of this chapter, I cannot possibly do justice to all the arguments in Tooley's book. Instead, I should like to raise for discussion some questions related to his theme.

First: Even if infanticide is not morally wrong, should we refrain from it just because a lot of people in our society would be upset at the killing of young children? The answer that springs to mind is 'Yes – respecting the feelings of others is the decent thing to do'. However, that this answer is not unproblematic can be seen if we try to answer some rather similar questions. For example, some people are deeply offended by the practice of slaughtering animals for human consumption, and are disgusted at the sight of meat hanging up in butchers' shops. So, should we ban butchers' shops out of respect for the feelings of those people? Again, many people are upset that those who commit rape are not executed, or at least castrated. So, should we institute such measures out of deference to those sentiments? There are great dangers in forsaking moral argument in favor of sentiment. Suppose my neighbors and I are upset at the prospect of more whites moving into the neighborhood – we know that there's nothing morally wrong with whites or with them coming here, it's just that we have a blind dislike of them. Should the municipal authorities ban the entry of whites into that district? If you have answered 'Yes' to all these questions, I should say that you are a rather strange person. If you have answered 'No' to any, but 'Yes' to the one about infanticide, then you owe us a principled account of the critical difference between the problems. Remember that your reason cannot be that infanticide is different in being morally wrong since, for the purpose of this exercise, we are not assuming that it is. If you believe that the important thing is to show that infanticide is morally wrong, then you should begin by answering Tooley's arguments.

Second: If abortion and infanticide are to be permitted then who should decide which foetuses and babies are to be destroyed? Here again, the answer that you are first inclined to give may not be the one with which you will stick. It is, perhaps, natural to think that decisions of this kind must ultimately rest with the parents. Yet the parents are probably in a state of emotional turmoil, and so in a very bad position to make a cool, sensible judgment. Further, consider two sets of parents each with an infant, and that the two infants are both grievously disabled to the same extent and can only live (in great pain) for a maximum of two years. One set of parents, perhaps because of religious beliefs, effectively condemns its child to two years of acute suffering, while the other parents put their infant out of its misery. (Alternative description: the first parents grant their child the great gift of life; the second murder theirs.) What gives a parent, who has no experience of managing this order of illness and pain, the right to determine the fate of the innocent infant? To answer that the child belongs to the parent seems unsatisfactory, because we are surely not talking property rights. Yet the spectre of doctors or state officials removing children for disposal against the parents' wishes is chilling.

Third: Since some higher-order, non-human animals seem to possess some of the psychological capacities necessary for having wants of the kind that, according to Tooley, gives creatures the right to life, is it wrong for humans to kill those animals for food? And if certain animals do have rights, then how can we possibly justify the kind of research done for the drugs and cosmetics industries which involves the infliction of prolonged suffering on such animals?

Fourth: I have been talking a lot about rights, and, in particular, about the right to life, presupposing that these are intelligible concepts. But are they? In our society we have certain legal rights, but is there any sense in the notion of a moral right? Well, it could be argued that many of our legal rights derive from our moral rights, and that, although there may not be universal agreement about what these rights are, that there are some is indisputable. If asked for examples of human rights, many people would, I'm sure, put the right to life on top of their list. Yet the existence of this right may be more problematic than that of all the other candidates. It is certainly true that being alive is a precondition of being able to enjoy most rights. But it does not follow that continuing to be alive is itself a moral right.

Notes

Michael Tooley, *Abortion and Infanticide* (Oxford: Oxford University Press, 1983). See also Tooley's reply (9-14) to a review of this book by Mary Anne Warren in *Philosophical Books* 26/1 (January 1985), 1-9.

There has been a welter of articles opposing Tooley's position. One that I found particularly persuasive is P. Montague, 'Infant rights and the morality of infanticide', *Nous* 23 (1989), 63-81.

A thorough and excellent discussion of issues dealt with in this chapter, as well as of related matters such as surrogacy and foetal research, is R. Hursthouse, *Beginning Lives* (Oxford: Blackwell, 1987).

There is a chapter on infanticide in J. Glover, *Causing Death and Saving Lives* (Harmondsworth: Penguin, 1977), pp. 150-69. Glover includes quotations from parents of children with spina bifida, and with doctors who have been confronted with the decision of whether to save life or let die.

A good philosophical discussion of suicide and other non-natural terminations of life is J. Rachels, *The End of Life: Euthanasia and Morality* (Oxford: Oxford University Press, 1986).

The case for animals is presented in P. Singer, *Animal Liberation: Towards an End to Man's Inhumanity to Animals* (London: Jonathan Cape, 1976); T. Regan, *The Case for Animal Rights* (London: Routledge & Kegan Paul, 1984). An opposing view is defended by R. G. Frey, *Interests and Rights: The Case against Animals* (Oxford: Clarendon Press, 1980); Frey, *Rights, Killing and Suffering: Moral Vegetarianism and Applied Ethics* (Oxford: Blackwell, 1983).

It is interesting that Frey, who argues for meat-eating, received a drawerfull of hate mail from the general public, whereas Tooley, who argues for infanticide, didn't get any.

Questions

1   I said that there is a great danger in forsaking argument in favor of sentiment. That was tendentious. For most women, to miscarry at two to three months into a pregnancy is psychologically vastly different from suffering a stillbirth or having a late abortion. Such *facts* about the emotions have the same status as observational facts in a scientific investigation – they cannot be disregarded. Are women's experiences the most important guide in any serious discussion of these problems?

2   Should a decision on abortion or infanticide be based not on considerations of *rights*, but wholly in utilitarian terms, that is, by considering which course of action would minimize unhappiness?

3   Is an abortion justified in a case where only by sacrificing the foetus can the mother's life be saved? For further reading on this subject, I recommend D. Locke, 'The choice between lives', *Philosophy* 57 (1982), 453-75.

4   Do animals have the right not to be killed?

5   Does endorsing euthanasia for the old imply disrespect for them? Sidney Hook argues that it does not. In an exceptionally fine review entitled 'The uses of death', *New York Review of Books* 35/7 (28 April 1988), 22-5, he writes: 'On the contrary, it recognizes that the old suffer from greater hazards than others, that we respect the diversity and freedom of their choices, that we are not imposing a mandatory medical regimen on them from which they cannot escape, regardless of the degreee of their torment and physical (or mental) degeneration.' See also J. Rachels, *The Ends of Life*, and R. Campbell and D. Collinson, *Ending Lives* (New York; Blackwell, 1988), pp. 121-68.

Chapter fourteen

Patriotism and racism

Violence at international football matches is now commonplace in Europe and in many other parts of the world. The scenario is sickeningly familiar: Supporters of the visiting team have made the long journey because they are patriotic, and want to cheer their team to victory. Their team, however, loses. The visiting supporters then pour out of the stadium and go on the rampage, injuring people, damaging property, and heaping *racial* abuse on the terrified local inhabitants.

My problem is this: If patriotic fervor can be transformed so quickly into racist violence (and, of course, not only after football matches) then it is plausible to suppose that patriotism is not very different from racism. After all, to place one's own country ahead of all others is the same as placing all those other countries behind one's own. So favoring one's own country is correlative with despising (or, at least, disfavoring) all other countries. Now, we cannot despise people just because they happen to have been born in a foreign country, so we must despise people we don't know because they are different from us in certain other ways. And the most visible differences are racial ones. Therefore loving one's own country (patriotism) seems closely connected to hating other races (racism). Yet we find that patriotism is generally condoned, but racism is almost universally condemned. How can this be, if the two are so similar?

You might object that I have not succeeded in raising a genuine problem because my argument that the concepts of *patriotism* and *racism* are similar is not sound. You may point out that just as loving one's parents does not entail hating other adults, so loving one's country does not entail hating anything else.

The answer to this objection is that the love of one's parents normally springs naturally from the close personal relationship that exists during the years that a child is under parental care.

But love of one's country cannot arise in the same way, since we don't have a personal relationship with our country – countries are not persons. Countries, however, get *personified*. Germans refer to 'the fatherland', Russians to 'mother Russia', and it is easy to forget that such expressions are merely metaphorical. This paves the way to assuming that we can have the same sort of duties to our country as we do to our parents.

Yet this assumption is highly questionable. We can see why we should help and obey our parents, but are there similar reasons, or any reasons, for helping and obeying our country? Surely the kinds of helping and obeying involved are very different. Certainly we may develop a feeling for the country, for example the comfortable feeling of familiar surroundings, a way of life, the mother tongue, and a culture to which we have become accustomed. And certainly, in one sense of the word, 'patriotism' just denotes such a feeling. But 'patriotism', as the word is generally understood, denotes much more than a feeling. When somebody tells you to be patriotic, that person is usually telling you not just to *feel* differently, but also to *believe* and *act* differently. We are encouraged to be patriotic (or more patriotic) but I cannot sensibly exhort you to feel more deeply any more than I can exhort you to strengthen your liking for the taste of liver.

However, to pursue the analogy, there is an indirect means whereby your liking for liver may be increased. If you are persuaded that liver is better for your health than other meats, you may well eat it more often, and, after some time, it may actually come to taste better to you than it did before. Similarly your feeling for your country may be strengthened if you are persuaded that your own country is, in crucial respects, better than others. If exhortations to patriotism are not irrational, they depend, it seems, on getting people to recognize that their own country is superior to others, that is, that other countries are inferior to theirs. So patriotism of this kind is, I think, quite dissimilar to love of parents. You may love your father more than anyone else without believing that he is objectively better than every other person.

It is really quite easy for children to become convinced that they are living in the best country on earth. Most children have no first-hand knowledge of other countries. Their access to relevant information is through the distorting channels of the news media and possibly through history books. But even history books do not in general provide an undistorted account of events. If two countries, A and B, were once engaged in protracted conflict, the record of events in A's school history texts will usually look quite different from the record of events in B's. A's books will say that A was fighting for the good, and will emphasize A's victorious battles while belittling B's; and B's history books will be biased in the opposite direction. So, insofar as the patriotism of a child is founded on reasons, those reasons themselves may well be founded on prejudice and half-truths, although a child, or an unreflecting adult, may not realize this. And prejudice is a central characteristic of racism.

The dictionary provides further evidence for the closeness of the concepts of *racism* and *patriotism*. In Roget's *Thesaurus* (an encyclopedia of synonyms and near-synonyms) under the heading 'hatred', are listed the words 'racialism', 'racism', and 'prejudice'. Among the words listed under 'prejudiced' ('biased'), we find 'nationalistic' and 'chauvinistic', and under the general heading 'philanthropy', sub-heading 'patriotism', are listed 'nationalism' and 'chauvinism'. Governments that refuse to grant nationality to refugees typically offer all manner of rationalizations for the decision. But it is hard to escape the conclusion that, in most cases, the real reasons are racist ones.

Patriotism is a global phenomenon. A French patriot believes that France is best, a Chinese patriot believes that China is best, a Greek patriot that Greece is best, etc. They can't all be right – but they can all be wrong. This should be obvious to anyone who stops to think about it for one minute. Why, then, is patriotism so attractive to so many people; why do they preach or practice it?

Political leaders who overtly deplore racism frequently extol patriotism. One reason is expediency. Unpopular measures can be made more palatable if people can be persuaded that, by complying with them, they are acting patriotically. You may be willing to work for very low wages, or to go and fight against another nation if you are assured that this is 'for the good of the country'. You will fight for your country even if you think the case for war is morally indefensible, because patriotism means 'my country, right or wrong' (Roget, again). Politicians, then, can exploit patriotism, but they can do this only because the people to whom they are appealing are either already patriotic or can easily be moved to patriotism. We have already seen how individuals can become convinced of their own country's greatness, but it is not a necessary consequence of this that they will love their country. A psychological explanation is required.

One tentative explanation might run as follows: Each of us is just an isolated individual, one of the millions of creatures crawling on the face of this earth. We are insignificant – the death tomorrow of any one of us would have a negligible effect on the course of human history. To many people, this is a terrifying and depressing thought. We should like to be superior beings, esteemed by our fellows. But most of us are not great athletes, nor will we make any staggering contribution to science, nor write music that will be admired for centuries to come. By all measurable criteria, we are decidedly ordinary, yet we need to feel somehow special. There is also a deep human need to 'belong', since, for most people, to be alone, friendless, with nobody on whom to depend, is a frightening prospect. So we form groups and join clubs in order to be part of a community. Patriotism satisfies both of these cravings. Just as a boy may come to love a girl because she satisfies his emotional, or even just his physical needs, so too is love of one's country born.

Now, it is not in the least shameful to come to love one's country, and it may be right to defend one's country against those who seek to destroy it. But there is all the difference in the world between defending one's countrymen, one's values and one's way of life and trying to impose those values on others or even just in thinking that one's own values are superior just because they are the values shared by one's group.

Patriots see themselves united with their fellow countrymen in a common cause, and although, as individuals, they may have no particular talents, they can claim to be special by virtue of being a privileged member of the greatest country in the world. Needless to say, the criteria for greatness are nebulous immeasurables, such as being more civilized, more cultured, or possessing superior moral values. But, reverting to a point made earlier, the accident of having been born at a particular geographical location cannot be responsible for a person's possession of all these great-making attributes. So either people acquire such desirable qualities as a result of how they were brought up, or they were genetically endowed with them. The latter view is very popular, especially among racists, and historically has led to sustained attempts to destroy those races deemed genetically inferior (genocide).

I presume that few people reading this book are such extreme racists that they would advocate genocide. But less extreme versions of racism are quite prevalent. These include intensely disliking people from other races (while not being prepared to kill them), mistrusting without disliking them, and claiming to be racially unprejudiced while still treating those not of one's own race with condescension. Even if there were scientific evidence for the superior intelligence of one's own race, would that justify any of these attitudes?

Patriotism, as I have been suggesting, also comes in different shades, so, in contrast to the received opinion that patriotism and racism are quite distinct, the former good, the latter bad, I have been arguing that the terms 'patriotism' and 'racism' cover large and overlapping areas. However, I do not regard my arguments as conclusive. I have a suspicion, but only a suspicion, that if many people who regard themselves as patriotic carefully reviewed their position and its consequences, they would find themselves committed to racist attitudes of which they might be quite ashamed. Perhaps if people conducted such self-assessment tests they would discover a mass of conflicting moral attitudes.

Notes

Patriotism does seem to be generally regarded as virtuous. In the following famous passage from Edmund Burke we find it positioned on a continuum between love of one's friends and love of the whole of humanity:

> To be attached to the subdivision, to love the little platoon we belong to in society, is the first principle (the germ as it were) of public affections. It is the first link in the series by which we proceed towards a love of our country and to mankind. The interests of that portion of social arrangement is a trust in the hands of all those who compose it; and as none but bad men would justify it in abuse, none but traitors would barter it away for their own personal advantage.

(E. Burke, *Reflections on the Revolution in France* (Harmondsworth: Penguin, 1969) 1st edn 1790, p. 135)

I have sought to distinguish patriotism from affection for the social environment in which one was brought up. It is very likely true that we are all, to some extent, shaped by our cultures, and people attach great importance to their 'roots'. Children who are constantly being moved from one country to another may develop an 'international outlook' but probably suffer from not having the opportunity to develop a deep understanding of, and affection for, any particular tradition. The idea of a future world in which all humans are inhabitants of a global village may sound cosy but would probably mean a dismal homogeneity. For discussion of these issues, see S. Weil, *The Need for Roots* (London: Routledge & Kegan Paul, 1952); M. Midgley, *Beast and Man* (Hassocks: Harvester Press, 1978), pp. 285-317.

Related to the matter I raised concerning the treatment of refugees, see D. Miller, 'The ethical significance of nationality', in an issue of *Ethics*, 98/4 (July 1988), which is given over to a symposium on 'Duties beyond borders'.

For an essay that examines my suggestion that most of us harbor unacknowledged racist attitudes, I recommend I. Thalberg, 'Visceral racism' in R. Wasserstrom (ed.), *Today's Moral Problems* (New York: Macmillan Publishing Co. Inc., 1975), pp. 187-204. (Some of Thalberg's remarks seem to indicate that he is assuming an all-white readership of his article – a viscerally racist assumption of exactly the kind that he is attempting to expose!)

Questions

1 Does it follow from the fact that we value the differences between various cultures that we must respect the values of different cultures? A moral relativist will say (roughly) that the practices of any cultural group cannot be justifiably criticized by those outside the group. An opponent might claim that this position is wholly irresponsible, and shamefully neglects the many important ways in which we are all brothers and sisters.

2 Can patriotism be defended?

3 Is a scientist who publishes research on racial differences morally culpable if he or she can foresee that the media or other groups are liable to employ those findings in seeking to foster racist attitudes?

4 R. Bauman's study of oral narrative, *Story, Performance and Event* (Cambridge: Cambridge University Press, 1986), depends on the accurate transcription of storytelling and dog-trading conversations recorded in Canton, Texas. In his prefatory notes, the author mentions that he has attempted to capture features of local pronunciation by using such written forms as 'gonna', ''bout', 'sumbitch', and 'hunnerd', but he remarks: 'I have avoided, however, certain renderings of pronunciation that tend to evoke most readily features of negative stereotype, most notably "d-" for "th-" as in "dis" and "dat"' (p. x). Bauman is thus a scientist who, though courteously warning us of his intentions, is deliberately falsifying evidence in an attempt to avoid being racially divisive. Is this justifiable?

5 Should there be institutional 'affirmative action' in favour of disadvantaged groups? For a useful discussion, see Lisa H. Newton, 'Reverse discrimination as unjustified', in R. Wasserstrom (ed.) *Today's Moral Problems*, 1st edn. (New York: Macmillan Publishing Co. Inc., 1975), pp. 204-9, and for an opposing view, R. Wasserstrom, 'Preferential treatment, color-blindness and the evils of racism', *Proceedings and Addresses of the American Philosophical Association* 61.1 (September 1987), 27-42. Another interesting set of conflicting opinions is to be found in the 3rd edition of R. Wasserstrom (ed.),

Ethical and social issues

Today's Moral Problems (New York: Macmillan Publishing Co. Inc., 1985), section 2, 'Preferential treatment'.

6   What entitles a people to a land? (This question was raised by the editor of *Proceedings and Addresses of the American Philosophical Association* 61.5 (June 1988) in a report on a recent visit of his to Israel at the time of a Palestinian uprising.)

Chapter fifteen

Love and fidelity

The philosopher's task is not just to bend the mind, but also to bring into question entrenched preconceptions and to uproot deep but rotten beliefs. This can be of great practical value. Few other areas are richer repositories for moldy misconceptions than that of human sexual relationships, and a great deal of recent philosophical effort has been devoted to investigating such issues as pornography, prostitution, sexism, homosexuality, and love.

Love is delicate and unfathomable; it is spiritually uplifting and inspires tenderness and poetry. But love between persons also often leads to jealousy and pain. An emotion that is beautiful, wholesome, and good is replaced by something bad and destructive. In many cultures, love between two adults is commonly held to be exclusive in the sense that the intensity of the feeling between the lovers is supposed to preclude the possibility of either of them simultaneously enjoying similar feelings for somebody else. And because sexual intercourse is thought to be a major form of the expression of such love, a lover's discovery that his or her partner is having sex with another usually leads to the destruction of the relationship – the partners see each other in a less favorable light, or may stop seeing each other altogether. Is it, as it were, a law of nature that such non-exclusive relationships are unstable, or does the explanation lie in the influence of the prevailing conventional attitudes, certain assumptions about sex and love and about what constitutes moral and immoral behavior, and are these attitudes and assumptions justified?

Let us confine attention to the special case of adultery. Is adultery immoral, or are extra-marital 'affairs' morally neutral, or do they have positive moral worth? According to the norms of many societies, adultery is immoral. These norms are not, in general, merely reflections of taste or prejudice; they may be seen as conclusions consistent with other widely held beliefs about the nature of institutions such as marriage, and about the demands on personal conduct in the context of such institutions.

One reason for thinking adultery immoral is that the marriage ceremony includes the making of certain promises, so that, since having extra-marital sex involves breaking one of these promises, and promise-breaking is always wrong, the adulterer has committed a moral offence. A similar argument to the same conclusion has as its premises the truth that adultery frequently involves deception (about one's whereabouts or one's feelings), and the claim that deception is always wrong.

A response to these kinds of argument (one, roughly speaking, offered by Richard Wasserstrom) is that we should not invest marriage, and sex within marriage, with a significance so great as to make extra-marital sex appear sinful. Then the making of solemn promises about one's sexual behavior would be inappropriate, and no deception would be needed. After all, as Wasserstrom points out, parental love for a child does not imply exclusivity – if parents who have one child have five more, their love for each of these may equal their undiminished love for the first (p. 215).

However, although there is something correct in this response, it betrays, as does the argument for the immorality of adultery, the philosopher's characteristic unhealthy craving for moral generalities. Why should we think that all breaking of promises is morally wrong and that all marriages ought to be regarded as never of great moral significance? If promise-breaking were always wrong, then the only way for a potential adulterer to escape culpability would be to come to an agreement with his or her spouse that the promise of fidelity is to be mutually abandoned. However, an 'open' marriage may not be altogether too easy to achieve, and it is not clear that honesty is always the best policy. Surely a more satisfactory response is that it is not always the case that promise-breaking and deception are morally wrong.

Marriages are not, in general, lightly undertaken, but often the reasons for a couple marrying, for example, to avoid loneliness or to raise children in an 'approved' environment, have nothing to do with the promises they make at the wedding ceremony. A package of promises is made in a ceremonial or ritualistic setting. While clearly, for some people, this setting lends solemnity to the promises, from many, full and serious commitment to each promise is not realistically to be expected. In a Christian wedding, the couple promise to love, honor, and obey until separated by death – although the obedience clause is sometimes deleted. Yet, even when that clause has been included, a wife who occasionally acts against her husband's wishes may not always be blamed for breaking her ceremonial promise of obedience. And, when a couple divorce, their plight is often greeted with compassion rather than with a condemnation for failure to keep their promise to stay together. If, then, these promises are not regarded as absolutely binding, why should we regard as any more solemn the (unspoken) promise of fidelity?

Thomas Hardy makes the stronger claim that it is quite absurd to feel committed by marriage vows. The following passage is taken from *Jude the Obscure*:

> And so the two swore that at every time of their lives, until death took them, they would assuredly believe, feel, and desire exactly as they had believed, felt and desired during the preceding weeks. What was as remarkable as the undertaking itself was the fact that nobody seemed at all surprised at what they swore.
>
> (Cited in Mendus, p. 243)

One need not be cynical about making such undertakings at the time of making them for one may seriously and unconditionally commit oneself without so much as the thought that one's commitments might fade. But, if one's commitments do fade, then it is not clear exactly how bad it is to break a promise that was made when one's beliefs, feelings and emotional state were different.

Deception too, though not normally good practice may, under certain circumstances, be permissible ('white lies'). Suppose we are convinced that societal censure of extra-marital relations is not the expression of a well-founded moral value, but is merely a practical ploy to keep marriages together. Then, if a person has a strong desire for love and intimacy which is not restricted to one partner, he or she may let this desire override the principle that deception of any kind is wrong. An outraged response to this might be that a mere animal desire should never override an absolute moral principle. That response masks a number of questionable assumptions. Are there absolute moral principles? Is sex outside marriage merely the satisfaction of an animal desire? Even if animals cannot enjoy significant loving relations (as Roger Scruton claims, pp. 36–41) we have no reason to think that an adulterous relationship can aspire to nothing higher. More strongly, one may regard adultery as a significant good that should be pursued even in the face of adversity.

The immorality of deception cannot, however, be dismissed so easily. A society in which deception is rampant is wholly corrupt and unmanageable. Apart from moral reasons for keeping deception to a minimum, there are good pragmatic reasons too. But such considerations do not get to the heart of the matter. Deception is immoral and, one is inclined to say, it is particularly immoral and inexcusable when the person being deceived is the partner with whom one has built a shared life. This is a consideration that ought to be accorded great weight in arguing the case against adultery.

Many of the other arguments purporting to show that adultery is wrong can be rebutted quite easily. It is said, for example, that a supreme virtue of the institution of monogamous marriage is that it provides the ideal environment for bringing up children, and that extra-marital affairs are somehow threatening to this environment. The answer to this is that the adultery is detrimental to the environment only if too much time is spent on it – but if the adulterous parent spent the same amount of time out at the local chess club instead, then the deprivation to the children would be just the same. 'No', you might say, 'chess is not corrupting, but adultery is.' But adultery is corrupting only if adultery is corrupt, and this has yet to be proved. It is true that, through adultery, some people make an appalling mess of their lives. But that just shows that some people do not have the resources or the resourcefulness to make a success of an adulterous relationship. That doesn't make adultery bad. (We don't say that marriage is bad just because it has ruined some people's lives.)

Much of the language used to describe an adulterer's partner (e.g. 'a bit of fluff', 'a floozy', 'a bit on the side,' 'a fancy man') reflects the feeling that an adulterous relationship cannot be a deep and loving one, but must be tenuous, exploitative, or cheap. Yet this is falsified by the fact that what starts as adultery sometimes leads to a second marriage much more rich and loving than the first. There is no reason to suppose that a quantum leap in the quality of the relationship must attend its change of status. Besides, even if it were true that no adulterous relationship can attain the peaks of love, warmth, and friendship found in the best marriages, this does not show that adultery is an evil. The Beatles may not be as good as Beethoven, and a detective story may not attain the profundity of *War and Peace*, but that doesn't mean that the Beatles or the thriller are bad, or that indulging in them will impair our taste for what is better.

Perhaps the most serious argument for thinking that adultery is bad is that it is threatening to the non-adulterous partner who may be 'left in the lurch' if the adulterer leaves the marital home.

It is certainly true that in many cases this is a real risk. But should all risks be avoided? It may be only a slight risk, especially if children are involved or if the marriage bond is strong. And if the marital bond is not strong, why shouldn't it be broken? One may think the risk worth running if one regards adultery not as shameful, but as an activity that has positive value. It could be argued that there is something profoundly unhealthy about the traditional association of love and marriage with concepts of possession and ownership of (sexual) property (think of dowries and the significance of wedding rings). By freeing ourselves of the notion that love entails shackling our sexual possessions, we may come to regard adultery as promoting romantic passion and as a means for enabling people to lead richer, happier, less restricted lives. On the other hand, it is surely a part of loving someone not to cause that person fear or harm. And the fear of losing a partner who is expected to be a companion for life cannot be easily written off as silly or irrational.

Richard Taylor, in the introduction to *Having Love Affairs*, praises extra-marital love in extravagant terms. He writes:

> . . . the joys of illicit and passionate love, which include but go far beyond the mere joys of sex, are incomparably good. And it is undeniable that those who never experience love affairs, and who perhaps even boast of their faultless monogamy year in and year out, have really missed something. Virtuous they may be – even this can be questioned – but truly blessed they are not quite. Such a person lives in a kind of lifelong total eclipse, or a house without windows. He is like someone who has never heard a nocturne of Chopin's, tasted caviar, or beheld the Alps – except that what he has missed is something with which these tepid things do not even begin to compare. (p. 12)

Taylor makes the point that, while all sorts of forces operate to hold marriages together, the same sort of forces work to drive love affairs apart. In an enduring love affair, it is principally just the strength of passionate love that withstands the pressure of such forces and this in itself is a testimony to the desirability of that love.

These conclusions were arrived at after an extensive empirical study of love affairs which Taylor undertook. His research began with an advertisement he repeatedly inserted over the course of three years in the classified section of five newspapers in three cities. It read:

> Professor researching causes and consequences of extramarital love affairs wishes to contact persons willing to answer questionnaire or be interviewed. Confidentiality assured.
> Write: Prof. R. Taylor,
> Dept. Philosophy, University of
> Rochester, NY 14627. (p. 13)

Each respondent was sent a questionnaire and on the basis of completed questionnaires, Taylor invited those that he judged were genuinely involved in serious extra-marital affairs for one-on-one interviews with him over cocktails or dinner. His book is built around the accounts people volunteered. Most of the respondents seem to have been middle-class, well-educated Americans and, since his sample was also self-selecting, one should be most wary about generalizing his results to the whole of the human race.

Some of Taylor's conclusions are not altogether surprising. He found, for example, that women who, as children, received little paternal warmth, often sought affection, in their teenage years, from older, married men. His findings supported the proposition that men and women are, in very basic ways, quite different in their needs, responses, and desires. For example, Taylor's results show that a woman will frequently desert a lover if she discovers that he is married, and will not tend to seek a lover if she herself is happily married. Whereas married men, or at least many of them, seek new lovers even when their domestic situation is quite satisfactory, a wife will most often be looking for a lover not because she has a healthy interest in the qualities of other men, but as a reaction to certain deficiencies she perceives in her husband. For example, Taylor cites one account of a woman married to an upright, dutiful, industrious man. She took a lover simply because she found her husband totally boring. It is typically only some kind of dissatisfaction with her marital partner that prompts such action in a woman.

Although Taylor depicts extra-marital love affairs in glowing terms, and a superficial reading of the various accounts he retails may give the impression that all the participants regarded their affairs as having pure unsullied value, one may detect, I think, something a little distasteful in the behavior of many of the people involved. A lover is treated not as an end in him/herself, in affirmation of the belief that loving someone is intrinsically valuable, but as a means to an end – as compensation, for example, for a neglectful father or husband. The partner is used to satisfy certain psychological and biological needs (these needs need not be for sexual gratification – Taylor cites evidence that, in many cases, women are quite content with an impotent partner). There seems to be a disparity between regarding love affairs as satisfying such needs and regarding them, in Taylor's way, as great goods. The disparity is not resolved by claiming that love affairs are good because they satisfy such needs – this would be to relegate love to the level of food and shelter. Something which is necessary is not necessarily good.

Taylor has what I consider to be a rather bad argument to explain men's relative gregariousness. It is to the effect that, while by nature, a man can sire over one hundred children a year, women can only manage about one, so the man has impulses consonant with that power. This must be invalid: a man is naturally endowed with the ability to strangle over one hundred people a year but that does not necessarily give him the desire to do so. A better explanation is that the men who engage in love affairs (as opposed to mere sexual liaisons) do really conform to Taylor's romantic ideals:

> Men who become involved in serious and lasting love affairs almost always have one thing in common, particularly if they are married. Their chief characteristic is that they are quite genuinely caring persons. When women describe their utter devotion to such men, the very same words constantly recur – such words as 'observant', 'considerate', 'attentive', 'interested in me' and, most of all, 'caring'. (p. 111)

The implication is that men (*some* men) regard intimate relationships as goods in themselves and so seek out such relationships rather than *resorting* to them when something has failed; the same is not true, to the same extent, of women.

If love affairs really are uplifting and high expressions of what is worthiest in the human spirit then a thinking person should resolutely disregard the censure of traditional morality. Yet this is far easier said than done. In most civilized societies, freedom of sexual expression is limited by taboos, conventions, and legal restrictions. In theory, restrictions on human action may be justified only when unrestricted forms of that action are liable to lead to harm or damage – yet sex between normal consenting adults is not intrinsically harmful, and therefore it should not be subject to restrictive rules. One could argue quite plausibly that under many circumstances where such behavior does lead to damaging consequences, this may be attributed to the very presence of those restrictions – it is the proscriptions that are harmful, not the behavior proscribed. However, it is the behavior that is condemned from the pulpit, from the pages of the gutter press, and from the mouths of the heroes and heroines of popular soap operas.

In the case of the media, the process is particularly vicious. If, for example, some newspapers sell themselves on scandal, then it is financially advantageous for that section of the press to promote a very censorious moral climate, thereby creating a background against which certain kinds of behavior will be counted as scandalous. Small wonder, then, that a rather traditional set of rules for sexual conduct is inculcated, gets entrenched, and is reinforced.

Where there are rules, legal or informal, regulating a practice, breaking the rules tends to produce shame and guilt even when the participants hold those rules in low regard. The rules act as a powerful deterrent and it seems that women generally defer to their authority, unless unhappy circumstances provoke them to break free. Of course, a woman will not generally see herself as constrained by such authority; she may say things such as, 'I am happily married and I don't want to sleep with another man.' But it is interesting to consider whether, or to what extent, such attitudes are shaped by pressures to conform to societal standards.

In most cultures, it has somehow come about that men who flout the traditional code of sexual morality are less strongly condemned than women who do. This, I believe, is symptomatic of the second-class citizenship that women are still accorded. The situation is deplorable, but will not be changed by sanctimonious pronouncements about treating women equally. What is called for is a thorough investigation of the origins of our current rules of law and of traditional morality, and a further examination of the arguments that might be thought to justify a particular code of sexual conduct. Some people believe that if we were to abandon our sexual mores society would degenerate into uncontrolled licentiousness and turpitude. It is therefore interesting to investigate whether other societies with very much more relaxed attitudes towards sex than our own are in fact hell-holes of vice and iniquity. A classic study of natives of the Trobriand Islands in north-west Melanesia by B.Malinowski provides some evidence that they are not.

Notes

R. Wasserstrom, 'Is adultery immoral?' in R. Baker and F. Elliston (eds), *Philosophy and Sex* (Buffalo, NY: Prometheus Books, 1975) pp. 207-21.

Many of the articles in the Baker and Elliston collection are accessible to beginners, and are fun to read. I got the Hardy quote from S. Mendus, 'Marital faithfulness', *Philosophy* 59 (1984), 243-52; which takes a line rather different from mine.

A book which is learned and clever, but which came in for some (mostly undeserved) abuse in newspaper reviews is R. Scruton, *Sexual Desire: A Philosophical Investigation* (London: Weidenfeld and Nicolson, 1986).

For the analogy between cheap thrillers and cheap thrills, see J. Wilson, 'Logic and sexual morality' in Lawrence Habermehl (ed.), *Morality in the Modern World* (Encino, Calif.; Dickenson Publishing Co. Inc., 1976) and, for plain sex, try A. Goldman, 'Plain sex', *Philosophy and Public Affairs* 6 (1977), 267-87.

Much empirical evidence on love affairs is documented in R. Taylor, *Having Love Affairs* (Buffalo: Prometheus Books, 1982), although this book is somewhat marred by the scarcity of good, solid, philosophical arguments to support the many interesting claims, and by the inclusion of a bunch of rules about love affairs with no guidance on how to abide by them.

For a guide to the Trobriand Islands, see B. Malinowski, *The Sexual Life of Savages* (London: Routledge & Kegan Paul, 1960).

A useful interdisciplinary reader is J. H. Geer and W. T. O'Donohue (eds), *Theories of Human Sexuality* (New York: Plenum Press, 1987).

Questions

1   One major objection to non-exclusive sexual relationships is that some non-exclusive partners may be consumed by painful jealousy. Is the proper reply to this simply that, in a more enlightened world, jealousy would vanish? Some serious indications that this is *not* an adequate reply are supplied by J. Neu, 'Jealous thoughts' and L. Tov-Ruach, 'Jealousy, attention and loss' in A. O. Rorty (ed.) *Explaining Emotions* (Berkeley, University of California Press, 1980), pp. 425-63 and 465-88 respectively.

2   Comment on the following remark: 'If marriages were equal relationships, then the changing of the relationship later on may be less serious. But clearly one problem today is that many marriages are not equal. Women make sacrifices far greater than men, and then are often left dangling after a man decides he prefers a new relationship.' For reading on this and on other topics discussed in this chapter, I strongly recommend J. F. M. Hunter, *Thinking about Sex and Love* (Toronto: Macmillan of Canada, 1980). On the question of whether men and women ought to be treated differently in virtue of being different, see J. R. Richards, 'Separate spheres' in P. Singer (ed.), *Applied Ethics* (Oxford: Oxford University Press, 1986), pp. 185-214.

3   One proposed definition of love is this: X loves Y if and only if whatever Y wants, X wants Y to have it just because Y wants it. If this definition is correct, then it would be impossible for a person to deceive a loved one, except in the unlikely event of the loved one wanting to be deceived. Is it true that we cannot deceive those we genuinely love, or is the proposed definition of love defective?

4   In Ibsen's *The Doll's House*, a wife walks out on her smug, domineering husband, and abandons her children in pursuit of what she calls 'her duty towards herself'. Ibsen portrays her as extremely courageous. Is her action morally admirable? (This question surfaces in a review by David Gallup of J. F. M. Hunter, *Thinking about Sex and Love*, in *Dialogue* 22 (1983), 113-23.)

Chapter sixteen

How (if at all) should we be governed?

One popular way of drawing a political map of the world is to classify countries as falling within either the capitalist or the socialist folds. Yet the terms 'capitalism' and 'socialism', and many of the other classifiers used in political science are, or have become, incredibly vague. It is often not even clear whether what are being referred to are economic systems, political systems, or both. The *Macmillan Contemporary Dictionary* defines 'capitalism' as an *economic* system in which capital goods and the means of production and distribution are privately owned, the wealth and goods passing freely between producers and consumers, with the competition between producers determining the price. The *Random House Dictionary* (College Edition) offers a similar definition. Yet both of these dictionaries define 'socialism' as a theory or system of *social* organization.

What are the distinctive features of capitalism and socialism considered as political systems? There is no general agreement amongst theorists as to how this question should be answered. Let us make two simplifying assumptions. First, that a capitalistic political system is one that promotes a capitalist economy and that a socialistic political system promotes a socialistic economy – one in which the community as a whole owns and controls industry, capital, land, and the basic means of production. Second, that when supply is limited, there will be competition for resources and for the power to control them. This second assumption may be simplistic as well as simplifying, since it has been argued that competitiveness is not a natural condition for individuals, but is a vice fostered by certain kinds of political system. However, one may become disposed towards accepting the second assumption, too, by observing the behavior of animals and infants, and by investigating corruption and private enterprise within long-established communist states.

A socialist system, in so far as it seeks to control the

distribution of wealth and power, must employ means to limit success in the competition for resources. Thus it will in some way be restrictive. But restrictiveness can assume different degrees of virulence, ranging from violent oppression to gentle paternalism. Capitalism finds nothing wrong with the stratification of society resulting from the unequal distribution of wealth, and hence does not oppose competition. But there are many types of non-opposition, and no state, so far as I know, is completely non-interventionist.

We see, then, a spectrum of political systems in the midst of which gently paternalistic socialist systems are, in practice, almost indistinguishable from strongly interventionist capitalist systems. This represents just one kind of ordering of political systems along one dimension (the socialist–capitalist). There are, of course, many alternative parameters that one might use as a theoretical instrument to identify and distinguish possible political systems. Only a small subset of such possible systems have historically been realized in the governance of states.

Suppose that one were given the task of dismantling a certain political regime and designing a new one to replace it. What is the optimum design for a system of government? Well, doesn't that depend upon what the community wants? Not according to some political theorists (Plato is a notable example) who argue that what ordinary, unsophisticated people want is quite irrelevant to determining the optimum form of government. Political science, so the argument goes, is, like any other science, the province of experts. The untutored may simply not know what is good for them. Marx explicitly added the corollary that, in the course of time, ordinary people would come to want the kind of political system he advocated (in the *Communist Manifesto*, he indicates that they already want it).

It is easy to see the merit of Plato's view. One doesn't expect ordinary aircraft passengers to be consulted on the design of the airplanes they are using. This is left to experts in aerodynamics and engineering. It is, of course, true that passengers might usefully be consulted on the design of aircraft seats, but this is because one can let a passengers sit in a variety of seats to test which is most comfortable. We can't let people try out a large variety of political systems to assess which they are most comfortable in.

If people don't know what they really want, or want what's not good for them, then one can hardly take the satisfaction of people's desires as the goal for our construction of a political system. However, something of worth might be achieved by looking not at people's positive desires, but at their aversions. If it is agreed by political theorists that there are certain things that people in general definitely don't want, and are right not to want, then we can consider what political theories can be faulted for promulgating conditions that people rightly want to avoid.

People do not want to be oppressed and stifled. This is not to say that there is a general demand for complete, absolute freedom. The only political system compatible with that demand is, as R. P. Wolff shows, no government at all, that is, anarchy. The word 'anarchy' is frequently used in a pejorative sense because of a tendency to associate unrule with unruliness. But it is by no means clear that the absence of law breeds disorder. Could one contend, more positively, that the promotion of justice depends on the abandoning of law? The idea has not won widespread acceptance. It is not just those on the political right who baulk at anarchy. Liberals enamoured of the idea that a state should care for its citizens 'from cradle to grave' recognize that public funding of welfare projects implies incursion into private wealth and thus involves the state in some coercion of the reluctant wealthy. But to accept the need for some degree of state intrusion into the private lives of citizens just is not the same as favoring oppression. A system of differential taxation will be oppressive only if the taxing authority takes an adversarial stance towards a particular section of the taxed population.

Given, then, that freedom from oppression is a reasonable desideratum, can we find any brand of political theory that, in principle, cannot deliver a society embracing this fundamental freedom? It has often been pointed out that in practice systems informed by Marx's thought do not deliver. The authoritarianism of regimes in the eastern bloc is often cited as evidence that this is the direction in which the directives of Marx inevitably lead. But, apart from committing the fallacies of moving from particular to general, and of *post hoc ergo propter hoc*, this argument can be refused for at least three reasons. First, it could be claimed that all socialist revolutions to date have occurred prematurely – before conditions were ripe for a relaxed, democratic communist system to flourish. Marx himself was aware that without achieving a certain level of education the proletariat would be unable properly to take on the task of law-making. Second, it could be claimed that the burgeoning of communism is not necessarily a *rapid* process and that some harsh transitional stages (some of which we are now witnessing) have to be traversed. Third, defenders of Marx's views could, with justification, argue that, in all past cases, the emergent ideologies were informed not by those views but by one or other perversion of them. So the kind of empirical evidence we have cited is not decisive.

It has been argued, however, that *in principle* certain essential characteristics of Marxist political theory are incompatible with those ideals of freedom from oppression that Marx himself espoused. One such trait, it has been claimed, is Marxism's 'Messianic aspiration for a society of perfect unity' (Femia, p. 223) which seems to militate against the participatory procedures modern Marxists almost unfailingly profess to desire.

Marx envisaged a communist society as being one in which antagonism between people was absent, where the traditional dominance of the bourgeois mercantile class over the working class was broken and where the political views of all individuals perfectly coincided (hence, as Engels remarked, the state as an instrument of power would become redundant and would wither away). In regarding unity and harmony as desirable and achievable ends, Marx is in agreement with Confucianism: 'Ten thousand eyes with one sight, ten thousand ears with one hearing, ten thousand powers with one purpose in life' (Liang Qichao). Some may find such words stirring; others will find them frightening.

As a bit of optimistic speculation, this idea of a unity of minds may be quite harmless, and it is possible that the human race will naturally develop in this way. But if a communist society is a desirable end, then, so the argument continues, we should not just sit back and wait for it to happen, but should actively seek it. Here lies the danger. For in order to hasten a condition of uniform opinion one must either repress dissenting voices or 'educate' the nonconformists. Mao Tse Tung favored the first course:

> What should our policy be towards non-Marxist ideas? As far as unmistakeable counter-revolutionaries and saboteurs of the socialist cause are concerned, the matter is easy: we simply deprive them of their freedom of speech.

Similar views are to be found in Lenin. This is the price to be paid for trying to bring about the ideal of unity. Kolakowski makes the point tellingly:

> The dream of perfect unity may come true only in the form of a caricature which denies its original intention: as an artificial unity imposed by coercion from above, in that the political body prevents real conflicts and real segmentation of the civil

society from expressing themselves. This body is almost mechanically compelled to crush all spontaneous forms of economic, political and cultural life. (p. 34)

I mentioned education as an alternative means for promoting uniformity of political opinion. Although apparently less drastic a policy, this is actually far more insidious than the blatant crushing of free expression. So-called 'civic education' is foisted on children, and this typically consists of instructing them in approved modes of behavior, coupled with warnings about the penalties, such as social ostracism, for not thinking and acting in the prescribed ways. Needless to say, discouraging children from dissent, and from acting differently from the majority, has the effect of a general stifling of creativity. Passive children are more easily fashioned into citizens obedient to the state.

The minimum requirement of any decent system of government, so I have been arguing, is that it tolerates a plurality of voices and encourages free debate. For unless these requirements are satisfied, the danger of oppression is omnipresent.

Notes

Plato, *The Republic* in B. Jowett (ed.), *The Dialogues of Plato* (New York: Random House, 1892).

On the question of the justification of intrusion by the state into the lives of citizens, see R. Nozick, *Anarchy, State and Utopia* (Oxford: Blackwell, 1974); R. P. Wolff, *In Defence of Anarchism* (New York: Harper & Row, 1970). Wolff's defence has been repeatedly attacked in the literature. A good, judicious assessment of the debate is provided by K. Graham, 'Democracy and the autonomous moral agent' in K. Graham (ed.), *Contemporary Political Philosophy* (Cambridge: Cambridge University Press, 1982).

The pronouncement of Liang Qichao is cited in A. J. Nathan, *Chinese Democracy* (New York: Alfred A. Knopf, 1985), pp. 57-8. I mentioned a remark from Mao Tse Tung, 'On the correct handling of contradictions among the people', *Five Essays on Philosophy* (Beijing: Foreign Languages Press, 1977), p. 117. This might be compared with the views expressed in V. I. Lenin, *What is to be Done?* (Moscow: Progress Publishers, 1967).

Two attacks on Marxist theory on which I drew are L. Kolakowski, 'The myth of human self-identity' in L. Kolakowski and S. Hampshire (eds) *The Socialist Idea* (London: Weidenfeld & Nicolson, 1974), pp. 18-35, and Joseph V. Femia, 'Marxism and radical democracy', *Inquiry*, 28 (1985), 293-319 (which drew a reply by J. O'Neil, *Inquiry* 29 (1986), 345-54).

Marx's extensive writings are assembled in K. Marx and F. Engels, *Collected Works* (Moscow: Progress Publishers, 1975-85). These are best approached through secondary sources, such as L. Kolakowski, *Main Currents of Marxism: Its Rise, Growth and Dissolution*, 3 vols. (Oxford: Clarendon Press, 1978); J. Mepham and D. H. Ruben (eds), *Issues in Marxist Philosophy* (New Jersey: Humanities Press, 1979); T. Campbell, *The Left and Rights* (London: Routledge & Kegan Paul, 1983); J. Roemer (ed.), *Analytical Marxism* (Cambridge: Cambridge University Press, 1986); J. Elster, *An Introduction to Karl Marx* (Cambridge: Cambridge University Press, 1986).

Questions

1 Where does benevolent state care end and the interference of the state in private lives begin? A relevant section (chapter 7) of Nozick, (*Anarchy, State and Utopia*) is reprinted in J. Perry and M. Bratman (eds) *Introduction to Philosophy* (New York: Oxford University Press, 1986), 659-66, which contains also a critique of Nozick by Kai Neilsen, pp. 667-80).

2 How can a democracy protect the rights of minorities?

3 Must a socialist state inevitably be oppressive? Femia ('Marxism and radical democracy') would be a good starting-point for this question.

4 Is it desirable for the judiciary to be, as far as possible, independent of the government?

Part five

Science and metaphysics

Introduction: thinking about reality

'As soon as what we would now call speculative physics had given us alternative pictures of reality, metaphysics was in place. Metaphysics is about criteria of reality. Metaphysics is intended to sort good systems of representation from bad ones' (p. 142). This quotation, from Ian Hacking's *Representing and Intervening*, is the best account I have encountered of metaphysics and its relation to science. Hacking's idea is that humans are, first and foremost, *depicters*. Prehistoric people painted pictures, carved sculptures, and imitated sounds before there was any such thing as a human language. These representations were intended as likenesses of reality. Early language (according to Hacking's 'philosophical anthropology') must have contained words that people used for acknowledging certain representations as faithful likenesses. We might translate these words as 'That's how it is!' or 'Real (man)!' The pre-Socratic philosopher–scientists offered competing 'pictures' of the world, different representations of reality. Democritus (*c*.460–*c*.370 BC), for example, advocated the view, which must have seemed very strange in his day, that the world consists of atoms swirling in a void. Later scientists have offered alternative theories. Thus Einstein, in his famous paper of 1905 introducing special relativity theory, offers a revolutionary picture which incorporates a dramatically new perspective on the nature of *time*. We can ask whether these are useful and productive representations, whether any are for real.

'Useful and productive'? Surely, a representation is useful and productive only to the extent that it is *true*. Isn't all this talk about different pictures of reality intolerably vague and unscientific? Well, consider the following argument: When humans perceive the world, they notice sounds and colors, the boundaries between solids and liquids, a diversity of tastes and smells, etc.

But suppose that we were creatures with totally different perceptual mechanisms. Suppose that we were built in such a way that we passed through solids just as easily as we now pass through air, that we made few of the perceptual discriminations that we now make but many that we now don't. What is the world? Is it what we perceive, or what is perceived by these hypothetical selves? Or by some other creatures like bats or goldfish? And what is 'the truth about the world' that science is supposed to deliver?

You may wish to say that there are many 'worlds of appearance' but these must be distinguished from the world as it is in itself – the real world that gives rise to, but should not be mistaken for, the different kinds of appearances to which different kinds of creatures are subject. What science seeks to discover, you may say, is the world behind the appearances. Well, if that is the aim, then scientists will not achieve it by observing the world, for all observation, including that in which scientific instruments are used, reveals only appearance. So the layman's notion that scientists achieve true theories about the world by making scrupulous observations is undermined.

The preceding discussion, brief and simple though it has been, has brought us face to face with both metaphysical and methodological issues. We have broached the metaphysical question of whether there is a reality behind all appearances – a way the world is *really* as opposed to how, to different perceivers, it appears to be. (The issue is pursued further in chapter 19.) A positive answer to this question is known as *scientific realism* which, following Bas van Fraassen, we may characterize thus: 'Science aims to give us, in its theories, a literally true story of what the world is like; and acceptance of a scientific theory involves the belief that it is true' (p. 8). For a scientific realist the unobservable or theoretical entities postulated by a true theory really exist. This is a view which appeals to untutored common sense, and much of the most interesting work in recent philosophy of science (including van Fraassen's book) is devoted to trying to show that it is false.

There is, then, an interface between science and metaphysics. The metaphysician enquires whether there are substances, whether there are properties which are not particular entities but which can inhabit many different particulars at once (the 'problem of universals'), whether our familiar metaphysical categories, such as *objects, events* and *persons* are indispensable, whether any change can occur uncaused, whether time can go into reverse, etc. Such questions, like those previously touched upon, while clearly related to scientific enquiry are of a more abstract kind than those that a working scientist typically addresses. But it is also true that some of the deepest metaphysical conundrums have emerged from activity at the cutting edge of science, and particularly from twentieth-century physics. One needs a fair amount of scientific training in order to be able to engage philosophically in such issues as wave/particle duality, indeterminism, the curvature of space, and the direction of time. Some recent texts, such as one by Peter Gibbins on quantum mechanics and one by Jonathan Powers which is strong on relativity theory, heroically attempt to provide non-scientists with the requisite background. But I suspect that Hacking (and others) are right in urging that, for aspiring philosophers of science, there is no real substitute for time spent *in the laboratory*.

Another set of questions of interest to the philosopher of science concerns the way in which science develops – how, and for what reasons 'alternative pictures' come into being. How do theories come to be formulated, how are they confirmed or disconfirmed, how do they figure in explanations, how do they come to be abandoned or superseded? These are questions about the nature of science and the methods that scientists employ. At first sight, they invite straightforward answers: scientific theorizing is a process of accumulating laws, and laws are discovered by making numerous observations of a phenomenon – the scientist proposes a general law to which all the observed cases appear to conform. The theory is confirmed by further relevant observations consistent with the proposed law, disconfirmed by any that are inconsistent with it. A phenomenon is explained if it can be deduced from a body of laws.

This whole bundle of ideas has been overturned by recent work in the philosophy of science. The notion that we can validly, or even rationally, proceed to general laws from (a multiplicity of) particular observations – a process called *induction* – has been shown to be riddled with difficulties (some of which are discussed in chapter 17). A famous alternative, championed by Karl Popper, holds that theories can never be established as true, but that progress towards true theories can be made only by seeking rigorously to *falsify* all serious contenders for the title of 'law'. The idea is that a hypothesis *can* be established as *false* if one or more of the consequences it predicts does not square with what we observe; and refuting a hypothesis clears the way for some bold new conjecture. One problem with this view is that, as a large number of case studies have shown, historically, science just does not seem always to have proceeded that way. A reason for this is that any scientific field at any given time plays host to a whole network of *interrelated* hypotheses and assumptions. So, when what is predicted by a theory fails to materialize, the blame cannot in general be pinned on an isolated hypothesis. (This, in rough terms, is what is called the Quine–Duhem thesis.) And when the recalcitrant evidence starts piling up, the whole edifice of hypotheses *cum* assumptions may start to wobble.

The view of scientific development just hinted at was worked out in a book now regarded as a classic – Thomas Kuhn's *The Structure of Scientific Revolutions*, first published in 1962. Kuhn, who was trained as a physicist, claims that scientists are mostly engaged in fairly routine work – 'normal science', as he calls it (p. 10). In a period of normal science there are, to be sure, plenty of problems to be solved, but these arise within a framework of concepts and approved methods – the 'paradigm' or 'disciplinary matrix' that the scientific community at that time accepts. However, after a time some scientific experiments may begin to throw up anomalous results – anomalous, that is, by the lights of the existing paradigm. For a while, various *ad hoc* manoeuvres are used to explain away the anomalies, but, as more of them appear the situation becomes increasingly uncomfortable until a *crisis* is reached. At this point, the time is ripe for what Kuhn calls a *revolutionary* change, a dramatic upheaval. The old paradigm is jettisoned and a new one, that is, a completely new way of thinking then becomes the norm.

An even more radical position is taken by Paul Feyerabend in a beautiful, learned (though some find it infuriating) book called *Against Method*. Feyerabend thinks that there may at any time be a multiplicity of different theories running alongside each other in any given scientific area, that theories do and should proliferate, that there is no unique 'scientific method' that guides the development of theories but that fruitful inspiration may come from anywhere, including ancient superstitions, political ideologies, and voodoo. Consistency with established beliefs should certainly not be regarded as a desideratum, since that has the effect of conserving the old and stifling the new. Feyerabend goes so far as to argue that there is no unique standard of rationality.

Sometimes, when reading Feyerabend, one is unsure whether he means some of his more outrageous suggestions to be taken seriously. His wild writing seems to be following his own anti-prescription, 'anything goes', and one might therefore congratulate him for his consistency – except that, as we have seen, consistency is no great virtue in Feyerabend's book. Feyerabend's work has come under heavy attack by authors like Larry Laudan and John Krige, and not too many philosophers seem to have been won over by his arguments. However, there is at least one respect in which his case seems highly plausible: Models and analogies play an essential, and not merely decorative, role in scientific thinking. Now, the models and analogies one employs in a scientific explanation are not themselves deduced from any scientific laws; the choice of them is determined by almost *artistic* considerations about what is thought to be elegant, appealing and compelling. So here one might expect the pluralism of theories and metaphysical views of which Feyerabend speaks, a pluralism which, he claims, 'is not only important for methodology, it is also an essential part of a humanitarian outlook' (p. 52).

Kuhn and Feyerabend, together with N. R. Hanson and a number of other writers accept, as a consequence of their views on the emergence of theories, that certain theories will be not incompatible, but incomparable or, in their favored term, 'incommensurable'. That is, one theory cannot be said to be more nearly true than the other, or even to conflict with the other, so far as considerations of truth and falsity are concerned. What lies behind this claim is the argument that, although two theories may contain the same scientific terms (e.g. 'mass', 'length') those terms *mean* different things in each theory, because what a theoretical term means is a function of the theory in which it is embedded. The word 'combustion', for us, means 'the combination of a substance with oxygen or another element accompanied by light and heat' (Odham's *New English Dictionary*), but it obviously meant something different in the days before the discovery of oxygen. (An even clearer case, for those who know some relativity theory, would be the meaning of the word 'simultaneous' in classical and in twentieth-century physics.) So to try, for example, to measure classical mechanics against relativity theory (both of which contain the terms 'mass' and 'length') would be to commit a fallacy of equivocation.

This conclusion may sound preposterous. 'Surely', it will be said, 'there is a perfectly straightforward way of comparing two theories, namely, see which one of them best squares with our experimental observations.' There is, however, a reply to this reply, and it is one most convincingly defended by Hanson (*Patterns of Discovery*, pp. 4-30): Observations themselves are not neutral between theories; the very observations we make are 'theory-laden', so we cannot use observations to adjudicate between incommensurable theories. In some ways, the view that observations are suffused with theory is trivially true. I cannot make the observation that the galvanometer reading is 40 milliamps unless I know some theory of electricity. And the calibration of measuring instruments is itself determined by theory. For example, a spring balance is calibrated in accordance with the principle that the extension of the spring is linearly related to weight; no measurements by such a balance are going to show that Hooke's law is wrong. Further, a trained observer of (say) a photomicrograph of neurons in a cross-section of the cortex will be able to see several distinct layers that an observer who knows no neurophysiological theory is simply unable to detect, even when the layers are labelled. The latter just sees a mass of blobs. Whether any of these considerations is sufficient to justify the theory-ladenness thesis in the strong form required by the incommensurability claim is a problem that I shall here leave open. There is a question at the end of chapter 19 that invites readers to pursue the matter further.

Aristotle's *Metaphysics* was so called simply because, in the opinion of an early editor of Aristotle, it was the book which was written after the *Physics* ('meta', in Greek = 'after'). We have argued that the content of modern metaphysics is such as to make the subject contiguous with science, but there is also a sense in which metaphysics deals with questions which go *beyond* science. Questions concerning the freedom of the will, the void beyond death and the possibility of a supernatural being are usually assigned to this category, and I have devoted a chapter to each of these.

References

Barnes, J. (1982) *The Pre-Socratic Philosophers*, rev. edn, London: Routledge & Keegan Paul. (Chapter 17, pp. 342-77 for Democritus.)

Duhem, P. (1954) *The Aim and Structure of Physical Theory*, Princeton: Princeton University Press. Originally published 1906.

Einstein, A. (1905) 'On the electrodynamics of moving bodies', in H. A. Lorentz, A. Einstein, H. Minkowski, and H. Weyl (1923) *The Principle of Relativity, a Collection of Original Memoirs on the Special and General Theory of Relativity*, translated by W. Perrett and G. B. Jeffrey, London: Methuen.

Feyerabend, P. K. (1975) *Against Method*, London: New Left Books.

Fraassen, B. C. van (1980) *The Scientific Image*, Oxford: Clarendon Press.

Gibbins, P. (1987) *Particles and Paradoxes: The Limits of Quantum Logic*, Cambridge: Cambridge University Press.

Hacking, I. (1983) *Representing and Intervening*, Cambridge: Cambridge University Press.

Hanson, N. R. (1972) *Observation and Explanation*, London: Methuen.
Krige, I. (1980) Science, *Revolution and Discontinuity*, New Jersey: Humanities Press.
Kuhn, T. S. (1970) *The Structure of Scientific Revolutions*, 2nd edn, Chicago: University of Chicago Press.
Laudan, L. (1977) *Progress and its Problems*, Berkeley: University of California Press.
Popper, K. R. (1963) *Conjectures and Refutations*, London: Routledge & Kegan Paul.
Powers, J. (1982) *Philosophy and the New Physics*, London: Methuen.
Quine, W. V. (1964) 'Two dogmas of empiricism', in Quine, *From a Logical Point of View*, 2nd edn, Cambridge, Mass.: Harvard University Press, pp. 20-46.
Sambursky, S. (ed.) (1974) *Physical Thought from the Presocratics to the Quantum Physicists*, London: Hutchinson, pp. 55-7.

Introductory texts

Philosophy of science

Barrow, J. D. (1988) *The World within the World*, Oxford: Oxford University Press.
Bechtel, W. (1988) *Philosophy of Science: An Overview of Cognitive Science*, Hillsdale, NJ: Lawrence Erlbaum Associates Inc.
Bhaskar, R. (1975) *A Realist Theory of Science*, Leeds: Leeds Books.
Brody, B. A. and Grandy, R. (1989) *Readings in the Philosophy of Science*, 2nd edn, Englewood Cliffs: Prentice Hall.
Buchdahl, G. (1969) *Metaphysics and the Philosophy of Science*, Oxford: Blackwell.
Cartwright, N. (1983) *How the Laws of Physics Lie*, Oxford: Oxford University Press.
Chalmers, A. F. (1982) *What Is This Thing Called Science?*, 2nd edn, Milton Keynes: Open University Press.
Cohen, L. J. (1989) *The Gradation of Certainty: An Introduction to the Philosophy of Induction and Probability*, Oxford: Oxford University Press.
Hanson, N. R. (1958) *Patterns of Discovery*, Cambridge: Cambridge University Press.
Harré, R. (1972) *The Philosophies of Science: An Introductory Survey*, Oxford: Oxford University Press.
Heisenberg, W. (1959) *Physics and Philosophy*, London: Allen & Unwin.
Hempel, C. G. (1963) *Aspects of Scientific Explanation*, New York: Free Press.
Lakatos, I. and Musgrave, A. (eds) (1970) *Criticism and the Growth of Knowledge*, Cambridge: Cambridge University Press.
Nagel, E. (1961) *The Structure of Science*, London: Routledge & Kegan Paul.

Science and metaphysics

Nidditch, P. H. (ed.) (1968) *The Philosophy of Science*, Oxford: Oxford University Press.
Popper, K. R. (1959) *The Logic of Scientific Discovery*, London: Hutchinson.
Smart, J. J. C. (1968) *Between Science and Philosophy*, New York: Random House.

Metaphysics

Armstrong, D. M. (1978), *Universals and Scientific Realism*, Cambridge: Cambridge University Press.
Aune, B. (1986) *Metaphysics: The Elements*, Oxford: Blackwell.
Carr, B. (1987) *Metaphysics: An Introduction*, London: Macmillan.
Hamlyn, D. W. (1984) *Metaphysics*, Cambridge: Cambridge University Press.
Taylor, R. (1974) *Metaphysics*, 2nd edn, Englewood Cliffs: Prentice-Hall.

Chapter seventeen

The myth of simplicity

William of Ockham, who lived about AD 1290–1349 (it is probable that he died in the plague known as the Black Death) was one of the great logicians of the middle ages. He is popularly known for a principle called 'Ockham's Razor'. The principle as it occurs in his writings reads (in translation): 'It is unnecessary to do with more what can be done with fewer.' (p. 74)

This is a principle of *scientific explanation*. It does not tell us that the world is a simple place, but it tells us that when we are devising scientific theories about the world, we should make our theories as simple as possible. However, it is not easy to see what should count as a simple theory in science, as I hope to show.

Recall some of the scientific experiments we performed at school. One may have had to find out how the distance an object falls is related to the time it has been dropping; or to find out how the radiation from a body is related to its temperature; or to find out how the frequency of vibration in a piece of stretched wire varies with its tension. In each of these experiments there are two variables, and the aim is try to find out how they change relative to each other.

Such an experiment typically involves the making of a succession of observations in which measurements of various kinds are taken. Let us suppose that, on the basis of these measurements, you formulate a hypothesis about what relationship exists between the variables; that is to say, you attempt to state a scientific law. You may then make further observations to test your hypothesis, or you may use your proposed law to make predictions about circumstances that you have not observed, or cannot observe.

Your measurements may be recorded as points on a graph. The shortest distance of a point from one axis represents the value that one variable has when the other variable has the value represented by the shortest distance between the point and the

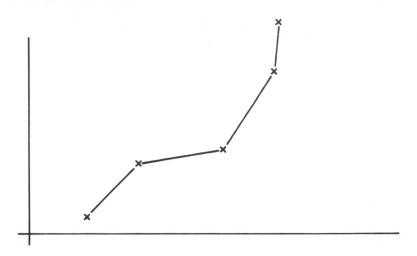

Diagram 1

other axis. Unless you have cheated, the points will probably be scattered so that, if you joined them up, you would get a jagged line such as is illustrated in diagram 1.

But you don't simply join up the points. You have probably been told to draw the smoothest possible curve so that all the points you have plotted are either on or near it. So you do something similar to what I have done in diagram 2.

From this curve, you read off pairs of values for the variables between and beyond those that you obtained by observation in the course of the experiment.

Two questions now arise: (i) Why should we draw a smooth curve rather than one that wriggles in such a way that it comes closer to the points plotted? (ii) How should we continue the curve outside the range of the plotted points? Let's take the second question first. Suppose that Carol has done an experiment in which she heats a fixed volume of gas and at each 5° rise in temperature she measures the pressure. She plots her readings on graph paper and, as shown in diagram 3, draws the solid line which nicely fits her experimental results. On the basis of these results she concludes that there is a linear relationship between pressure and temperature, that is, if she extends her straight line in both directions she will be able to correctly predict what would

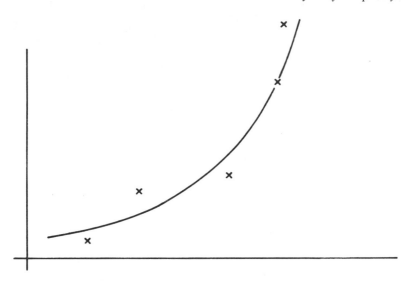

Diagram 2

be the pressure of the gas at temperatures beyond those at which she took readings. Such extrapolation from the observed to the unobserved is known as *induction*. Can the procedure be justified? Or, to put it another way, can we show that it is right to do things Carol's way – extending her straight line in a straight line – rather than, given exactly the same data, extending it in some more fancy way, for example, as shown by the dotted line in diagram 3?

Someone who proposed the dotty continuation would be suggesting that the simple, regular relationship established between temperature and pressure over the range observed in the experiment fails to hold outside that range. But why is that conjecture more unreasonable than Carol's, remembering that, *ex hypothesi*, neither has made any observations outside the range recorded by the points on the graph? One answer might be that every time (or almost every time) in the past when we have done such experiments and projected our results in the straightforward way, subsequent experiments have confirmed that that projection was correct, so we shall not go wrong by doing likewise (like-Carol-wise) this time.

Now look carefully at that answer. It is a bit of inductive reasoning! It says in effect that doing X in the past has always

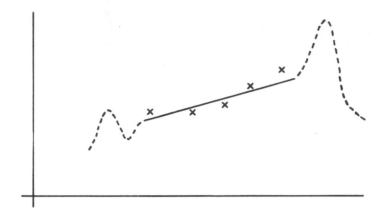

Diagram 3

worked, so it will continue to work in the future. So we have used induction in the very process of trying to show that the use of induction is justified. That won't do at all, will it? Yet we have a gut feeling that Carol's procedure is reasonable, and that the proposed alternative is barmy. (But not *completely* barmy – the graph of temperature against volume for ice has a strange kink in it at about −4°C, which keeps plumbers in business.) Is there some other way, then, of justifying induction? Question (ii) has led us to a couple of very awkward questions, and I am going to take the cowardly course of dropping the subject and reverting to question (i).

Question (i) states: Why go for the visually and algebraically simpler curve rather than a more complicated curve that better fits the plotted points? What this question presupposes is that, allowing for experimental error, there is some way of determining the simplest law consistent with a bunch of experimental data. It's this presupposition that I want to query.

Consider the graph we obtain from an experiment on objects falling freely through the air. If we let the distance from the y-axis represent elapsed time, and the distance from the x-axis represent distance fallen, then the measurements you take of distance fallen against time, when plotted graphically, should fall,

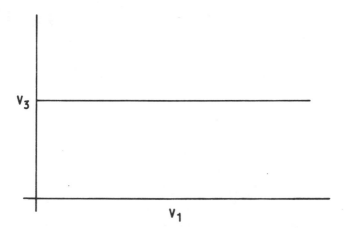

Diagram 4

roughly, on a parabola – similar in shape to the curve in Diagram 2 – which is expressed algebraically as the equation

$$y = kx^2$$

Suppose, however, that if, instead of using the distance from the x-axis to represent distance fallen, we use it to represent that distance divided by the square of the elapsed time, then the graph we obtain is simply a straight line, as shown in diagram 4, and this looks even simpler than the curve in diagram 2.

You may object that this is a trick performed, in effect, by introducing a strange new variable (distance divided by the square of time) which is represented by the distance from the x-axis. My reply is, first, that this variable is not so strange – it's known as *acceleration* – but second, even if it were, this should not trouble us. For one of the ways in which science progresses is by the introduction of 'strange' new concepts. Many of the concepts that are the common currency of modern physicists were simply not available to previous generations of scientists.

By a suitable transformation of the variables any curve can be similarly transformed into a simple straight line. For example, using the same observations as were recorded in diagrams 1 and

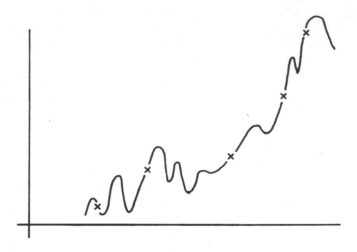

Diagram 5

2, we might suggest that the relation between the variables is that shown by the curve in diagram 5.

Suppose that this curve has the equation $y = f(x)$. We have plotted the pairs of values obtained by our experimental observations, but obviously the pairs of values for the variables between and beyond those so obtained that can be 'read off' this curve differ greatly from those read off diagram 2. So which curve makes the right predictions? If you favor the curve in diagram 2 because it is 'simpler', just consider that the very different predictions shown in diagram 5 can be expressed as a straight-line graph if, instead of plotting the values of V_1, we plotted those values divided by $f(x)$, where x takes the values of the variable V_2. Since you are keen on simplicity then, on that account, you should not be prejudiced against the latter alternative.

Again you may respond that to perform this transformation, we have had to introduce a rather unnatural new variable. Again I reply that if science restricted itself to terms that now seem natural and well entrenched, it would stagnate.

So here is the problem: We make a finite number of observations and record these on a piece of graph paper. Yet there is an infinite number of curves that can be drawn which pass through or close to all of these points. But which of these curves is the right one expressing a scientific law on which we can reliably base predictions if none of the curves can be singled out as being the simplest?

This problem is dramatically highlighted in a chapter called 'The new riddle of induction' from Nelson Goodman's *Fact, Fiction and Forecast*. I shall use, but slightly modify, Goodman's own example (pp. 73–5):

Suppose that all emeralds observed up to the present time have been green. On the basis of these observations, we may be strongly inclined to accept the hypothesis that all emeralds are green. But now let us introduce a new adjective 'grue', which applies to all those things that are examined before AD 2000 and are green, and to all other things not so examined that are blue. Let's also have an adjective 'bleen' which applies to all those things that are examined before AD 2000 and are blue, and to things not so examined that are green. (Looking out of my window now, I see a clear bleen sky.) Anyone who has befriended such exotica as bosons, charm quarks and super-symmetry won't bat an eyelid at grue and bleen.

Since all the emeralds observed up to now are grue, the hypothesis that all emeralds are grue is as strongly supported as the hypothesis that all emeralds are green, yet these hypotheses are *incompatible* – they yield different predictions. So which hypothesis should we trust? You might say that 'grue' is such an unnatural, contrived, complicated adjective that we can safely discard the hypothesis that all emeralds are grue. But just imagine that there is a tribe who do not possess our color words, but who do have words like 'grue' and 'bleen' in their vocabulary. People in that tribe would complain that it is our words 'green' and 'blue' that are complicated. One tribesman explaining the word 'green' to another would say, 'It's a strange adjective which applies to all those things that are examined before AD 2000 and are grue, and to all things not so examined that are bleen.'

What this shows is that our 'green' is just as complicated for this tribe as their 'grue' is for us. So we cannot favor, on grounds of simplicity, our hypothesis which predicts that emeralds examined after AD 2000 will be green to the 'grue' hypothesis which predicts that they will be blue.

The problem raised by Goodman is quite general: What reason do we have for relying on our current scientific hypotheses when, by employing different variables, we can generate incompatible hypotheses *that are equally well supported by the evidence*?

Notes

The quotation from William of Ockham is taken from M. J. Loux (trans.), *Ockham's Theory of Terms: Part I of the Summa Logicae* (Indiana: University of Notre Dame Press, 1974).

The *locus classicus* for the problem of induction is D. Hume, *An Enquiry Concerning Human Understanding* (La Salle: Open Court), Sections 4 and 5.

Karl Popper has been a lifelong enemy of induction, taking an even more skeptical line than Hume. See, for example, K. Popper, *Objective Knowledge* (Oxford; Clarendon Press, 1972), pp. 1-31.

The conundrum about justifying inductive arguments by means of an inductive argument and other issues on which this chapter touches are dicussed by several of the contributors to the following two collections: P. H. Nidditch (ed.), *The Philosophy of Science* (Oxford: Oxford University Press, 1968); R. Swinburne (ed.), *The Justification of Induction* (Oxford: Oxford University Press, 1974).

The *locus modernus-classicus* for the 'new riddle of induction' is N. Goodman, *Fact, Fiction and Forecast*, 2nd edn (Indianapolis: Bobbs Merrill Co. Inc., 1965), chap. 3, Sect. 4, esp. pp. 73-5.

My inspiration for this chapter came from G. Priest, 'Gruesome Simplicity', *Philosophy of Science* 43 (1976), 432-7.

The complexity of the issue of simplicity is brought out in E. Sober, *Simplicity* (Oxford: Clarendon Press, 1985).

Questions

1 Can inductive arguments be justified? We saw that one attempt at justification appeared to be circular, but it has been argued that certain 'self-supporting' inferences are legitimate. See the debate between Max Black and Peter Achinstein, reprinted in R. Swinburne (ed.), *The Justification of Induction*. Various other means of justifying or vindicating induction are proposed by contributors to this volume. See also D.C. Stove, *The Rationality of Induction* (Oxford: Clarendon Press, 1986).

2 Could 'All emeralds are grue' be a law of nature? There is a vast literature on laws of nature. You might try P. Achinstein, *Law and Explanation* (Oxford: Clarendon Press, 1971), chapters 1–3 and D. M. Armstrong, *What is a Law of Nature?* (Cambridge: Cambridge University Press, 1983).

3 We supposedly confirm a scientific hypothesis of the form 'All Xs are Ys' by finding examples of Xs which are Ys. Thus we would confirm the hypothesis 'All ravens are black' by finding ravens which are indeed black. (The discovery of ravens which are not black would *disconfirm* the hypothesis.) But now, consider the hypothesis 'All non-black things are non-ravens.' This is equivalent to the first hypothesis, and here the Xs

are non-black things. So, apparently, in order to confirm this hypothesis, we need only find non-black things that are not ravens. But my red carpet is a non-black thing, and it is not a raven. So my red carpet is a confirming instance of the hypothesis 'All non-black things are non-ravens', and hence also a confirming instance of the *equivalent* hypothesis, 'All ravens are black.' But can it *really* be true that a scientific hypothesis about ravens can be confirmed by finding such things as red carpets, green apples, etc.? That would make the business of theory-confirmation a bit too easy. In order to confirm 'All neutrinos lack mass', we wouldn't need to set up any complicated experiment; we should only need to look around for objects that have mass and are not neutrinos – again, we should need to look no further than red carpets and green apples. This puzzle is known as Hempel's paradox, and was discovered in 1948. The paper is reprinted in C. G. Hempel, *Aspects of Scientific Explanation* (New York: Free Press, 1965). There are a great many discussions of the problem, including one in a useful book by Mary Hesse: *The Structure of Scientific Inference* (London: Macmillan, 1974), pp. 155-62.

Chapter eighteen

Free action in a material world

Every day we make decisions. We consider alternatives and choose to do one thing rather than another. Occasionally, a person is forced to do what he or she does not want to do, but usually people act out of their own free will.

That, at least, is what we like to think. But consider this: the body of a human being is a marvellously complicated organism, but it is composed only of physical particles. Now, physical particles do not act freely – their behavior conforms to the laws of physics. Therefore a human being, because just a mass of such particles, must always behave in accordance with physical laws, and so cannot act in any way different from what is determined by these laws. In other words, a human being does not act out of free will.

This is a very strange conclusion. For isn't it obvious that, at this very moment you are reading this chapter because you decided to do so, and right now you are free to continue reading or to stop – the choice is yours. It seems silly to say that all your actions are predetermined and that we only have the illusion of freedom.

Some people have said that there is a mistake in the reasoning that I have just sketched. They point out that, according to some widely accepted claims of modern physics, not all physical laws are deterministic – there is a certain essential unpredictability or randomness in the behavior of physical particles. Therefore the behavior of persons is not rigidly predetermined.

Now, even if such indeterministic theories are accepted (they have been disputed by many physicists, including Einstein) we do not have a solution to our problem. For we wanted to show how it is possible for there to be free human action in which we have control over what we do. But if some of our behavior is random and unpredictable by us, that means precisely that we do not have control over it.

Another popular attempt to solve our problem consists of denying my assumption that a human being consists solely of physical particles. The suggestion, which we have already encountered in the first section of this book, is that a human being consists of a physical body and a non-material mind or soul, and that it is the presence of this mind or soul that accounts for our ability to act freely.

The trouble with this suggestion is that it has no explanatory value. For, when we enquire what this mind or soul is, no description is forthcoming. All we are told is that it is whatever is responsible for our free actions. This is just like the situation in Molière's play *Le Malade Imaginaire* when the physician is asked why opium puts people to sleep. He replies 'Because it has a dormitive power.' But a 'dormitive power' is just the power to put people to sleep. So the physician's 'explanation' amounts to this: 'Opium puts people to sleep because it has the power to put people to sleep' – and this is clearly no explanation at all.

A much more interesting way out of our difficulties has been suggested by the modern philosopher Donald Davidson. In order to understand Davidson's solution, let us first take another look at our problem.

Those human actions that we are inclined to call 'free' arise from decisions, choices, desires – let's call such psychological occurrences 'mental events'. (We shall not think of these as events in a non-material mind; indeed Davidson believes that all mental events are physical.) Mental events (e.g. wanting a swim) often cause physical events (e.g. diving into the pool), and physical events (e.g. sitting on a pin) frequently cause mental events (e.g. feeling a pain).

Scientific causal laws are general – they do not deal with singular occurrences, but state relations between *types* of event. For example, one of the laws that we all learn at school is that the heating of metal – any heating of any metal – causes expansion (in direct proportion to the increase of temperature). Scientific laws allow us to predict the effects of certain *kinds* of event.

Now, if there are psychophysical laws – laws that connect types of mental events to types of physical events – then all of our actions will be predictable. For, if you are affected by a physical event of some type, a psychophysical law will determine what type of mental event will be produced in you, and another psychophysical law will determine your behavior caused by that type of mental event.

Davidson argues that while *particular* mental events do cause

177

particular physical events and vice versa, there are no psycho-physical laws connecting *types* of mental events to *types* of physical events. This is because it is extremely unlikely that the particular mental events that group together as a psychological type will also form a unified physical type of the sort that could be related by a causal law to another physical type. For example, if, on different occasions, several mental events occur in me that from a psychological point of view are similar in that they could all be classified as *wanting a banana* then, if each of those mental events is a physical event (something taking place in my brain) then those physical events might be so *dissimilar* that no neorophysiologist would say that they belong to a single type. In other words, each time I want a banana, the relevant configur-ations of neural activity inside my head might be different – in fact so different that they don't even come close to exemplifying a common pattern. And when you want a banana on a given occasion, the inside of your brain might, again, look quite different from mine when I want one.

The following diagram may help to make this difficult idea a bit clearer:

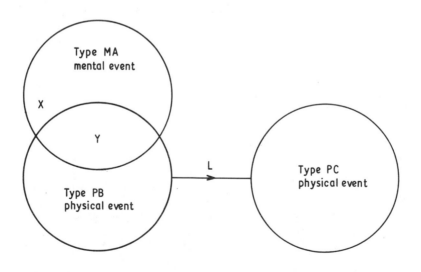

Here X and Y are particular events of the same mental type (MA), but only Y belongs to the type of physical event (PB). There is a causal law (L) that links physical events of type (PB) with physical events of type (PC), but there is no psychophysical law linking (MA) to (PC) or to any other type of physical event.

If Davidson's argument is correct, it seems to follow that psychology cannot be reduced to the science of neurophysiology. And free action is shown to be possible in this sense: Our actions do not occur haphazardly – we have control over them in that we ourselves (our mental events) cause our behavior. Yet our behavior cannot be predicted by scientific law, since there are no psychophysical laws dictating that a certain kind of behavior inevitably follows a certain kind of mental state.

The position is decidedly subtle. On the one hand, Davidson will concede that every individual event is caused, and to some people this concession seems to close the door on free will. On the other hand, if Davidson is right, our thoughts and actions are not subject to causal laws, so it would seem that those that are not random, haphazard, or reflex must be free.

But is Davidson's argument convincing? Many attempts to refute it have been made in the literature. I shall offer one objection with the help of the diagram below:

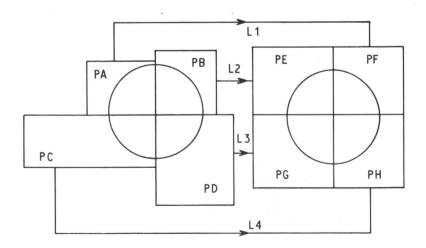

The left-hand circle represents a type of mental event (ML), and we shall suppose that there are just four types of physical events (PA), (PB), (PC), and (PD) – these are represented by rectangles – which together exhaust (ML). Now could it be that (PA) is connected to (PF) by the law (L1), that (PB) is connected to (PE) by (L2), (PD) to (PG) by (L3) and (PC) to (PH) by (L4), as shown, and that (PE), (PF), (PG), and (PH) together form a unified, natural type of physical event (PR)? If so, then we have here a psychophysical law connecting (ML) to (PR).

Moreover, if we say that the right-hand circle on the diagram represents a type of mental event (MR), then we obtain a (highly simplified and idealized) model of the non-uniform relation between types of mental events. For example, sometimes a mental event, such as hearing a noise in the dark, will cause a certain psychological state, such as fear; but sometimes, under similar circumstances, a similar mental event will have no such effect.

Notes

The view that it is our possession of minds or souls that opens the possibility of our acting freely dates from Socrates or earlier. Its most famous defense is by Descartes, and there is, of course, much more to be said for the theory than I have said. J. Ferguson, *Socrates* (London: Macmillan, 1970), e.g. p. 129; R. Descartes, *Meditations on First Philosophy*, in G. E. M. Anscombe and P. T. Geach (eds), *Descartes: Philosophical Writings* (London: Nelson, 1954).

For the dispute between Einstein and Bohr over indeterminism, see P. A. Schlipp (ed.), *Albert Einstein: Philosopher-Scientist*, 2nd edn (La Salle: Open Court, 1951), pp. 201-41.

On illusory explanations: J. Molière, *Le Malade Imaginaire* (Paris: Bordas, 1980).

Davidson's 'anomalous monism' is presented in 'Mental events' repr. in D. Davidson, *Essays on Actions and Events* (Oxford: Oxford University Press, 1980), pp. 207-7. Some of this article is too difficult for beginners, but essays 12 and 13 in the same collection (pp. 228-59) provide considerable clarification.

For short criticisms of Davidson's position, see C. McGinn, *Character of Mind* (Oxford: Oxford University Press, 1982), pp. 16-36; D.W. Hamlyn, *Metaphysics* (Cambridge: Cambridge University Press, 1984), pp. 161-86.

Another argument against Davidson is advanced in A. J. Ayer, *Philosophy in the Twentieth Century* (London: Weidenfeld & Nicolson, 1982), pp. 187-9. Earlier in this book (p. 17), Ayer says that he doubts whether he would wish to give up his current attitudes to himself and his fellow-men in favor of a strictly scientific approach even if it were in his power to do so. He thinks 'that there is a case for retaining a muddled concept of free will, just in so far as the myths it engenders are salutary'. Ayer was certainly an older, and possibly a wiser, man than me, but I would not commend to anyone this counsel of self-deception.

For a defense of a conclusion similar to Davidson's, and a reply to the kind of objection I raised in the text, see H. Putnam, 'Philosophy and our mental life' in Putnam, *Philosophical Papers*, vol. 2 (Cambridge: Cambridge University Press, 1975), pp. 291-303.

Readers may feel that I have been too swift to espouse physicalism (the doctrine that everything that occurs in the world can be explained in terms of the concepts and laws of whatever turns out to be true physics). For a concerted, sophisticated attack on physicalism and an impressive discussion of free will and ethics, see T. Nagel, *The View from Nowhere* (Oxford: Oxford University Press, 1986).

A good introduction to the free will problem is given in B. Aune, *Metaphysics – The Elements* (Oxford: Blackwell, 1986), pp. 187-225. Some useful essays on the problem are collected in G. Watson (ed.), *Free Will* (Oxford: Oxford University Press, 1984).

For an excellent account of the wrong directions that discussions of the problem of free will frequently take, read D. Dennett, *Elbow Room: The Varieties of Free Will Worth Wanting* (Oxford: Oxford University Press, 1984), esp. pp. 1-19.

Questions

1   Does Davidson succeed in showing that the possibility of free will is compatible with materialism?

2   In what sense, if any, is the possession of free will constitutive of our being human? A clearly written book on this subject is A. Donagan, *Choice: The Essential Element in Human Action* (New York: Routledge & Kegan Paul, 1987).

3   Is determinism a defensible doctrine, and is it compatible with free will? P. van Inwagen, *An Essay on Free will* (Oxford: Clarendon Press, 1983) argues that free will and determinism are incompatible. The doctrine of determinism is defended in T. Honderich, *A Theory of Determinism: The Mind, Neuroscience and Life-Hopes* (New York: Oxford University Press, 1988), an important book to an examination of which an issue of *Inquiry*, vol. 32 (March 1989), has been devoted.

Chapter nineteen

The world as we perceive it and as it really is

It is often naive questions about things we normally take for granted that lead to fruitful investigations. One classic, but perhaps apocryphal, example is the question 'Why do apples fall *down* from trees rather than *up*?' This is the question that is said to have occurred to Isaac Newton, prompting his enquiry into the nature of *gravitation*.

Here is another naive question. Every object can be divided and subdivided until we get down to its indivisible constituent particles. Now suppose I take a twig in one hand and hold it out horizontally in front of me. Why don't the particles of which the twig is composed simply fall away? What holds them together so that the twig in fact remains rigid? It's no use answering that the particles must be held together by some sort of glue, because glue itself is just a substance consisting wholly of minute particles, and we are left with the question of what holds *these* together.

Notice that the answers to these questions are highly non-naive. For example, the idea that objects many miles apart with nothing between them can nevertheless influence each other by strange 'forces', such as that of 'gravitation', must have appeared astonishing when it was first proposed. Similarly, the idea that the piece of twig in front of me is really a miniature system of orbital systems is so exotic as to be almost unbelievable.

What I am suggesting is that by reflecting on certain simple, everyday facts we can acquire some appreciation of how difficult is the physicist's task of providing a coherent explanation of how things are in the physical world. The world as it really is is quite different from what an ordinary person, unaided by experiment or theory, might suppose it to be. As Bertrand Russell said, 'The truth about physical objects *must* be strange. It *may* be unattainable' (p. 19).

Is Russell exaggerating here? We are aware that, in the upper reaches of modern physics, some pretty exotic ideas are floating around – antimatter, black holes, a twelve-dimensional universe, time flowing backwards, etc. But surely there are some simple truths about physical objects that we can discern just by looking? Can't we perceive many of the properties of the real world? Indeed, doesn't the ability to experimentally test our more exotic scientific hypotheses depend on just the ability to make mundane observations of the world around us?

The most radical *negative* answer to these questions was given by Bishop Berkeley, who argued that there are *no* objective properties – that the material world is a figment of our imagination, a fiction constructed from our subjective impressions. *Esse est percipi* – to be is to be perceived. In putting forward this view, Berkeley claimed to be *defending* common sense. Berkeley's position, known as *idealism* (or, better, *immaterialism*) was attacked by Immanuel Kant, although Kant himself held that we can never observe the real ('noumenal') world. All that is available to experience are 'appearances', never 'things-in-themselves'.

These views may appear to you somewhat fanciful, so it will be worth considering some evidence that tends to show that the real, mind-independent properties of things (if any there be) may be quite different from how they appear to us.

The first case is the illusion known as 'apparent motion'. We are presented, in rapid succession, with a pair of similar diagrams or pictures in which some of the shapes in the second are somewhat displaced from their position in the first, and we mentally construct motion – we see the displaced shapes as *moving* to their new position, as, for example, in movie films. What is presented on the screen are 'stills', but, because they are presented in rapid succession (twenty-five frames per second) then, so long as the differences between successive frames are not great, what we see is not a jerky flickering but continuous, smooth motion.

It is, of course, interesting to discover how it is that our visual system can be thus 'fooled', and a lot of experimental work has been done on the phenomenon. In the simplest type of experiment, a single colored spot is flashed briefly on a screen, followed by another flash of a similar spot a short distance away. If the time between flashes is sufficiently short (between 10 and 45 milliseconds) then what we perceive is a spot moving from the first position to the second. Now although, in some sense, this provides a miniature illustration of our perceptual experiences at the movies, it explains nothing. In fact the experiment suggests a perplexing question: We 'see' the spot moving between the two positions, so we must see it in an intermediate position at a time intermediate between that of the two flashes. So we see it in that position before the second flash. But until the second flash occurs, the observer does not know the position of that flash relative to the first. So how can the observer 'see' the intermediate spot in the correct position before knowing the direction of the second spot relative to the first? Had there been just one flash of light, there would obviously be no 'intermediate' spot. So the intermediate spot results from the second flash, yet it *precedes* it. Backward causation??!! If we wish to avoid that option, we shall need to contrive a fairly fancy theory that distinguishes between the occurrence of a physical event, our conscious awareness of that event, and possibly our preconscious registering of it.

Variations on the simple version of this experiment immediately suggest themselves. We might try making the second spot different in shape from the first. What happens here is apparent motion *and* shape deformation, where the spot, while moving, gradually changes from the first shape into the second. Or we could put a barrier on the screen between the first spot and the second (the moving spot hurdles it), or flash two or more spots after the first one, or flash two groups of spots, each group containing the same components, but in a different order; or replace the first spot with a larger one in the same position. All these experiments have been done, and, in all cases, a *gradual* transition takes place.

What do you think happens when spots of different shape *and* color are flashed succesively a short time and distance apart? One would expect a smooth transition of both shape and color. This expectation is shattered. I quote from Nelson Goodman's *Ways of Worldmaking*:

> Flash a small red square and then a large green (or pink) circle, within the specified time and distance limitations, and we see the square, while smoothly moving and transforming and growing into the circle, *remaining red until about midcourse and then abruptly changing to green (or pink)*. (p. 84)

Smooth change of shape, sharp change of color. What is the explanation? The answer can be seen by contrasting our everyday experiences with shapes and colors. We move around objects, and many objects move around, so we are familiar with gradual perceptual change in shape and size. By contrast, perceptual changes in color tend to be abrupt – there are generally sharp boundaries between pairs of colors. A glance around your room will confirm this. And we are accustomed to rapid changes in the perceived color of objects – as Goodman points out, 'an object does not lose its identity as it passes through dappled sun and shade' (p. 87). Further, when we see an object as moving, abrupt changes of color occur at the leading and trailing edges; a fixed point in the visual field changes from background color to the color of the object and back to the background color as the object passes across. So our experience of real-motion perception primes us, when it comes to apparent motion, to contrive smoothly changing intermediate shapes but to accept with equanimity color jumps. The experiments on apparent motion illustrate, says Goodman 'how perception makes its facts' (p. 89) – a claim in the tradition of Kant, even though the phrase is highly reminiscent of Berkeley.

Apparent motion does not occur 'out there' in the world; it is a construct of our minds. This may cause us to wonder to what extent we ever have access to 'objective' (mind-independent) properties of the world or, indeed, whether there are any such properties. Take blueness, for example. What enters our eyes – the blue light – is simply (objectively) electromagnetic radiation. Yet the electromagnetic radiation is not blue. Color has at least three dimensions – hue, brightness, and saturation – and four of the hues – red, green, yellow, and blue – are *primary*, that is, visibly non-composite. There can be reddish blues, but no yellowish blues or reddish greens. Yet such characteristics of *color* are not characteristics of electromagnetic radiation. For example, no unique wavelength can be identified with a unique hue, since *identical* color experiences may be produced by *different* combinations of wavelength. So light of any particular wavelength cannot be identified with a color, that is, light is not colored.

Blueness, then, is not a property of electromagnetic radiation. Perhaps it is a property possessed by blue objects, that is, a property that they possess whether or not anyone is looking at them. But are objects intrinsically colored? There is a strong temptation to suppose that all the objects that we perceive as blue have something, for example a certain molecular surface structure, that makes them so. Yet, when we actually conduct a detailed analysis of the different kinds of blue things that we see, it soon becomes clear that this supposition is incorrect. The blueness of the sky is due to the scattering of white light by particles of a certain size, and the same cause is responsible for the blueness of the eyes of some Caucasians and of the facial skin of many monkeys. But the blue of a rainbow has quite a different cause from that of the blueness of certain stars. And what makes sapphire blue is quite different from what makes some birds blue, and both are different from what causes the blueness of certain beetles.

It would be inappropriate to give here the scientific accounts of all such different causes of color, but anyone who is sufficiently interested could consult a text such as Leo Hurvich's *Color Vision*. The point that I wish to stress is, since there is nothing common to all those things we see as blue, blueness, or, more generally, color, is not an objective property of things. There are different features of different things that cause us to see them all as blue; no doubt if our visual apparatus was slightly different, then we would no longer see some of those things as blue. Putting this in Kant's terms, the world *as we see it* (the phenomenal world) is a colorful place, but the world as it really is, in itself, is colorless.

Thinking back, now, to the discussion of apparent motion, it will be recalled that we drew the tentative conclusion that, in perception, we do not acquire pure unvarnished information about the world, but an interpretation based on our transactions with things (our experiences) and what one might call common-sense theories, in that case concerning the different ways in which rapid changes in shape and color indicate continuity or non-continuity.

I want to consider another way in which, so it is claimed, some observations fail to supply us with objective information about the world. Have a look at the diagram below (you've probably seen this kind of diagram many times before) and check which of the two horizontal lines seems to you the longer.

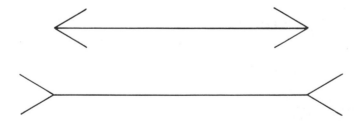

This is the famous Muller-Lyer illusion. Both horizontal lines are in fact of equal length, but the top line looks shorter. The usual explanation for this is that we unconsciously interpret the top line as the outside edge of a convex corner, and the bottom line as the inside edge of a concave corner. So the bottom line looks further away. But the images of both lines on the retina are of equal length, so our three-dimensional interpretation of the figures causes us to see the bottom line as longer.

We seem to have here confirmation of the claim that perception is *interpretation*, an exercise in problem-solving based on beliefs, expectations, and background knowledge – in this case knowledge that comes from our experience of three-dimensional objects and perspectival representations. Experiments show that children who have had less relevant experience are not so susceptible to the Muller-Lyer illusion. However, in a challenging paper called 'Observation reconsidered', Jerry Fodor draws exactly the opposite conclusion from these examples.

Fodor points out that the Muller-Lyer is an illusion with which many of us are very familiar – it is part of our 'background theory' that the horizontal lines in Muller-Lyer diagrams turn out, on measurement, to have equal length. Then 'why', asks Fodor,

> isn't perception penetrated by THAT piece of background theory? Why, that is, doesn't *knowing* that the lines are the same length make it *look as though* the lines are the same length? (For that matter, since one knows perfectly well that [the diagram] is a drawing in two dimensions, why doesn't *that* information penetrate perception, thereby blocking the three dimensional interpretation and cancelling the illusion?) (p. 34).

In opposition to the view that what we perceive is dependent on what we know, Fodor suggests just the reverse: 'that how the world looks can be peculiarly unaffected by how one knows it to be' (p. 34). He concludes, 'all the standard perceptual illusions exhibit this curiously refractory character: knowing that they *are* illusions doesn't make them go away' (p. 34). The contrast between Fodor's position and Goodman's is altogether sharp. And, having been strongly drawn towards Goodman's anti-objectivism, we may now find ourselves being pulled the other way. Fodor's explanation of the Muller-Lyer illusion would presumably make no reference to our experiences with convex corners. And presumably his explanation of the illusion on the following page, would not advert to our experiences of rings lying on striped surfaces.

This may seem to be depriving us of perfectly plausible explanations, until we reflect on the fact that there is *nothing* about our experiences or expectations that would lead us to predict that the apparent ring would seem *whiter* than the white background.

Notes

My quotation from Russell on the strangeness of the physical world comes from B. Russell, *The Problems of Philosophy* 1st edn 1912 (Oxford: Oxford University Press, 1973), p. 19. The first four chapters (pp. 1-24) of this classic introduction to philosophy deal with several of the issues (appearance and reality, matter, idealism) with which I am concerned in this chapter.

The most accessible source for Bishop Berkeley's 'immaterialism' is G. Berkeley, 'Three dialogues between Hylas and Philonous' (first published 1713) in G. J. Warnock (ed.) *The Principles of Human Knowledge* (London: Collins, 1962), pp. 147-259. On the question of whether color is part of the natural order, see C. L. Hardin, 'Are "scientific" objects coloured?' *Mind* 93/372 (1984), 491-500.

There are many excellent books providing information on color, perception, and visual illusion, but I'll mention just four: L. Hurvich, *Color Vision* (Sunderland, Mass.: Sinauer Associates, 1981); E. H. Gombrich, *The Image and the Eye* (Oxford: Phaidon Press, 1982); R. L. Gregory, *Eye and Brain: The Psychology of Seeing*, 3rd edn (London: Weidenfeld & Nicolson, 1977); C. L. Hardin, *Color for Philosophers. Unweaving the Rainbow* (Indianapolis: Hackett, 1988). Gregory captures the mystery of perception quite nicely: 'We are given tiny distorted upside-down images in the eyes, and we see separate solid objects in surrounding space. From the patterns of stimulation on the retinas we perceive the world of objects, and this is nothing short of a miracle' (p. 9). He is also particularly good on visual illusions and has a useful section (pp. 142-57) showing why various theories purporting to account for these illusions have to be rejected.

An intriguing but neglected work on color by a great philosopher is L. Wittgenstein, *Remarks on Colour* (Oxford: Blackwell, 1977).

On the question of whether observation is 'theory laden', I mentioned J. Fodor, 'Observation reconsidered', *Philosophy of Science* 51 (1984), 23-43.

A detailed philosophical investigation of each of the senses is conducted in M. Perkins, *Sensing the World* (Indianapolis, Hackett, 1983).

On 'apparent motion' (the seeing of change that is not there), see P. A. Kolers, *Aspects of Motion Perception* (Oxford: Pergamon Press, 1972).

A survey of recent experiments on this phenomenon is provided in V. S. Ramachandran and S. M. Anstis, 'The perception of apparent motion', *Scientific American* 254/6 (June 1986), 80-7.

For a philosophical discussion of Koler's work, see N. Goodman, *Ways of Worldmaking* (Hassocks: Harvester, 1978), pp. 71-90.

Questions

1   N. R. Hanson, in his *Patterns of Discovery* (Cambridge: Cambridge University Press, 1958) defends the view that all observation is 'theory-laden'. He says, 'there is more to seeing than meets the eyeball' (p. 7). Is there? For an elementary introduction to this question, see A. F. Chalmers, *What is this thing called Science?*, 2nd edn. (Milton Keynes: Open University Press, 1982), pp. 22-37. Also useful is I. Hacking, *Representing and Intervening* (Cambridge: Cambridge University Press, 1983), pp. 167-85.

2   A related question concerns the *realist* view of perception. Does perception purport to be of features of the actual world which are independent of perception itself? I have adapted this characterization from Mohan Matthen, 'Biological functions and perceptual content', *Journal of Philosophy* 85 (1988), 5-27: a difficult paper. The realist position is opposed by Clyde Hardin, 'Are "scientific" objects coloured?'; *Color for Philosophers* (see notes p. 188); and 'Qualia and materialism: closing the explanatory gap', *Philosophy and Phenomenological Research* 48 (1987), 281-98. The neurobiologist J. Z. Young also favors the anti-realist position, which he formulates in terms very similar to Goodman's: 'The world we see is largely of our own making . . . The very daylight we see is our own creation' in his *Philosophy and the Brain* (New York: Oxford University Press, 1987).

Chapter twenty

Is it rational to fear being dead?

We live in the present. The past is gone and irretrievable. The future awaits us, and is unknown. But human beings (and possibly some other animals) have the amazing ability, as it were, to, bring the past and future into the present: We can vividly *remember* things that happened, sometimes many years ago, and we can *envisage* how certain things will be in times to come.

These abilities are useful, for without them we should never be able to learn from experience nor should we be able to make any plans. We should not be able to lead the lives that we do if we were unable to remember and envisage. But, if these abilities are a blessing, they are also something of a curse. The reason is that they are *defective*. We do not have perfect recall, nor are we able to foretell the future.

In the case of a somewhat imperfect memory, the consequences are not so grave. It is merely irritating to forget things we once learned. In the case of our imperfect ability to see into the future, we have to suffer the uncertainty of not knowing how things will turn out. Some people are optimists – they are confident that everything will turn out well. However, such confidence is not justified. For example, we are all growing older; our mental and physical faculties will decline. Most old people I know agree that being old is not nearly as enjoyable as being young. We can be fairly certain that we shall grow old, but how it will be for us when we are old is quite uncertain. And, for many people, such uncertainty is a source of fear.

Other people worry about the process of dying. We know that many deaths are slow and uncomfortable, so it is quite natural to wonder, 'Will my own death be like that?' Yet the process of dying may not be as worrisome as the prospect of being dead. As Thomas Nagel memorably said, 'I should not really object to dying if it were not followed by death.' (p. 3, fn) The question I want to ask is not about the process of dying, but about being dead – no longer existing. As I've said, it is quite natural to fear the process of dying, but my question is: 'Is it reasonable to fear death?' – that is, should we fear simply not existing in the distant future? The word 'fear' – which connotes a gut-wrenching feeling – is not crucial in this formulation. My question is whether it is rational to contemplate with disquiet the prospect of one's own death.

I shall not accept the answer that we never really die, but live on as spirits or are reincarnated, since to answer that way is just to refuse to accept the terms of the question. The question asks us to assume that ceasing to exist will be something final, so there can be no experiencing being dead. Experiencing needs an experiencer, not a corpse.

Ceasing to exist is one of those things that all people can be sure will happen to them, so that, unlike in the previous cases we have considered, uncertainty would not be the source of the fear. And if we are certain that death is inevitable, why worry about it? Shakespeare is addressing this point when he writes:

> Of all the wonders that I have yet heard,
> It seems to me most strange that men should fear;
> Seeing that death, a necessary end,
> Will come when it will come.
>
> (*Julius Caesar*, II. ii. 34-7)

But the idea being expressed here – that it is irrational to fear the inevitable – seems wrong. If it is inevitable that something extremely pleasant will happen to you, it is only natural, and not irrational, to be delighted at the prospect. And if you can revel in the thought of some future good, you can certainly be dismayed at the thought of some future evil. Something inevitably bad is no less bad for being inevitable. Fear of the unknown is often said to be irrational, but fear of the predictable is quite intelligible when what is predicted to happen is something that is extremely unpleasant.

Up till now, I have simply been assuming that ceasing to exist is something bad, and, if this assumption is correct, then it would be quite reasonable for people to be horrified at the thought of their own future non-existence. But is the assumption correct? Can it be *justified*? Many people would say that it is just good to be alive even though there are few pleasures and much pain. Their claim is that just being able to experience the world around us, being able to do things, and to think thoughts, is what makes life worthwhile. This is a fairly widespread view which, if rarely explicitly stated, is nevertheless reflected in the fact that few

191

people seriously contemplate suicide. However, how can we prove to those people who hate life and wish they were dead that they are wrong? I confess that I do not have an answer to this question.

Now, a person who hates life would presumably welcome death, and not regard it as a deprivation. Then why don't all these people take their own lives? There are, of course, many reasons – fear of the process of dying, religious scruples, the desire not to be a cause of grief, etc. – but there is a rather more abstract reason, and this is that the thought of the world continuing to exist without oneself in it is somehow terrifying. This thought is not, of course, restricted to those needing reasons to deter them from suicide; for many people, the thought of themselves as no longer being around is a frightening one.

But is it rational to be appalled at the prospect of oneself ceasing to exist? A negative answer to this question may be found (depending on how we interpret the text) in Book 3 of *De Rerum Natura* by Lucretius, who lived in the first century BC. His argument is this:

> Again, look back and see how the ancient past of everlasting time before we are born has been nothing to us. Nature then shows us this as a mirror of future time after our final death. Does anything appear horrible there, does anything seem sad? Does it not stay steadier than any sleep?
>
> (Sorabji, p. 176)

What Lucretius appears to be saying is that since it is not horrible to think of ourselves not existing in the past, before we were born, then it is equally not horrible to think of ourselves not existing in the future.

My guess is that Lucretius' argument has not enabled many people to free themselves from the fear of death. One objection to the argument that I can think of is, if people do regard life as worthwhile, then they are unhappy about death setting a finite limit to the enjoyments and satisfactions that life has to offer. They would like life to go on forever. But suppose it were absolutely certain that the world was going to come to an end in six months' time. Then people might bitterly regret that they had not been born a lot earlier. In other words, they would think it horrible that the time before they were born did not contain them.

Why is it, then, as Lucretius says, people are not generally sad about not being around in times long past? I can think of three reasons. First, people tend to regard the old days as bad – no television, poor transportation, no fast food, dingy gaslight, etc. – so that, given a choice between extending one's life into the future or into the past, most would opt for the former. Second, it doesn't take much thought to realize that adding a bit onto the end of one's life (in the sense of prolonging one's life) is a piece of cake when compared with adding a bit on at the beginning. Besides, there's not much to be said for more time in the womb nor for a lengthy spell as pre-foetal. Third, it is impossible to turn the clock back, to travel backwards in time, and a sane person knows that it is useless to think of undoing the past and dropping oneself into it.

In short, the answer to Lucretius is that we *would* be sad about missing out on the past if we thought that it was full of good things that we might then have been able to obtain but which are unavailable now and in the future. Perhaps Lucretius is right in saying that we don't much mind not having lived through the 'ancient past of *everlasting* time' – but you can have too much of a good thing. I conclude that Lucretius' argument fails to show that it is irrational to fear being dead.

Another suggestion sometimes made is that there is a kind of logical error involved in the fear of one's own death. The argument is that if death is regarded as a misfortune, there must be someone who suffers the misfortune. Yet a person when alive can hardly be said to suffer the misfortune of not being alive, and a person when dead cannot be said to suffer anything. Thomas Nagel provides what I think is a powerful refutation of this argument by comparing the fate of someone who dies with the fate of someone who suffers a different drastic change of state: Imagine that an adult suffers acute brain damage and, as a result, is reduced to the state of a contented infant. Before the injury, the adult cannot be said to have suffered the misfortune of being injured. But after the injury, the brain-damaged person is in no fit state to mind the new condition and is *ex hypothesi* perfectly contented, so it is incorrect to say that this 'infant' is sad at some misfortune (pp. 5-9). Nevertheless, something unfortunate has occurred, and we pity people who have been stricken this way because of the fact that they have been reduced to this state, even though they themselves are in no position to mind their condition.

Similarly, the misfortune of someone who has died is not a current attribute of that person, but resides in the fact that there is no more life left for that person to lead. Since this is a misfortune that confronts all of us who enjoy life, then, unless we are short-sighted or can successfully deceive ourselves, we may anticipate the state of affairs with some misgiving.

Notes

Lucretius' argument is discussed in R. Sorabji, *Time, Creation and the Continuum* (London: Duckworths, 1983), pp. 174-190.

The argument by Thomas Nagel that I mentioned is contained in an article called 'Death', reprinted in T. Nagel, *Mortal Questions* (Cambridge: Cambridge University Press, 1979), pp. 1-10. That dying is a misfortune, but one that can be ameliorated, is argued in S. Luper-Foy, 'Annihilation', *Philosophical Quarterly* 37 (1987), 233-52.

For reasons why living very long may be too much of a good thing, see B. Williams, 'The Makropulos case: reflections on the tedium of immortality', reprinted in Williams, *Problems of the Self* (London and New York: Cambridge University Press, 1973), pp. 82-100.

The argument that to fear death involves a logical mistake is defended by S. E. Rosenbaum, 'How to be dead and not care: a defence of Epicurus', *American Philosophical Quarterly* 23 (1986), 217-25.

For an attack on Lucretius, see A. L. Brueckner and J. M. Fischer, 'Why is death bad?', *Philosophical Studies* 50 (1986), 213-21, where reasons are offered for treating prenatal and posthumous non-existence asymmetrically. Further arguments against Lucretius, intended to show that the quality of a person's life can (at least in principle) be adversely affected by his or her death, are presented in D. Grover, 'Death and life', *Canadian Journal of Philosophy* 17 (1987), pp. 711-32.

A philosophical work covering many death-related issues is J. F. Rosenberg, *Thinking Clearly about Death* (New Jersey: Prentice Hall, 1983).

Questions

1   Imagine that you were confronted with a suicidal person, who was obsessed with the idea that, whatever our ambitions and achievements, we all ultimately crumble to dust, so that life is meaningless. How would you persuade this person that life really is worth living? Some useful reading: O. Hanfling, *The Quest for Meaning* (Oxford: Blackwell, 1987); Hanfling (ed.), *Life and Meaning* (Oxford: Blackwell, 1987); W. H. Davis, 'The meaning of life', *Metaphilosophy* 18 (1987), 288-305.

2   If immortality took the form of infinitely repeating identical 6-month cycles, then, undoubtedly, it would wear thin after a time. But, given a less rigid pattern, would immortality necessarily be tedious? Refer to the Williams paper on the Makropulos case, see above.

3   Nagel, in his introductory book *What Does it All Mean?* (Oxford: Oxford University Press, 1987), p. 94, expresses puzzlement that the prospect of one's own non-existence can be positively alarming to oneself. Do you think that he is right to be puzzled?

Chapter twenty-one

Arguments for and against God's existence

'And don't tell me that God works in mysterious ways, Yossarian continued, hurtling on over her objection. 'There's nothing so mysterious about it. He's not working at all. . . . Good God, how much reverence can you have for a Supreme Being who finds it necessary to include such phenomena as phlegm and tooth decay in His divine system of creation? What in the world was running through that warped, evil, scatological mind of His when He robbed old people of the power to control their bowel movements? Why in the world did He ever create pain?'

'Pain?' Lieutenant Scheisskopf's wife pounced upon the word victoriously. 'Pain is a useful symptom. Pain is a warning to us of bodily dangers.'

'And who created the dangers?' Yossarian demanded. He laughed caustically. 'Oh, He was really being charitable to us when He gave us pain! Why couldn't He have used a doorbell instead to notify us, or one of His celestial choirs? Or a system of blue-and-red neon tubes right in the middle of each person's forehead. Any jukebox manufacturer worth his salt could have done that. Why couldn't He?'

'People would certainly look silly walking around with red neon tubes in the middle of their foreheads.'

'They certainly look beautiful now writhing in agony or stupefied with morphine, don't they? What a colossal, immortal blunderer!'

(Joseph Heller *Catch-22*, p. 194)

The belief that there must be a supernatural, extremely powerful being has existed for thousands of years. It is not difficult to see why this belief should be so appealing. For early humans, the falling of rain, the rising of the sun, the roaring of thunder, and the flashing of lightning must have seemed deeply mysterious happenings. Ordinary people cannot cause such events, so it may have appeared obvious that an *extraordinary* but invisible being or beings was responsible for bringing about massive occurrences of this sort.

In the Christian tradition, the supernatural, all-powerful being is called 'God'. Christians believe that God created the world, and that, as well as being omnipotent, He is all-knowing (omniscient) and entirely good (omnibenevolent) – in short, He is the greatest. Christians believe that by coming to recognize the existence of God and to worship him, people will lead better lives. So Christians have always regarded it as important to try to persuade non-believers that God really exists. Yet this is a difficult task, for God cannot be *observed* in any of the normal ways; He cannot be detected by any of the five senses.

It is often said that God's existence cannot be *proved*, but must be accepted as a matter of faith. If this were true, then the chances of *converting* a person to belief in the existence of God would be slight. For how could that person be led to acquire the necessary faith? So, for many hundreds of years, thinkers have searched for a decisive *argument* to prove that God exists. One of the earliest arguments, and, to my mind, one of the best, was devised in the early medieval period by St Anselm of Canterbury (AD 1033–1109). The argument has attracted a great deal of interest in recent philosophy, and various attempts have been made to tighten it up. Before looking at the argument in detail, I want to comment on its *structure*.

St Anselm provides a *reductio ad absurdum* argument, that is, an argument in which a tentative assumption is shown to lead to a contradiction or to an absurdity, and which must therefore be *rejected* as false. The assumption that St Anselm makes at the beginning of his argument is that a greatest being does not exist in reality, but only in our minds. It is this assumption that he will try to show, by a *reductio ad absurdum*, is false.

In order to grasp the argument, you must be very clear about the difference between *existing merely in our minds as an idea* and *existing in reality*. There are many ideas that we have which do not correspond to anything in reality. For example, you may have an idea of a mountain made of gold, but no such mountain really exists. You may have the *idea* of a prime number larger than all others, but it can be proved that there is no such thing. But St Anselm thinks that he can show that our having the *idea* of a greatest being entails that such a being really exists. The argument is ingenious.

A greatest being is such that it is impossible to think of

anything greater than it. Each of us (and even a fool, so St Anselm says) has the *idea* of a greatest being. So the *idea* 'something such that it is impossible to think of anything greater than it' exists in our minds. Now, for the purpose of our *reductio ad absurdum* argument, let us make the *assumption* that this greatest being exists *only* in our minds, but not in reality. However, what exists both in our minds and in reality is greater than what exists in our minds only. For example, a golden mountain existing in the real world is greater than one existing just as an idea in our minds. So, if we have the idea 'a certain object that exists only in our minds' we can have the idea of something greater – that object existing *both* in our minds and in reality.

Now we made the assumption that the greatest being exists only in our minds, but we have just shown that we can think of something greater, namely that the being exists also in reality. So we would be thinking of something greater than the greatest being – greater, that is to say, than something such that it is impossible to think of anything greater than it. And this is clearly absurd. So our original assumption – that the greatest being exists only in our minds but not in reality – must be rejected as *false*, since it leads to an absurdity. The conclusion is that this greatest being – God – exists in reality.

Do you find this argument convincing? The earliest known objection to St Anselm's argument was put forward by Gaunilo, a monk of Marmoutiers. Gaunilo claimed that if the form of St Anselm's reasoning were correct, then we should be able to 'prove' the existence of a great many things. For example, we have the idea of a perfect island, so, by arguing in a way similar to that of St Anselm, we conclude that this perfect island must also exist in reality. So the kind of argument used by St Anselm produces conclusions that are *false*. This shows that his argument is not valid. (See D. P. Henry, *Mediaeval Logic*.)

St Anselm, however, has an additional argument designed to show that, unlike the perfect island, the greatest being (God) cannot be thought not to exist, and anyway, since a perfect island is not something such that it is impossible to think of anything greater than it, the conclusion that this island must exist does not follow.

There are further objections that we might raise against St Anselm. First, he supposes that all of us (including fools) have the *idea* of a greatest being. But do we? I have listed some of the qualities that go to make up greatness – omnipotence, omniscience, and omnibenevolence – but what other qualities must a being possess in order for it to be the greatest? If we do *not* have the idea of a greatest being then St Anselm's argument breaks down at its very first step.

Second, St Anselm assumes that *existing* is a kind of quality, and that an object is made greater by having this quality added to it. Now, we can certainly think, for example, of a woman having the quality *beauty*, but losing it as the result of a car accident. The woman would survive the accident but lose her beauty. But can we think of an object losing the quality of *existence*? *What* would survive? There is, then, some doubt as to whether it can be right to say that existence is a quality that makes an object 'greater'. This point was first raised by Immanuel Kant in his monumental treatise *Critique of Pure Reason*, but Kant's discussion of this issue is somewhat unclear.

At least one modern writer thinks that a modified version of St Anselm's argument does succeed in demonstrating God's existence. Other writers have felt that there are much simpler ways of establishing the same conclusion. For example, it has been claimed that the abundant evidence of design in nature shows that there must be a Great Designer. Another argument starts from the principle that there is some explanation for the existence of anything whatever (this is known as the principle of sufficient reason) and ends with the conclusion that the only thing that can explain the existence of *the world* is God. This argument is certainly well worth discussing, but, since there already exists a discussion of it by Richard Taylor (*Metaphysics*), pp. 103–5 that I cannot better, I do not have sufficient reason for examining it here.

What I want to do, however, is to give an argument on the *opposite* side. My discussion will take as its starting-point an argument that has always seemed to me a very strong one against God's existence, the argument from evil. What the argument from evil seeks to establish is that the presence of evil in the world is inconsistent with the proposition that there is a being who is omnipotent, omniscient, and omnibenevolent – those characteristics traditionally thought to be essential to God's nature.

It's quite simple: if there is some evil about to happen, then that being, because he (or she, or it) is omniscient, will know about it and, because omnipotent, will be able to prevent it happening and, because good, will do so. But evil occurs. Hence no such being exists.

A common response to this argument is that evil doesn't *really* exist – what looks thoroughly evil to us does not look that way to

God. It's just that we mere humans are not clever enough to realize that what seems to us bad and disgusting is actually a good which contributes to making this the best of all possible worlds. I must say that I find in this objection further evidence of evil – the wicked perversity of the objector. For surely one must be culpably egocentric to take so distant a view of the pain and suffering of other people that one can sincerely claim that all of that suffering is good – if you only look at it the right way. The world is full of vile iniquities, and anyone who denies this is either dishonest or naive.

When casting about for examples of obvious evil, one thinks first of children in poor countries dying of starvation and disease. I am reminded of a line from Christopher New's book *Goodbye Chairman Mao*, where the author is writing about the passengers in a modern jet flying over the central plains of India, gorging themselves on excessive quantities of airline food, while below the Indian peasants 'looked up vacantly and starved' (p. 1). Countless billions of dollars are spent on producing weapons of mass annihilation. A fraction of that expenditure would alleviate hunger worldwide, yet the rulers of rich nations callously disregard the sufferings of the poor.

It is this disregard for the welfare of one's fellows that I find the most depressing kind of evil. Worse than indifference is the savagery and barbarity in which some men seem to delight. Think of the pillage, rape, and murder perpetrated by the armies of Attila the Hun or of Genghis Khan; think of the medieval torture industry. Unfortunately, bestiality of this kind is not a thing of the past. Indeed, a mass of evidence clearly shows that it has now reached epidemic proportions. Everywhere we find people harming, hating, and exploiting. Yet it is said that God created us. How could a perfect, all-loving God have done such a thing?

The standard rejoinder to this last point is that God gave us free will, so that we can choose how to live our lives, can choose to be good or bad. But, in reply, we may first point out that there are some obvious evils suffered by animals in their natural state (e.g. blindness, disease, painful death) which are clearly not brought about by the free choice of *humans*. Second, if a person in choosing to be bad causes suffering to a helpless and blameless victim, how can we make sense of the fate of that victim? The victim neither chose, nor deserved, to suffer pain. Consider the calamities that befall innocent people – for example babies who have not even had the opportunity to do anything blameworthy, yet whose short lives are tormented and terminated either by grotesque disease or by maltreatment. Is the existence of such unjustified suffering consistent with the existence of a good, supreme deity? Surely a just God would not punish the innocent.

It seems to me that there is only one possible reply that someone who believes in an almighty God can make here; namely that the suffering of an innocent person is God's punishment, not for anything that the person did in this life (since, as we are assuming, the person did nothing blameworthy in this life), but punishment for what that person did in a *previous* life (or, more improbably, for what that person will do in a *subsequent* life). Hence someone who believes that a good God allows evil to occur is committed to a doctrine of spirits that precede (and may survive) the human bodies that they temporarily inhabit. The version of this doctrine most commonly embraced is *reincarnation*. Let us, then, investigate the possibility that an innocent man A is punished for the wrongdoing of person B, a previous embodiment of A's spirit (though my argument applies equally if A's spirit is unembodied except when embodied in A).

Some philosophers claim that the doctrine of reincarnation is incoherent on the grounds that we cannot know that A and B share a spirit when there is neither bodily continuity between A and B nor any shared psychological features (e.g. memories common to both). In my view, this does not constitute a refutation of the doctrine, since it has not yet been shown impossible that A and B may share a spirit even though nobody, including A, can identify A's previous personae. In other words, we must distinguish the question of whether A and B share a spirit from the question of whether anyone *knows* this. However, the question of whether A knows anything about his previous selves becomes absolutely critical when we are considering the justification of punishing innocent A for something he did when he (or his spirit) was B.

For if A is innocent, and knows that he is innocent, then it is cruel and unjust to punish him – that would be punishment without a crime. If, however, A knows that he is paying for a wrong perpetrated by B, then he can at least see the reason why pain is being visited on him (but how many of us know the deeds of our previous selves?) If, alternatively, A knows nothing of B's deeds but, as a believer in divine justice, believes that to merit his current suffering he *must have done something wrong* in a previous life, then his punishment makes some sense, at least to him (others might question his stoical quiescence).

Neither of these alternative explanations, however, can

account for those instances of infants dying in torment, since here the children are certainly physiologically equipped to experience pain, but do not possess the conceptual apparatus needed to rationalize their suffering in terms of *punishment, previous selves, must have done*, etc. So in cases like this we simply cannot claim that the suffering can be explained by saying that the sufferer recognizes that he is receiving just punishment for the misdemeanors of a previous self of which he is the current reincarnation.

The conclusion is that there is unjustifiable evil in the world. If this evil is perpetrated by some powerful being, then that being cannot be omnibenevolent. If there is some higher being who, although he does not perpetrate the evil, either does not know of its existence or is unable to prevent it, then that being is either not omniscient or not omnipotent. In short, there is no omnibenevolent, omniscient, omnipotent God.

The argument from evil, and my development of it, amounts to what I think is a fairly strong case for the conclusion that a perfect supreme being does not exist. This leaves open the possibility of a not-entirely-perfect God – a supreme but not entirely flawless being. To my knowledge, few orthodox religions embrace this conception, but I have yet to see an argument demonstrating that the idea is incoherent or even suspect.

There are those who wish to reject the argument from evil, but I must confess that I have not encountered an effective counterargument. In an article by Thomas Morris entitled 'A response to the problem of evil', I found this:

> And surely it is a deeply religious insight that the goodness of God is at times manifested in the suffering we are allowed to endure as well as in the more immediately pleasant of his gifts to us. (p. 183)

If this insight is deep, it is too deep for me to comprehend. It is reminiscent, rather, of the rationalizations of Lieutenant Scheisskopf's wife. The idea that suffering is a gift that we are privileged to endure (or enjoy) seems very odd, but I would not wish to discourage anyone from trying to explain it.

Notes

An English translation of the relevant section of St Anselm's Proslogion side by side with the Latin original is provided in D. P. Henry, *Mediaeval Logic and Metaphysics* (London: Hutchinson, 1972), pp. 101-17.

Science and metaphysics

In an excellent article written in his characteristically happy style, O. K. Bouwsma says of St Anselm's argument that 'no more splendid headache has ever been composed' (p. 41): O. K. Bouwsma, 'Anselm's argument', in J. L. Craft and R. E. Hushvit (eds), *Without Proof or Evidence: Essays of O. K. Bouwsma* (Lincoln: University of Nebraska Press, 1984), pp. 40-72. *

A thorough discussion of the argument, together with a comprehensive bibliography, is contained in R. Brecher, *Anselm's Argument: The Logic of Divine Existence* (Dorset: Blackmore Press, 1985).

There are numerous expositions of Kant's criticism of the ontological argument, but these should be consulted only after looking at I. Kant, *Critique of Pure Reason*, edited by N. K. Smith (London: Macmillan, 1929), A592/B620–A602/B630

For what he claims is a 'victorious version' of the ontological argument, see A. Plantinga, *The Nature of Necessity* (Oxford: Clarendon Press, 1974), pp. 213-21, but be warned that this is fairly tough going. Other arguments for the existence of God are reviewed in many texts on the philosophy of religion. One which contains a discussion of Plantinga is B. Davies, *An Introduction to the Philosophy of Religion* (Oxford: Oxford University Press, 1982), pp. 27-37.

The proof of God's existence from the principle of sufficient reason is discussed in R. Taylor, *Metaphysics*, 2nd edn (New Jersey: Prentice Hall, 1974), pp. 102-20. I cited, as an attempt to solve the problem of evil, Thomas V. Morris, 'A response to the problem of evil', *Philosophia* 14 (1984), 173-85.

The two works of philosophical fiction from which I quoted are Joseph Heller, *Catch-22* London: Jonathan Cape Ltd, 1961; Christopher New, *Goodbye Chairman Mao* (New York: Putnam Publishing Group, 1979).

For a Christian's defense of the existence of pain, see C. S. Lewis, *The Problem of Pain* (London: Fountain Books, 1977).

There is an entry under 'Evil, the problem of' by John Hick in P. Edwards (ed.), *The Encyclopaedia of Philosophy*, vol. 3 (New York: Macmillan, 1967), pp. 136-40. Although this encyclopedia is over twenty years old, it remains a useful tool, and many of the entries are truly excellent introductions to their subjects.

The problem of reincarnation receives an extended examination in P. Edwards, 'The case against reincarnation', *Free Inquiry* (Spring 1987), pp. 38-49.

For a discussion of the possibility of a less-than-perfect God, see William James, *Essays in Radical Empiricism; A Pluralistic Universe* (New York: Longman Green and Co., 1943). James writes, 'The God of David or of Isaiah . . . is an essentially finite being in the cosmos, not with the cosmos in him . . . I hold to the finite God' (p. 111). See also P. T. Geach, *Providence and Evil* (Cambridge: Cambridge University Press, 1977); T. P. Flint and A. J. Freddoso, 'Maximal power', reprinted in T. V. Morris (ed.), *The Concept of God* (Oxford: Oxford University Press, 1987), pp. 134-67; P. J. McGrath, 'Evil and the existence of a finite God', *Analysis* 46 (1986), 63-4, with a reply by R. Crisp on p. 160

of the same issue, and a rejoinder: P. J. McGrath, 'Children of a lesser God? A reply to Blake and Crisp', *Analysis* 47 (1987), 236-8.

Questions

1 One argument for the existence of God that has widespread appeal is the 'Argument from design'. It receives its classic statement (and criticism) by David Hume in *Dialogues concerning Natural Religion*, edited by R. H. Popkin, Indiana: Hackett, 1980). The argument begins from the observation that the world is like a vast, beautiful, complex machine in which even the most minute parts, in Hume's words, 'are adjusted to each other with an accuracy which ravishes into admiration all men who have ever contemplated them'. Can this great design be anything other than the work of a great designer – God? A powerful answer in the negative is provided by the zoologist Richard Dawkins in his *The Blind Watchmaker* (New York: W. W. Norton and Co., 1986). Dawkins' book bears the subtitle *Why the Evidence of Evolution reveals a Universe without Design*. A good critical survey of several of the major arguments for God's existence is provided in A. Flew, *An Introduction to Western Philosophy* (London: Thames and Hudson, 1971), pp. 180-221.

2 Another famous argument, known as the 'Cosmological argument' takes as its starting-point the premise that everything has a cause, and ends with the conclusion that there must be a first cause, namely God. Can this argument go through? The argument was formulated by St Thomas Aquinas in his *Summa Theologica* (edited by T. Gilbey, New York: McGraw-Hill, 1963) and has, of course, received extensive discussion in the literature. A recent article that contains a neat demonstration which seems to establish that the argument is valid is R. Meyer, 'God exists!', *Nous* 21 (1987), 345-61. But this article is accessible only to those who possess some knowledge of logic and axiomatic set theory.

3 Is the existence of God compatible with the existence of evil?

4 Can a being who is not omnipotent be God?

5 At the end of a chapter on the existence of God, L. Goddard, in *Philosophical Problems* (Edinburgh: Scottish Academic Press, 1977), concludes 'What is beyond the possibility of experience is beyond our comprehension. If God does exist, we cannot know it; and if he does not, we cannot know that either.' (p. 87). Is such skepticism justified?

Index

Index

Index

Elster, John 158
emotion 31, 37, 55, 95, 115, 125, 127, 133–4, 145
emotivism 124–5
emphasis 65
empirical 89, 98, 114–16, 155
empiricism 96–7
endorphin 12
Engels, Friedrich 156, 157n
English 54, 62
entailment 86–7, 91, 93, 108–9, 125
environmental protection 127
Epimenides 74, 75n, 76n
epistemology 95–9
esse est percipi 183
Etchemendy, John 75n
ethics xvi, 123–52, 181n
Euclid 87
euthanasia 123, 135

——

faith 196
fallacy 90, 155, 163
falsification 161
fear 15, 31
feeling (touch) 37
feeling: *see* sentiment
Feigl, Herbert 58n, 75n
Feinberg, Joel 128n
Femia, Joseph 156, 157n, 158
Ferguson, John 180n
Feyerabend, Paul 67, 162–3, 164n
fidelity 143–52
Fischer, J.M. 194n
Fisher, Mark xi
Flew, Antony 203
Flint, T.P. 202n
Fodor, Jerome 28n, 29, 67, 116, 120n, 187, 188n
foetus 130, 132, 134 & n, 193
Fogelin, Robert 13
folk psychology 27, 28n
Føllesdal, Dagfinn 28n
Foot, Philippa 128n
form of knowledge 114–16
form of life 55
Foulkes, D. 20n
foundationalism 98, 111
Fox, R.M. 128n
Fraassen, Bas van 160, 164n
Frazer, J.G. 106
Freddoso, A.J. 202n
free will 176–181, 199n
freedom 126, 155–6, 164

Frege, Gottlob 42–5, 48n, 52, 88, 90, 92n, 93n
Freud, Sigmund 15, 19n, 20–1, 31
Frey, Raymond 134n
functionalism 4, 13
Furth, Montgomery 93n
future 42, 131, 170, 190–3

Gallup, David 152
game 54
Gardner, Howard 39n, 116, 120n
Gaunilo 197
Geach, Peter 4n, 48n, 98n, 180n, 202n
Geer, J.H. 151n
general 42
genetic 61, 64, 66, 139
genocide 139
geography 112
George IV 45
gestalt 55
gesture 42
Gettier, Edmund 108–11
Genghis Khan 199
Gibbins, Peter 161, 164n
Gilbey, T. 203
Gillies, Frank xi
Glover, Jonathan 134n
goal 33
God 126, 195–203
Goddard, Leonard 203
Gödel, Kurt 76n
Goldman, Alan 151n
Goldman, Alvin 99n
Goldstein, Laurence 75n, 111
Gombrich, E.H. 188n
good 123–4, 127, 149, 199
Goodman, Nelson 66n, 67, 173, 174n, 184–5, 187, 189 & n
Graham, Keith 157n
grammar 42–3, 52, 55–6, 58n, 61
Grandy, Richard 28n, 93n, 165n
Grayling, Anthony 48n
Green, A. 117, 120n
Greenfield, S. 4n
Gregory, R.L. 188n
Grelling, Kurt 77
Grice, Paul 56, 58n, 59
Grover, Dorothy 194n
grue 173–4
Gruneberg, M.M. 11n
guilt 150
Guttenplan, Samuel 28n

Haack, Susan 48n, 75n, 94

208

Index

Index

speech act 42, 53
spina bifida 134
Spinoza, Benedict de 96
spirit 3, 191, 200
Stalnaker, Robert 25, 28n
statement 26, 42, 55, 69–76, 125
stealing 126
Steinberg, D.D. 59
Sterelny, Kim 29, 42, 58n, 67
stereotype 141
Stevenson, C.L. 93n
Stich, Stephen 28n
Stock, Saint George 75n
Stove, D.C. 174
Strachey, J. 19n
Strawson, Peter 49n, 59, 76, 93n
Stroud, Barry 99n
subjective 125
substance 160
suffering 10, 199–200
sufficient reason (principle of) 198, 202n
suggesting 56
suicide 134n, 192, 194
superstition 162
surgery 7–9, 11, 17
Surinan 66
surprise examination paradox 100–1, 104n, 105n
surrogacy 127, 134n
Sutherland, Stuart 39n
Swinburne, Richard 174 & n
symbol 86–7
synonymy 47
syntax 23–4, 50, 66, 87
synthetic 97

taboo 149
tachometer paradox 85
Tarski, Alfred 51, 58n, 71–2, 75n, 89
Taylor, Richard 147–9, 151n, 166n, 198, 202n
technology 118
Teichman, Jenny 5n
tense 65
Thalberg, Irving 141n
theoretical entity 160
theory 27, 47, 51–2, 54, 86, 95, 160–4, 167
there 55
Theseus 85
thinking, thought 2–4, 14, 22–9, 47, 53
Thomson, J.A.K. 127n
threat 53

time, temporal 27, 114, 159–60, 193
Titus 74
Tooley, Michael 130–2, 133n, 134n
toothpaste 26
Tour de France 45
Tov-Ruach, L. 151
toxin puzzle 165
Traiger, Saul 105n
transcendental 115
transfinite 73
translation 47, 61, 91
transplant 18
Travis, Charles 28n
Trobriand Islands 150, 151n
Truman, Harry 125
truth 47, 71–3, 75, 113, 125, 159–60, 163
truth-value 44, 92
Twin-Earth 46

unconscious 21, 186
understanding 4, 31–40, 41–2, 68, 91, 114
universal 55, 61, 66n, 91, 115, 133, 160
universalizability 126
utilitarianism 126, 134
utterance 22, 53

vagueness 43, 72, 78–85, 89, 139
validity 90, 113, 161
value 147
virtue 127, 147
vision 8, 26, 183, 186
voice-onset time 62–3
volition 2
Volterra, V. 68
voluntary 1–3
voodoo 162

Waldrop, M.M. 39n
Wallis, Claudia 12n
Wang, Hao 83–4
warfare 123
Warner, Richard 28n, 93n
Warnock, Geoffrey 98n, 120, 188n
Warnock, Mary 120n
Warren, Mary Anne 133n
Wartofsky, Marx 84n
Wasserstrom, Richard 141, 144, 150n
Watson, Gary 181n
Weil, Simone 140
Weiskrantz, L. 28n
Weizenbaum, Joseph 31, 38n
Wettstein, Howard 46–7, 48n

214